THE FEDERALIST FRONTIER

THE FEDERALIST FRONTIER

Settler Politics in the Old Northwest, 1783–1840

Kristopher Maulden

UNIVERSITY OF MISSOURI PRESS
COLUMBIA

Publication of this volume has been supported with a gift from the
Kinder Institute on Constitutional Democracy

Library of Congress Cataloging-in-Publication Data

Names: Maulden, Kristopher, 1981- author.
Title: The Federalist frontier : settler politics in the Old Northwest,
    1783-1840 / by Kristopher Maulden.
Description: Columbia : University of Missouri Press, 2019. | Series:
    Studies in constitutional democracy | Revision of author's thesis
    (doctoral)--University of Missouri--Columbia, 2012, titled Federalist
    frontier : early American political development in the Northwest. |
    Includes bibliographical references and index.
Identifiers: LCCN 2019023512 (print) | LCCN 2019023513 (ebook) | ISBN
    9780826221964 (hardcover) | ISBN 9780826222855 (paperback) | ISBN
    9780826274397 (ebook)
Subjects: LCSH: Federal Party (U.S.) | Pioneers--Political
    activity--Northwest, Old. | Northwest, Old--Politics and government. |
    United States--Territorial expansion.
Classification: LCC F483 .M43 2019 (print) | LCC F483 (ebook) | DDC
    977--dc23
LC record available at https://lccn.loc.gov/2019023512
LC ebook record available at https://lccn.loc.gov/2019023513

Typefaces: Minion

STUDIES IN CONSTITUTIONAL DEMOCRACY

Jay Dow and Jeffrey L. Pasley, Series Editors

The Studies in Constitutional Democracy Series explores the origins and development of American constitutional and democratic traditions, as well as their applications and interpretations throughout the world. The often subtle interaction between constitutionalism's commitment to the rule of law and democracy's emphasis on the rule of the many lies at the heart of this enterprise. Bringing together insights from history and political theory, the series showcases interdisciplinary scholarship that traces constitutional and democratic themes in American politics, law, society, and culture, with an eye to both the practical and theoretical implications.

Previous Titles in Studies in Constitutional Democracy

For my nephew, Landon Allen Maulden

(May 2–May 15, 2015)

May you always be loved

Contents

Illustrations

Acknowledgments

First and foremost, I would like to thank you for picking up this book. Scholarship can often be a long, slow, lonely process, and we do it so others might be able to gain knowledge and understanding by reading our work.

As solitary as academic research can often seem, we always have plenty of people to thank for their help and support along the way. I want to thank my dissertation committee—Mark Carroll, Kerby Miller, Robert Smale, and W. Raymond Wood—for reading and commenting on this work in its infancy. The Interlibrary Loan staff at Ellis Library came through time and time again with rare and hard-to-find items, and it made my research much easier and richer. Thank you also to the University of Missouri History Department and the excellent group of graduate students who helped me hone my work on this work as a dissertation. In particular, Joseph Beilein, Josh Rice, Steven C. Smith, Mike Snodgrass, and Lucas Volkman provided especially helpful commentary and questions.

I would also like to extend a special thank you to my graduate adviser, Jeff Pasley, for his support and friendship over the years. His interest and insights show throughout this book, and I might have abandoned it a few times along the way if not for his encouragement. His suggestion that I send the book in for this series has also proven to be wise, and I hope it will live up to the standards set so far by the other series authors.

I would also like to thank those who commented on conference papers and articles that I have written over the years that helped me complete this book project. The Society for Historians of the Early American Republic and the Mid-American Conference on History were kind enough to welcome me in twice with my research, and I appreciate it greatly. Thank you also to my paper commentators over the years: Richard John,

Brad Lookingbill, Matthew Mason, Robert Owens, and the late Andrew
Cayton. Matthew Norman and LeeAnn Whites of *Ohio Valley History*
and the article commentators were helpful with my article, which in turn
has helped the early parts of this book.

I am grateful to the staff at many historical societies as well. The cour-
teous and professional work by archivists at the Ohio Historical Society
(OHS) in Columbus, the Indiana Historical Society in Indianapolis, and
the Abraham Lincoln Presidential Library in Springfield, Illinois, is much
appreciated, and I am glad to have gotten a chance to meet them and
work with all of them. Debbie Ross with the newspaper library at the
Abraham Lincoln Presidential Library and Museum was always helpful
and kind, and I am especially glad for the work she did finding just the
right items along the way. Finally, I want to thank the Filson Historical
Society not only for hosting me as I did research, but also for the Filson
Fellowship that made a longer research stay there—and consequently at
the OHS—possible.

The University of Missouri Press has been great as well. I deeply appreciate the work by Mary Conley and Gary Kass along the way, and their
suggestions and direction have helped me to get to this point. For that,
I cannot say thank you enough. Comments from an anonymous review-
er and John Lauritz Larson have also improved this work greatly, and I
can only hope that I would have a chance to repay them the favors they
have done for me. In addition, I want to say a special thanks to David
Nichols, who provided pointed and invaluable commentary on selected
chapters. The support academics give to one another can sometimes be
humbling, and I am so glad all three readers were willing to take their time
to help me.

Special thanks go to Steve Heying, who has lent me the office space
and computer software needed to create the maps in this book. I am
also indebted to him for his friendship and encouragement as this work
has proceeded.

I also want to thank friends I have made teaching over the years for
their support: Jonathan Winkler and Bruce Laforse of Wright State University; Craig Bruce Smith of the U.S. Army Command and General Staff
College; Terry Smith and Kennedy Amofa of Columbia College; and Jason
Vansell at Versailles High School have all been too kind throughout the
years. Without them, getting through the days before the long nights of
reading, research, and writing would have been so much more difficult,
and I am proud to have their friendships. I also want to say thank you to

the English teachers of Versailles High School—Natasha Anderson, Deborah Larson, Stacy Lawless, and Sandra Randall—for their suggestions as I have edited the manuscript. The students here at VHS have been wonderful as well; the interest and encouragement that many students from the Class of 2020 has offered this past year is heartening.

Last but not least, my family deserve a thank you. My parents Russell and Nancy always encouraged my interest in history, and for that I cannot be thankful enough. My brother Craig, his wife Maureen, and their daughter Nora have also offered a welcome respite from the stresses of work. Finally, I want to thank my partner Kara Hicks for her love and support. I would not be writing these acknowledgements without her, and finally, the long and winding journey behind this book is complete.

Abbreviations

AC — *Annals of the Congress of the United States, 1789–1824,* 42 vols. (Washington: Gales and Seaton, 1834–1856)

ALPL — Abraham Lincoln Presidential Library, Springfield, Illinois

ASP:IA — *American State Papers: Indian Affairs* (Washington: Gales and Seaton, 1832–1861)

ASP:PL — *American State Papers: Public Lands* (Washington: Gales and Seaton, 1832–1861)

FHS — Filson Historical Society, Louisville, Kentucky

IHS — Indiana Historical Society, Indianapolis, Indiana

NNV — A New Nation Votes: American Electoral Returns 1787–1825 (online database): https://elections.lib.tufts.edu/

OHS — Ohio Historical Society, Columbus, Ohio

THE FEDERALIST FRONTIER

The Log Cabin on Washington Street

Federalists and the Early American State in the Old Northwest

OHIO'S FIRST LAND office does not make a strong first impression. A fairly plain, one-room, split-log cabin occupying about five hundred square feet, the office now stands in the side yard of the Campus Martius Museum in Marietta. Small and simply built, the cabin is also a fitting metaphor for John Murrin's interpretation, previously a common one in early American history, which sees the U.S. government as "a midget institution in a giant land" that possessed "almost no internal functions." Similarly, Robert H. Wiebe argued that Westerners in places like Marietta formed "fluid societies of strangers" who often disregarded "distant seats of authority" across the Appalachian Mountains.[1] Compared to the more physically imposing military camps and Indian mounds nearby, the land office cabin is a tiny building within the vast expanse of the trans-Appalachian West.

However, the cabin's appearance does not reflect its true significance. The Ohio Company of Associates saw much more in their land office cabin, erected in summer 1788 on the south side of Washington Street. One of the first buildings they completed at Marietta, it sat a hundred yards from the military camp, Campus Martius. Moved across the street from the camp in 1791, the land office and Campus Martius ultimately stood atop a hill above the main docks along the Muskingum River.[2] Thus, when travelers and new arrivals disembarked at Marietta, the Ohio Company had two symbols of the company standing immediately above them. The blockhouse of Campus Martius signified military protection, while the land office showed civil authority at work. Crucially, it was the official gateway to acquiring land and, thereby, respectability in the Ohio Company's new, corporate West.

3

FIGURE 1. The Marietta Land Office, now at the Campus Martius Museum.
Photograph taken by the author.

Plans for the rest of Marietta also reinforced regular and orderly settlement, an overarching ideal for the Ohio Company. In addition to the
land office and Campus Martius, the company laid out sixty rectangular
blocks with streets running approximately parallel and perpendicular to
the Muskingum River as it emptied into the Ohio. In all, company plans
called for a new Western city containing roughly a thousand lots measuring 90 by 180 feet.[3] In the center of that planned community lay Washington Street, the main thoroughfare for this new town that would serve
as the capital of the Northwest Territory until 1800. People landing at the
town's main docks would disembark to Washington Street, and just a few
blocks away sat the land office in the center of town. There, parcels of land
sold according to company guidelines and as part of the national government's rectangular survey system. Fittingly, the office was the nerve center for distributing land in an orderly fashion in the middle of a planned
city meant to represent what the Ohio Company brought west.[4]
    That order created a sense of refinement that often surprised visitors.
In 1802, French botanist, Francois André Michaux, described a vibrant

and complaisant Marietta "which fifteen years ago was not in existence" but already contained a shipyard and two hundred houses "elegantly built . . . in front of the Ohio." Fortescue Cuming was similarly impressed in 1807, finding Marietta "finely situated" with many houses "large, and having a certain air of taste." Ohioans boasted about Marietta, too. Itinerant resident Jervis Cutler wrote glowingly about Marietta in his 1812 geographical tract: "The form in which the town is built, adds much to its elegance, and the gentle rising of the city ground back from the Ohio, affords an extended and delightful prospect of the rivers and distant hills." Overall, instead of landing at a crude river town, travelers to Marietta found sophistication and order that charmed them in the 1800s and remains impressive today.[5]

Marietta also signified wider ambitions for the Ohio Company that spread across the country. Company leader Manasseh Cutler imagined its efforts as the catalyst for "regular and judicious" settlement that would be "a wise model for . . . all the federal lands."[6] From Washington Street, the land office projected this model of settlement onto the countryside, and thus the humble cabin cast a figurative shadow across the entire continent. Further, the Marietta office was the foundation for one of the earliest national bureaucracies, as federal land offices across America oversaw a determined march over the diverse American landscape in the mile-long strides of the rectangular survey system. In addition to rationalizing American approaches to land and property, the rectangular system also left a more concrete but accidental legacy. Generally, country roads in the Old Northwest and towns built within rectangular townships aligned to section lines in rectangles. Thus, government surveys left subtle imprints on many American street corners.[7]

The institutional effects of the Marietta land office are noteworthy, but they occurred because of the men, nearly all of them Federalists and many of them former Continental officers, who built that cabin in 1788. Most Ohio Company members were Federalists, and its leaders were former Continental officers and members of the Society of the Cincinnati. To them, orderly and efficient land distribution was just the first step in reorienting American society. Ultimately, they hoped to create a nation "of well informed and well disposed Citizens," according to Rufus Putnam, Ohio Company stockholder, leader of the first settlers at Marietta, and operator of the company land office. He explained further that good government would "remove . . . a State of Ignorence" from white

Westerners and engineer a new American society that rejected the disorder of the 1780s.[8]

These Federalists joined other white settlers who advanced the American state through conscious choices. Settlers moving to the Northwest literally risked their lives to improve their circumstances, seek social advancement, and establish new communities. To achieve these goals, Ohio valley residents time and time again preferred, used, and advanced government institutions. They welcomed aid from the United States Army during conflicts with Indians, sought the security of federally backed land titles, looked to local and state authorities to provide education, and advocated for government spending to improve their transportation networks and economic opportunities. Too often, historical studies and modern political discourse treat government as an alien force countervailing the prerogatives of Americans. However, such a treatment fails to recognize the roles played by citizens in creating their circumstances. Living in a republic, Americans choose their government, after all, and in the Northwest, settlers often recognized and sought the benefits of government intervention.

In this vein, Federalist ideals drove the development of the early American state in the Northwest during the late eighteenth century, and Westerners advanced that agenda well into the nineteenth century. As a result, institutions created by Federalists persisted and moved westward well after the party disintegrated. Historians may limit effective Federalist political influence to the final dozen years of the eighteenth century, but the policies and institutions they created in the Northwest Territory largely remained in place throughout the next century. In the 1840s, aging Federalist Jacob Burnet of Cincinnati defended that legacy adamantly, noting that his party "established [the nation's] character—renovated her energy, and laid the foundation of all her subsequent prosperity." Further, he predicted that on some future day, history would "do justice to that abused, persecuted, misunderstood party" and acknowledge that "by their efforts and influence, the country was raised from poverty to affluence."[9] Stated simply, this book seeks to understand those Federalist efforts and influences.

Federalist Ideology and American Westward Expansion
To understand how Federalists affected early American westward expansion and the nation overall, especially as Burnet described, this book argues for two distinct legacies in Federalist-led westward expansion. First,

Federalists created many new institutions that oversaw the generations-long march of white settlers to the Pacific. The Marietta land office was but the first step in that process, and innovations supported by settlers and officials alike extended the depth and physical reach of those institutions in the young nation. Second, settlers in the Northwest came to appreciate how those institutions affected their lives, even as many of them preferred the libertarian rhetoric of Jeffersonian and Jacksonian democracy.

This grand dissonance of American political thought, in which Americans embrace government power in their actions but dismiss it through their words, has long obscured Federalist and statist influence in the early American West. White Westerners sought greater government intervention to save them from Indian violence in the 1780s, and they expressed sympathy for Henry Clay's American System even while many voted for Democrats over Whigs. Thus, even as settlers imagined themselves to be rugged individualists, they approved of state-driven approaches to frontier settlement that extended federal power across the continent. By the nineteenth century and the Market Revolution, the American state had become much more active and visible to its Western citizens, even while talk of liberty remained so alluring to voters. Ultimately, Federalist ideals continued onward not at the ballot box but through the institutional memory of its creations, keeping alive the spirit behind the humble log cabin on Washington Street.

Through this focus on Federalists and state power, this book seeks to make two contributions to the study of Federalists and the Northwest. First, this book analyzes the Federalist Party beyond its usual context of late eighteenth-century New England. Historians have rarely discussed Federalism after 1800, the point at which Linda Kerber argued in her study focused on New England that the party "had nothing to look forward to but its own disintegration," and John Miller claimed "The sun of Federalism had sunk forever."[10] Stanley Elkins and Eric McKitrick extended the lifespan of the Federalists to 1802, when Jefferson promised to "sink federalism into an abyss from which there shall be no resurrection for it." Even David Hackett Fischer, who found Federalists in important positions after 1800, claimed the young proponents of new-school Federalism still only brought "new life to a lost cause" that faded away by 1815. Donald J. Ratcliffe argued in *Party Spirit in a Frontier Republic* that in the 1790s, Ohio was a "bastion of Federalist strength," but by 1804 Federalists often failed to run slates of political candidates.[11] Such an observation is true but, this book argues, Federalism was more than a ticket in a newspaper. Indeed, the policies they implemented and institutions they created encased Federalist ideals in administration over westward expansion. Thereby, Federalist ideals survived much longer and enhanced the party's legacy.

Second, this book places government at the fore of American expansion in the Northwest, synthesizing and advancing a growing historiography of the early American state in the trans-Appalachian West. Earlier studies of public administration by Leonard White and Malcolm Rohrbough established that federal policy and administration had clear effects on Americans. In the economy as well, Charles Sellers and John Lauritz Larson observed state power used to advance transportation networks nationally; Larson has termed it fittingly, "the positive use of government power for popular constructive purposes." Recently, William Bergmann has focused on the role of federal power in aiding Western economic development as well.[12] In other areas like Indian trade and diplomacy, defining cultural boundaries of citizenship, and state politics, the respective work of David Nichols, Bethel Saler, and Silvana Siddali has continued to observe the importance of government in overseeing and even altering the lives of both white and Native American inhabitants of the West.[13]

The Federalist Frontier builds upon all these aspects while incorporating innovations made by locals, especially in using military power and support for public education. Further, this book offers these disparate elements an overarching ideology. In this view, an alternative political tradition emerges that sought to use government power to positive ends for white American settlers. This book joins a growing body of scholarship that explodes the myth of the lone pioneer on the prairie scraping together a living without anyone's aid. Quite to the contrary, early American Westerners understood and appreciated government involvement.

Returning to Washington Street, the Ohio Company buildings illustrate these intentions perfectly. Campus Martius and Fort Harmar, which sat a mile down the Muskingum River, showed the commitment of federal and local leaders to conquering Indians and protecting settlers. After Wayne's Legion removed Indian threats in 1795 and the Ohio Company disbanded, Rufus Putnam made the cabin his base for recording features of the Ohio valley landscape and then measuring them for sale as U.S. Surveyor General. In 1800 the cabin became the new federal land office. In these capacities, the cabin was crucial to proper administration. As Richard White summed up the role of the state in American postbellum expansion onto the Great Plains, "Armies of the federal government conquered the region, agents of the federal government explored it, federal officials administered it, and federal bureaucrats supervised (or at least tried to supervise) the division and development of its resources."[14] That model unmistakably traces back to Marietta. In all its uses, the humble cabin projected federal power not just locally but more broadly across the United States.

Overall, Federalist administration of the Northwest rested on three major tenets. First, Federalists wanted energy in government after the Confederation period, or as Fischer argued similarly, they preached "maximal rather than minimal government." Decisive, powerful action was a prerequisite for effective government, so they enhanced national power through their policy choices in matters like public credit, taxation, a national bank, and promotion of domestic manufacturing, all guided by Alexander Hamilton. Finance lay at the heart of the Hamiltonian program, with credit from the First Bank of the United States providing essential resources for American business and government. Meanwhile, revenue from import duties and excise taxes went to fund new federal institutions and projects, all meant to encourage Americans to think in national terms and forsake the "excesses" of democracy.[15]

Second, eschewing laissez-faire capitalism, Federalists oriented government to guide and protect the growth of commercial markets. As Hamilton argued in 1787, the Constitution was written to guarantee "the good will of the commercial interest" and make the federal government "capable of regulating protecting and extending the commerce of the Union." Four years later, he wrote in the Report on Manufactures that commerce, manufacturing, and large-scale farming "not only occasion a positive augmentation of the Produce and Revenue of the Society, but that they contribute essentially to rendering them greater." Federalists hoped to achieve through wise leadership a model for reliable economic development and eventual prosperity.[16]

Finally, Federalists shared a strong sense of social order. As Linda Kerber argued persuasively, Federalists were always vigilant against the disintegration of their carefully created and still-fragile social order that deserved to be led by, John Adams said in 1790, "nobility . . . founded in nature." They were keenly aware of the upheaval created by the American Revolution and, according to Gordon Wood, believed strong regulation could guard against the creeping dangers of self-interest and excess democracy that threatened to turn republican liberty into license and lawlessness.[17] In other words, Federalists saw government as the guarantor of

liberty, and good government had the ability to banish the evils of demagoguery and anarchy from the land. Within this conception, leaders served
a higher purpose than voters could ever confer, so many Federalists came
to develop a negative attitude toward popularity. As historian John Miller
noted, they took pride in their "disdain of 'the vile love of popularity'" and
decided "order and stability must prevail." In short, the electorate was
fickle but Federalist principles were not.[18]

In the Northwest, leaders and citizens expressed these three
principles—energy in government, neo-mercantilist economics, and
well-ordered republican liberty—in multiple ways. The desire for energetic government made Federalist administration of the Ohio valley a
state-building venture. They hoped to give settlers what Ohio Company
speculator Manasseh Cutler termed "examples of government" meant to
"revive the ideas of order, citizenship, and the useful sciences" and secure
the fragile American hold on the region. If "government will forever accommodate them as much as their brethren on the east," Cutler wrote,
Westerners would not be "forming schemes of independence, [or] seeking
other connexions." Meanwhile, the Federalist desire for guiding economic development led territorial officials and land speculators in Ohio to attempt consciously to attract capital and men of means. Policies aimed at
commodifying land, aggressively protecting property rights, and building
internal improvements served those goals well. For example, Rufus Putnam called for new post roads to aid commerce and mail service, and he
wanted a canal between the Potomac and Ohio Rivers, a pet project for
George Washington as well.[19]

Federalist leaders also saw government as vital to building a respectable society in the Northwest. Putnam extolled government as "absolutely
necessary for the well being of any people, and the General Happiness
of Society," and the Ohio Company supported commercial growth and
small-scale manufacturing on their lands. However, they also wanted development to be guided by a landed elite to save Western society from the
eventual disruptions economic development would create. Perhaps the
clearest sign of Federalist respect for social order came from the governor
of the Northwest Territory, Arthur St. Clair. As he told the Ohio state constitutional convention of 1802, he only wanted to ensure "laws have been
executed faithfully" to allow government to imbue in settlers "the spirit of
obedience . . . and a love of order."[20]

Executing all these ideals took a variety of forms in the Northwest. Embrace of the military was the most conspicuous sign of Federalist policy

and ideology. Presidents George Washington and John Adams both believed a powerful, disciplined army would offer not only national security but assurances for effective federal government. Federalists also consistently argued for enlarging the military and were happy to see it used in Indian wars and in suppressing rowdy frontiersmen, even sending the U.S. Army door to door to evict squatters in present-day southern Ohio in the 1780s. Elsewhere, Federalists advocated for using federal force against the moribund Whiskey Rebellion in 1794 as well as the French at New Orleans in 1802–1803.[21] In these various approaches, Federalists used the military not only to prove federal capabilities but also to preserve social and political order. By offering such services, Rufus Putnam said, the federal government proved itself "a terror to evil doers, and a protection to Such as Shall do well."[22]

However, republics are never built on force alone. In the Northwest, military strength provided the early American state what sociologist Michael Mann has termed the state's despotic power, defined briefly as its ability to monopolize force. However, building legitimacy in a republic like the United States requires that the state also show its ability to make the rules of society, termed by Mann a state's infrastructural power. After all, Mann states, officials in a republic cannot "brazenly expropriate or kill their enemies" legitimately, nor can they "overturn legal traditions enshrining constitutional rule."[23] Thus, after it forced out squatters and Indians, the U.S. government needed other means to establish legitimacy among the new settlers.

These efforts to establish infrastructural power in the Northwest resulted in a variety of new institutions to oversee the flow of settlement, protect commercial interests, and encourage social cohesion. The land office represented the clearest sign of state intervention in civil society, as Western settlers interacted personally with federal power there. In time, government became the font of legitimate ownership and residency, and visiting the federal land office became a normal part of moving west and seeking independence through land ownership. Overall, the land office was not just a business but an agent of social change. Federalist land policy established a bureaucratic institution that standardized land measurement and ownership in the West while extending federal power. Manasseh Cutler termed this wise distribution of land as "Next to its conquest . . . the most important exercise of governmental power ever exerted in laying solid foundations for the American Republic." With government-backed titles, "every man could sit under his own vine and fig tree, with none to molest or make him afraid." Thirty years later, an English immigrant to Illinois, George Flower, concurred about the land office in his diary, "Disputes about title are avoided by this simple orderly proceeding."[24]

Federalists championed many other causes in order to bring prosperity and order to the frontier. As was mentioned earlier, Federalist officials and citizens pressed for a comprehensive transportation network to help economic development and to spread governmental influence. To preserve peace and discourage liquor sales, Federalists also pushed to control the Indian trade through various means, especially through the trade factory system that saw its greatest financial success in the Northwest. Federalists also became staunch advocates for public education in the West, contending that widely available education offered, in the words of Manasseh Cutler, "a most favorable aspect upon the settlement" and led to "the acquisition of useful knowledge placed upon a more respectable footing here, than in any other part of the world." He took pride in their commitment to education, too, telling settlers in Marietta that emphasizing education was a sign of energetic government, but it would also "lay the foundations for a well-regulated society" by "mak[ing] subjects conform to the laws."[25]

By establishing new institutions throughout the Northwest, frontier Federalism left two distinct political legacies. First, Westerners developed a state-friendly style of politics, with settlers coming to expect government to aid citizens in their ventures. Nowhere is this approach clearer than in Western attitudes toward internal improvements even after the Revolution of 1800. In 1818, for example, the overwhelmingly Republican Congressmen from Ohio and Indiana voted nearly unanimously in favor of hotly debated resolutions about internal improvements in the U.S. House. Based on statistics compiled by John Lauritz Larson, Western Congressmen were the staunchest supporters of resolutions that Congress should build national roads and canals, national defense justified public funding for them, and the elastic clause allowed Congress to build them for commercial development. In those votes, the Northwest proved to be the best friends of internal improvements outside of Henry Clay.[26]

Further, state legislatures in the Northwest embraced internal improvements earlier than the rest of the nation and paid for them with funded debts through state banks, all very clearly Hamiltonian measures. Western legislators, even Democrats, had few qualms about confronting Andrew Jackson directly when they demanded federal aid for local internal improvements, largely because they believed almost universally that government should aid economic development as much as possible.[27] The real question was not whether representatives should support internal improvements, but rather how enthusiastic they should be about them. Overall, Westerners embraced government involvement in internal improvements and other services like public education largely because they had become accustomed to the benefits of an energetic government spearheaded by Federalists.

Even as Federalist election losses mounted, their second important legacy remained: their distinct pro-state ideology. Western citizens often argued for a more powerful state because they had higher expectations of their government, and over time the frontier Federalist strain underwent a series of mutations to evolve into Western Whiggery by the 1830s. Federalists arrived in the Northwest during the 1780s and 1790s to build new societies and a new American state, and Western Whigs ultimately broadcast a political vision back east that embraced government power. Thus, the attitudes behind frontier Federalism were hewn into the new Western Whig politics. Taking cues from Federalist ideology, Whigs promoted energetic government, centralized economic development, and respect for legal and social order against the alleged demagoguery of Jacksonian Democrats. When examined from the perspective of policy, Federalist ideals remained salient in the Northwest well beyond the party's life and reached well into the nineteenth century and across the continent.

The Federalist Frontier in Outline

This book will examine Federalist administration and the legacies it left behind through six chapters and an epilogue. Chapter One, "A Contested Land: The Old Northwest in the 1780s," establishes the Northwest as a desirable but chaotic region in which American settlers, Indians, and European officials were already engaged in a decades-long rivalry. The Confederation Congress proved unequal to the challenge posed by the Northwest. Indians formed a new confederacy to oppose American expansion, and the British continued to advance their designs on the region. However, those difficulties did not stop future Federalists from seeking stronger government capable of controlling the Ohio valley's inhabitants, while speculators organized to construct their version of an ideal republican society along the north side of the Ohio River. In both cases, those plans made the Northwest a laboratory in which speculators and

Federalist authorities could test the abilities of the new federal government to actualize their ideals.

The next two chapters focus on Ohio during the Age of Federalism. Chapter Two, "'To Show All Lawless Adventurers': The Northwest Indian War, 1789–1795" discusses the Indian war Federalists like Henry Knox and Alexander Hamilton championed in the George Washington administration and culminated in victory at the Battle of Fallen Timbers. In the early 1790s, the war was an important issue that separated Federalists and Republicans, and it allowed Federalists to refine their political positions against an emerging opposition. Further, Federalists used the war to capture under federal institutions, especially the U.S. Army, Indian wars that had been administrative nightmares in the colonial and Confederation eras. Such a move showcased the promise behind federal power to open new lands for settlement and protect settlers in the Northwest Territory from Indian or British threats. Defeating the Indians also let speculators and federal officials implement their plans for a new society in Ohio, as detailed in Chapter Three, "The Speculator's Republic: Federalists in Territorial Ohio, 1787–1803." Speculators and officials cooperated to realign the Northwest along their shared vision for the new republic, reining in the social implications of the American Revolution with new institutions that protected speculator interests, enhanced American state power, and laid the groundwork for an orderly society that recognized limits to liberty. Though they lost elections by the end of the territorial period, this chapter argues that Federalist ideals and policies left clear imprints on the political discourse in the Buckeye State and the rest of the Old Northwest for decades.

The next two chapters cover the period of Republican ascendance that eventually saw the Federalists cease to be a national party. Chapter Four, "Energy and Republicanism: Jeffersonian Administration in Indiana and Illinois," centers on territorial governments in Indiana and Illinois. While historians commonly associate the victory of Jefferson with shrinking federal power and expenditures, the energetic Republicans of these territorial governments expanded and articulated institutions created by Federalists to govern Indiana and Illinois. They repurposed and augmented services like the federal land offices and the Indian trade factories, by which these energetic Republicans strengthened the presence of government for both white settlers and Indians. Further, the governor of the Indiana Territory,

William Henry Harrison, used Federalist-style approaches to Indian policy and warfare he learned in the 1790s to clear Indian title and ultimately Indian people from the way of settlers. Through his work, the War of 1812 became a fight for regional security and an unmitigated victory for the United States in the war. Chapter Five, "'Our Strength Is Our Union': Federalists in Ohio, 1803–1815," shifts the focus to partisan politics in the new state as Republicans maintained power there. Overall, political discussions often occurred within the frame of Federalist policies, as both parties enthusiastically promoted public education and state-led economic development. Meanwhile, some Federalists continued pursuing their goals for civil society by establishing schools and libraries privately, while party members distanced themselves from their eastern counterparts on many issues that allowed them to survive beyond the War of 1812.

The final chapter and epilogue trace the legacies of Federalists in the Northwest and the emergence of a new political alliance in the Whig Party. Chapter Six, "From Frontier Federalists to Western Whigs: The Rise of a New Coalition," looks at the so-called Era of Good Feelings and the emergence of the Second Party System in the young states of Ohio, Indiana, and Illinois. Federalists had crumbled as a national party, but their approaches to active government intervention in the economy gained traction as the Panic of 1819 crippled countless businesses. By this period, Westerners clearly had a different relationship with government, as they had come to expect more from their government and continued to seek other avenues for state power to benefit citizens. Eventually, three distinct groups converged into the Whig Party in the Northwest: longtime Federalists who continued in Ohio (with some even winning office in the 1830s), energetic Republicans, and a new generation who benefitted from government institutions in the West. They united behind Federalist-tinged policies that supported economic development, transportation projects, public education, and a society that respected the rule of law. Those values were also broadcast nationally by the 1830s with Westerners gaining prominence on the national stage. The epilogue examines this Western Whig alliance's most successful scion in "Up the Capitol Steps: Abraham Lincoln and the New Western Whigs." In Abraham Lincoln, the old values of the Federalist frontier found a grand champion in the eventual President, and recognizing this relationship helps to reveal the long-range contributions of the Federalist Party to American politics and society.

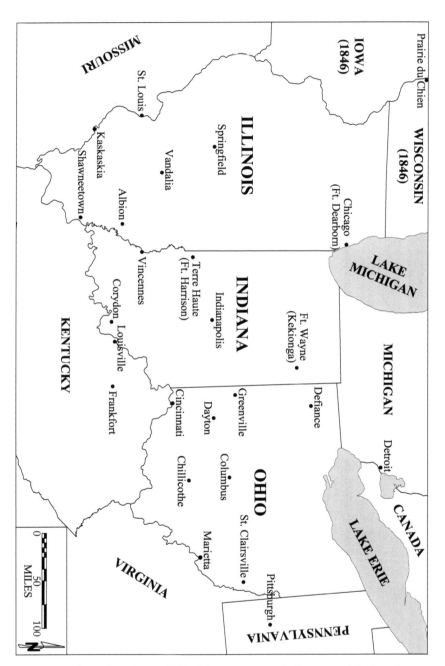

FIGURE 2. Ohio Valley Towns, 1830s. This map is a guide for many of the locations discussed in this book. The dates under Wisconsin and Iowa indicate their year of statehood, which came after the focus of this book. Map created by the author.

CHAPTER ONE

A Contested Land

The Ohio Valley in the 1780s

In the summer of 1786, the *Pittsburgh Gazette* published one of the wildest fishing stories in early American history. After a day of fishing in the Ohio River, a U.S. Army officer claimed to have caught a catfish twelve feet long and of extraordinary proportions. "His feet were two feet a part, and I judge his mouth must have been 13 inches in diameter," he recounted, "and surpassed every thing I ever heard of . . . the catfish of Ohio." Upon cutting open the fish, he discovered to his horror, "the thigh and leg of a man" complete with a boot, "a square canteen . . . [with] two bottles full of liquor, one of sherry wine, and the other of excellent spirit, with a number of other things." In a self-aware moment, the officer ended his story about this less fortunate Jonah in the great fish because he feared stretching the truth too much for his friend. After all, he admitted, "the story carries already a completion of improbabilities."[1]

The story also urged caution. The correspondent advised readers considering coming to the Ohio valley, "the greatest misfortune a man can experience on this river, is to fall from a steep bank into the hands of such an unmerciful creature." The end of his letter reinforced his call for care by recounting a murder in the area. The two accused men claimed that the victim died accidentally, but no one believed them. They had a simple motive of stealing servants, slaves, or "a sum of money with [the victim] to purchase some land."[2] In this letter, the Ohio valley appeared fraught with danger, and travelers to the region always had to watch for natural and human hazards.

These tales revealed the prevailing outlook that drove land speculation and attempts to govern what became the Northwest Territory in the 1780s. Soldiers, government officials, and speculators shared with the region's settlers an image of the Ohio valley as a land of plenty where prosperity awaited adventurers and entrepreneurs able to tame the land. The or giant catfish was a symbol of that promise, too.[3] Turning the waterways into productive commercial arteries offered more wealth than any pursuits back east during the depression of the 1780s, but the stories of the catfish and of the murder also relayed the peril of the enterprise. To be tamed, the Ohio River valley required decisive actions and wise government. Bringing order to the region and its new residents would be difficult for investors and prospective leaders of new Western settlements, but the potential rewards more than compensated for the risks.

However, those western lands Americans regarded with such enthusiasm were also the site of an intense, transatlantic contest in the 1780s. In addition to the Confederation Congress, squatters and New England speculators competed with one another to settle the land and form new states that reflected very different visions of an American future. Meanwhile, Indians and European powers hoped to retain their homes or regain their (often nominal) political control, respectively. British officials were already working with Indians to resist American settlement as well, maintaining posts on American soil as a sign to Indian allies that they were staying. Furthermore, many British officials hoped to establish a buffer state between British Canada and the United States, a project that continued until the War of 1812.[4] Driven by political and religious motives, Indians living north of the Ohio and east of the Mississippi sought to build a confederacy that could halt or even turn back the advancement of white settlers. Spain looked to seal off the Mississippi River from American trade as well, with an ultimate plan to impede American westward expansion and possibly even take U.S. territory west of the Appalachians. To that effect, Spanish officials corresponded in secret with Gen. James Wilkinson and federal judge Harry Innes into the 1790s, hoping to separate Kentucky from the United States.[5]

The officials who eventually formed the center of Federalist authority in the Northwest Territory believed that decisive and powerful responses were the only way to quell these challenges to American control northwest of the Ohio River. They argued that only a strong military would secure American control against the Indians and protect American claims against British and Spanish machinations. They also sought to replace those Indians with exemplary citizens through programmatic means. With plans to remake the Northwest Territory by defining respectability in everything from republican citizenship to living space, these officials understood the transatlantic contest for the Ohio valley as a challenge to American statehood. To emerge victorious, the new United States would have to build a stronger national state capable of regulating all the region's inhabitants and the events that occurred therein.

As a result, American officials in the contested Northwest pursued two major strategies in the 1780s. First, they attempted to assert control over the Indian inhabitants of the region, seeking to dispossess the native population and squeeze out foreign competitors who relied on Indian allies to achieve their policy goals. Because of their tactless approach to Indian diplomacy in the 1780s, however, American actions exacerbated resentment among Indians and contributed to unrestrained hostilities between Indians and settlers by the end of the 1780s. Second, the national government, speculators, and soldiers looked to control the settlers flocking into the region after the Revolutionary War. Demonstrating their authority over the settlers would establish the United States as the sole legitimate power in the Northwest. In pursuing this goal, national government officials laid the groundwork for an American state that would rise over the Northwest and all American westward expansion.

A Tale of Two Confederacies
Indians and the U.S. in the Northwest

When the United States gained what became the Northwest Territory in 1783, the new nation was merely the latest entrant into a bitter and complex contest for the region that was already a half-century old. American officials and soldiers joined Indian inhabitants, European officials, French settlers, and newly arriving American settlers in a struggle of competing visions that bred hostility. Securing this new territory for the United States government required assertive policies and decisive actions, but the Confederation Congress was not up to the task. Attempts to take a tough stance in Indian negotiations yielded few positive results, and unwittingly aided Indians in the Northwest who were seeking unity in a broad confederacy. By the late 1780s, the deteriorating situation underlined for many future Federalists that the region—and the nation at large—demanded a strong national state able to demonstrate its authority across the entirety of its territory.

The eighteenth-century Ohio River valley had become a refuge for various peoples displaced by British colonization. The Beaver Wars pushed most Indians out of present-day Kentucky and Ohio by the late 1600s, and some Native Americans returned early in the 1700s. Between 1730 and 1760, the Delaware, Mingo, Wyandot, and many other members of the eventual Northwest Indian confederacy migrated west into the Ohio valley after British colonists upset their trading and hunting patterns. By 1750, the Shawnee held major towns along the Ohio and its tributaries, resettling lands they had called home before the Beaver Wars.[6] The Ohio valley also held out promise for colonists. Small numbers of French settlers came to present-day Indiana and Illinois in the early 1700s, and British colonists of various ethnicities poured into the Ohio valley once Britain claimed most of North America after the French and Indian War. By the mid-1770s, up to fifty thousand squatters had settled along Ohio valley waterways, especially south of the Ohio River, in defiance of local Indians and the Proclamation of 1763.[7]

The Revolutionary War escalated the struggle for control over the Ohio River valley, and the fighting showed the need for a stronger American state presence. The war revealed the absence of state authority in the region, especially as British and American troops were sparse. Only around 500 British troops staffed Great Lakes posts at the outset of the war, while George Rogers Clark's expedition with 1,300 frontier militia represented the strongest American military presence in the Northwest. Meanwhile, the only clear effort from the new United States to administer and defend the region came from Virginia, which created a handful of new counties to allow locals clamoring for aid and protection to coordinate their defenses more effectively. However, no level of government could offer much to prevent violence against settlers. As a result, Indians and white Kentuckians attacked each other with greater ferocity as the war carried on, with Indians effectively closing the Ohio River to American traffic after 1779. In the end, the war did not clarify the claims the new nation held to the Northwest: British regulars remained at Detroit and elsewhere, and settlers remained imperiled.[8]

For the Indians of the Northwest, the Revolutionary War was much more consequential. From the start, both British and American commanders realized Indians were the linchpin to the war in the West, and they had to adhere to local Indian customs and understandings of diplomacy in order to compete for Indian loyalties. In fact, Washington wanted to capture Detroit to disrupt British supplies of gifts and weapons, which he believed would prevent an estimated 8,000 Indian warriors from joining the British. Such a campaign never occurred, but his assessments and his desire to attack so remote a location testified to the key role Indians played in the conflict. Given the incursions of American settlers, most Indians in the region sided with the British but never unanimously or consistently. Decisions over which side to aid—or to be neutral—divided nations in the Ohio River valley, and elevated war chiefs in Indian politics as they led warriors who supported them. Further, the irregular flow of European goods correlated to waxing and waning Indian support for both sides, with dependency on European weapons, alcohol, and other goods affecting choices as well.[9]

Ultimately, the Revolutionary War resolved little in the Northwest, and American officials took an aggressive diplomatic stance in hopes of bringing their authority to the region without bloodshed. The Treaty of Paris made no mention of Indians or their fate, leaving open the possibility of continued hostilities between settlers and Indians. British officials also promised Indians they were not leaving, giving evidence of their hopes to revive the Covenant Chain by maintaining their forts on American soil. Meanwhile, the continued arrival of American settlers—the pace of which increased during the war—directly threatened Indians of the Northwest. Hoping to defuse the situation, Congress declared an end to hostilities with Indian nations in April 1783, and the next month they sent diplomats to inform Ohio valley Indians of the war's end and the new authority of the United States. Borrowing the long-standing customs and language of the Middle Ground, the diplomats also told Indians that the Americans were their new "father."[10] Such a claim was a direct challenge to the British as well. By arrogating the title, Americans symbolically declared themselves the preeminent white interest in the Ohio valley.

These demands for respect from Indians dovetailed with American diplomatic claims to the Northwest based on the right of conquest. As George Washington explained the position to James Duane in September 1783, "after a Contest of eight years . . . Britain has ceded all the Lands of the United States," so the Indians who were British allies "share[d] their fortune." Therefore, Indians lost all claim to the Northwest, and thus "their true Interest and safety must now depend upon *our* friendship."[11] By mid-October, a Congressional committee that included Duane agreed, imagining the trans-Appalachian West as a site for settlement and trade that could also be a "bounty to their army" as well as "a fund towards the security and payment of the national debt." Noting the numerous wartime attacks on Western settlements and the expenses of retaliatory campaigns, the committee declared that Indians sided with Britain and had no "reasonable objections . . . to make atonement for the enormities which they have perpetuated" by accepting the boundaries laid out in the Treaty of Paris.[12]

This official attitude of the United States saw Indians of the Northwest as mere subjects of a superior U.S. government with no real right to refuse American demands, especially for land. As a result, treaties concluded just after the Revolutionary War employed stilted language investing all power in the United States. In the 1785 Treaty of Fort McIntosh, for example, the U.S. agreed to "give peace" to the Chippewa, Delaware, Ottawa, and Wyandot. Indian signers also agreed to negotiate solely with the U.S. and to be "under the protection of the United States, and of no other sovereign whatsoever." In return, the U.S. agreed to "allot" land between the Muskingum and Miami Rivers to the Indians.[13] This language did two things. First, it defined Indian affairs as an internal matter, giving a protection of international law (as it existed) for American dealings with Indians to the exclusion of European powers. Second, and more importantly, these treaties revealed that American diplomats steadily ignored Indian claims to the Ohio valley and their right to refuse American demands. Peace talks yielded little of substance, with Indians resuming raids on Ohio River travelers and Kentucky settlements by 1784 and negotiations largely faded away within the next few years.[14]

Treaties also proved ineffective because the national government was only one of many white voices in the region, leading to frustration Indians did not hide. In fact, the national government only participated in eleven of twenty-one treaties concluded between American representatives and Native people between 1783 and 1786, with the others made with state governments or private speculators. Meanwhile, treaties and signers often faced scorn in Indian communities. For example, many Iroquois castigated the signers of the second Treaty of Fort Stanwix in 1784, concerned that the signers abdicated both the leadership the Six Nations had among Indians in the West and the confederacy's role as mediators in white-Indian disputes. Indians of the Ohio valley also wanted to speak to a unified voice for American interests by the mid-1780s, hoping to create a lasting and binding peace with the white invaders. Such a unified voice would have been helpful, as David Nichols has recently argued effectively, with Indian peoples whose emotional wounds from war were yet to heal.[15]

Hoping to frustrate the naked ambitions behind American mandates and to counter American diplomatic tactics, Northwestern Indians had formed their own confederacy by 1786. Developing a trade and communication center at Kekionga along the Maumee River and building on the precedent of Pontiac and with British blessing, the confederacy adopted

simple principles to preserve their homes. They insisted most prominently on two items, that the Ohio River was the only proper Indian-white
boundary and that Americans negotiate with them in common. "All treaties . . . should be carried on with the general voice of the whole confederacy," they insisted in November, and they also asked the national
government to "order your surveyors and others, that mark out lands, to
cease from crossing the Ohio." Such demands represented their unity,
protected their land claims, and sought to avoid piecemeal cessions that
may or may not be signed by those who physically occupied the land. In
addition, the confederacy hoped negotiating as one would check the arro-
gant position of American diplomats, who they said "kindled your council
fires where you thought proper, without consulting us . . . and have entirely neglected our plan."[16] Unlike other pan-Indian movements of the
period, this confederacy happily received European goods and was open
to European influence, but member nations ferociously defended their
lands and political autonomy. In short, the confederacy was a pragmatic
political alliance with a distinct anti-American tincture that mirrored the
anti-Indian stance taken by the new American republic. Congress claimed
to be the sole legitimate power with Indians in the 1780s, and the nascent
Northwest confederacy countered by claiming to be the sole legitimate
Native negotiating entity.[17]

The continued immigration of American settlers fractured the already
difficult diplomatic relationship even further. After all, each settler's arrival meant more forest cleared, more crops planted, and more competition
for hunting. Settling mostly in present-day Kentucky, these settlers came
in numbers alarming to Indians. For example, between October 1786
and June 1788, American officers stationed along the Ohio River counted
more than 630 boats and over 12,000 settlers heading west. These new
settlers exacerbated the interracial violence that the U.S. government was
failing to contain. One resident of Vincennes testified to the vacuum of
authority when he asked Army commander Josiah Harmar for a garrison
because residents were "ignorant of what authority we lived under," nor
did they wish to "be prey of vagabonds." An American traveler remarked
that Vincennes residents "appear rather to favour the Indians than the
Americans" after a winter "more troublesome . . . than I ever knew." Major
John Hamtramck assessed simply that American government was "in great
confusion. . . . I never saw so injudicious administration."[18] In every sense,
the national government had failed in the Northwest. Indians, Europeans,

and even American settlers pursued their own agendas without regard to national officials, and the results were disastrous.

In response, officials needed a new direction to build legitimacy in the Northwest, which many historians have seen as a kinder diplomacy style after 1786. Conquest diplomacy failed, as Dorothy V. Jones argued in a typical example of this interpretation, because Americans could not "Pressur[e] the Indians into agreements that would allow for white expansion" on equitable terms. Instead, the U.S. made appeals as "one sovereign group to other sovereign groups."[19] American diplomats indeed offered to buy land after 1786, and Congress appropriated $14,000 in 1787 to "extinguish the Indian claim" by charging Arthur St. Clair with the task of concluding new treaties in the Northwest.[20] While a few gifts and land purchases represented a cosmetic shift in Indian policy, American officials did not abandon the underlying assumption that Indians were subordinate. Purchase may have been more equitable, but according to American understanding, those negotiations were hardly between equal sovereign powers.

That incongruity showed in arguments for enlarging the military to pacify the Northwest. Henry Knox asked continually for a larger, professionalized military capable of ending violence in the Ohio valley since his appointment as Secretary of War in 1785, and by March 1787 he wanted new posts along the Ohio River to "induce a confidence in the protection of the United States" against Indian raids. By July, Knox took a binary position on the growing violence: "Either one or the other party must remove to a greater distance." To defeat the Indians, he wanted to increase the size of the U.S. Army to 1,500 men who would occupy forts running the entire Ohio River and ensure "complete protection of the frontiers, and other objects . . . in the western territory." That show of force, he argued, would at once "awe the savages, cover the surveyors and . . . prevent intrusions on the public lands."[21] For Knox, the simmering conflict offered a clear opportunity to assert American power and bring order to its unruly Western lands.

Unfortunately for Knox, the national government was simply unequal to the task. The Secretary of War lamented the national government's weakness and anticipated federalist arguments after the Constitutional Convention. He believed his plan "the most rational that can be devised," but the "embarrassed state of public affairs and entire deficiency of funds" for the Confederation Congress made it impossible. Given the political situation, he observed, "An indian war of any considerable extent and duration would most exceedingly distress the United States."[22] With a national government too ill-equipped to bring order to the Northwest, Knox had to make do with six hundred men in what the *Boston Gazette* called a "a feeble line . . . from Fort-Pitt to the [Ohio] rapids" at Louisville.[23] Worse, that paltry force was overwhelmed by the massive influx of white squatters, and it could not police against Indian raiders effectively. To Knox, the conflict in the Northwest demanded a forceful response, which the national government could never offer.

White Westerners linked Indian policy to a stronger American military presence, too. In January 1786, a Western correspondent to the *Pennsylvania Mercury* of Philadelphia wished for "such a force against the savages as will awe them to peace" to avoid "abandon[ing] their views of surveying and selling the foederal lands on the north-west of the Ohio River."[24] Colonel Josiah Harmar agreed, telling Knox that Indian raids left Kentuckians "in great dread of the savages." The solution was simple: "a respectable garrison of regular troops established in the heart of the Indian country . . . would keep the Indians in awe." He added a few months later that "troops will have a peculiar good effect" on the public order of the region. After all, soldiers could "deter several people from Kentucky and other parts from taking up the public lands," which he saw as a key source of conflict.[25]

Western settlers also found the situation simply becoming too desperate to allow events to continue as they had by 1787, and they sought state help to guarantee their survival. Indian attacks on settlers around Louisville prompted a petition signed by fifty-four people to neighboring counties begging for "aid to revenge the injuries we have already suffered and to prevent those with which we are every day threatened." They only asked, they said, "in defense of the lives of ourselves, our wives and helpless infants, who without your friendly interposition will most probably fall a prey to Savage Barbarity." Another settler warned Virginia governor, Edmund Randolph, of the "distressed situation of this part of the State." He feared that any "farther Temporizing of any kind with the Indians" would lead to "Inevitable Destruction." After all, "Numbers have been massacred" and those not yet evacuated "are Collected in Forts, so that it is entirely out of their Power to Raise any thing for the support of their families."[26] These settlers did not ask the national government for help, whether because of recent U.S. Army evictions of squatters or because they did not believe the national government could do much. Regardless, the lack of security and appeals for aid did not bode well for American prospects in the Ohio valley.

Congressional feebleness led future Federalist administrators to feel a sense of urgency, and they argued vigorously that Congress must act quickly and decisively in the West. In pursuit of their goals, they developed concrete positions in favor of enlarging the military, guaranteeing public order in the Ohio valley, and quickly expropriating Indian lands. As early as 1783, George Washington wanted a stronger military to "give security to our frontiers" as well as "awe the Indians, and more than probably prevent the murder of many innocent families."[27] In 1786, the *Pennsylvania Mercury* published similar arguments for stronger government over the Northwest, reflecting Knox's advice to Congress for an enlarged regular army. Further, the newspaper, which later became a staunchly pro-ratification newspaper, opined that "some confederation" was needed in the national government to "effect this force, and give a tone to our treaties."[28]

John Jay and Alexander Hamilton joined the chorus by 1787, arguing in the *Federalist Papers* that the Constitution would allow a stronger government presence in the Northwest and elsewhere. Jay illustrated his complaints about the national government in *Federalist* number 3 by arguing that Congress was impotent in restraining Western violence, with Indian raids "provoked by the improper conduct of individual States . . . unable or unwilling to restrain or punish offenses" that led to "the slaughter of many innocent inhabitants." He also believed the West was particularly vulnerable because of its proximity to British and Spanish colonies. Settlers would have "a quick sense of apparent interest or injury" and would "most likely . . . excite war with those nations." The cure was simple. As he declared, "nothing can so effectually obviate that danger as a national government."[29]

Hamilton offered a stronger case for energetic national government to control the West in *Federalist* numbers 7 and 24. Like Washington and Jay, Hamilton believed national power would prevent the region from becoming "an ample theater for hostile pretensions without any umpire" in which "the sword would sometimes be appealed to as the arbiter of their differences." In *Federalist* number 24, he interlinked westward expansion, a larger military, and energetic government explicitly. Potential British and Spanish competition for western territories necessitated giving the new government the ability to create a national military, as closing out that competition required a muscular Indian policy that employed the military. To prevent "a common interest" from forming between European powers and Indians in the Ohio valley, Hamilton thought that "The savage tribes on our Western frontier ought to be regarded as our natural enemies . . . because they have the most to fear from us."[30]

Hamilton had a clear vision for the new American army, too: "small garrisons on our Western frontier" in a series of forts staffed by either state militias or a "permanent corps in the pay of the government." However, he reasoned based on his Continental Army service, militiamen would not serve longer tours of duty far from home. Worse, taking them from home would harm economic development because "the loss of labor and disconcertion of the industrious pursuits" would prove "ruinous to private citizens." Therefore, Hamilton settled on a peacetime standing army that could grow when "expedient . . . in some ratio to the force by which our Western settlements might be annoyed" as well as "facilitate future invasions" to assert American control in the Ohio valley.[31] By Hamilton's reckoning, the new Constitution meant not only an orderly form of government but also the army Henry Knox had always wanted.

The conflict for the Ohio River valley had become a quagmire for the United States in the 1780s, and future Federalists like Hamilton, Jay, and Knox responded in two ways. First, turmoil proved the need for enhanced national power. Problems in the Western territories only grew worse under the existing national government, and solving those problems required a strong central government. Second, the Northwest was a good place to start establishing the power of the new U.S. government and extending its influence. As historian Max Edling noted in his study of government finance in the 1780s and 1790s, proponents of a strong central government had to build one without raising the ire of voters in the original thirteen states. Thus, the state had to be "both inconspicuous and light." Quite simply, building federal institutions hundreds of miles away was very inconspicuous, and there the U.S. government could prove its capabilities while impacting relatively few citizens.[32]

The Ohio valley had been a primary theater in which the national government proved its incompetence in the 1780s. Congress barreled into the Northwest with a forceful Indian policy but no military force to back it, and it was unable to prevent its own citizens from further harming the situation. In turn, the national government's ineptitude in understanding or controlling the long fight for the Northwest created a precarious moment. A new Indian confederacy had formed, British traders and officials were still operating freely, and settlers begged for help that did not come. In such a seemingly hopeless situation, future Federalists saw an opportunity. The Northwest may have suffered from a humiliating series of mistakes at the hands of the national government, but it could soon become the site of a grand victory for federal power and the American people.

Schemers and Dreamers
Settlers, Speculators, and the State in the 1780s

While the Confederation Congress formed its plans for the Northwest in 1783, Colonel Rufus Putnam was already working with other Continental Army officers on plans to remake the region and strengthen the new American government. Assessing the future of the army after the war, he recommended a series of Western forts "To keep the Western savages in awe, [and] to protect and regulate our Trade with them." Even better, that military presence would provide protection and "Incouragement not only to those who have lands on this Side the Ohio but also to Such as may obtain grants on the other Side." In turn, using the army to control Western residents of all races would allow the U.S. to take advantage of the Ohio valley's farmland. "Within a few years," he hoped, farmers there might "Feed all our Garisons in the Western World," who would in turn "render that whole Frontear perfectly Secure against every forreign Enemy and the Savages."[33] Years before he headed west to Marietta with the Ohio Company of Associates, Putnam was already agitating for a powerful military—and thereby, a conspicuous government presence—in the trans-Appalachian West.

In June 1783, Putnam sent a petition to General Washington that also suggested a maximalist approach to governing the Northwest. Timothy Pickering (later Washington's Secretary of War in 1795 and Secretary of State for Washington and John Adams from 1796 to 1800) had gained signatures from 288 other officers and asked Congress to grant land in the eastern half of present-day Ohio to "Such of the army as wish to become adventurers in the new government." It was meant to help settlers, too, by including "conditions of settlement, & purchess, for public securities" for grantees. These payments in land would offset debts to creditors and veterans as well. Soon after, these grantees would seek statehood and make the Northwest "of lasting consequence to the *American Empire*."[34]

Washington approved, extoling to Congress the coherent plan to "connect our Governments with the frontiers" and implant the national government in numerous affairs. The petition also called for a government-sponsored system of trading posts to regulate the Indian trade and encourage commerce for white settlers. The petitioners even recommended what became the rectangular survey system, dividing the land into townships of six mile squares with portions of each township given to aid education and churches.[35] Congress never acted on it, but clearly, Putnam and Pickering were already imagining the Northwest as a venue for establishing and expanding American state power. Undeterred, they kept alive their hopes to build a commercial empire in the Northwest via land speculation throughout the 1780s.

These officers proceeded with their plans based on their conceptions of public service and republicanism. On one level, they saw Western lands as due compensation for wartime service. Many Continentals were owed back pay, and officers served anyway while making further sacrifices; Arthur St. Clair, for example, spent $1,800 of his own money to pay re-enlistment bonuses in 1776. In a sense, the plan made land in the Ohio country acceptable payment in lieu of cash from a deeply indebted U.S. government. In addition, their upbringing taught them that they could reasonably expect gratitude from a Congress and a nation they had self-lessly served for years. As Gordon Wood summarized well, Americans of the Revolutionary era regarded service to government as "personal sacrifice required of certain gentlemen because of their talents, independence, and social preeminence."[36] Socially and politically, their sacrifices made officers into gentlemen worthy of respect from Congress and their fellow citizens.

These self-styled respectable men had to suffer the further indignity of watching squatters occupy the Ohio valley in ever larger numbers and brazenly seek statehood for their illegal settlements. By 1782, squatters along the Muskingum River and in Kentucky talked about forming new states, and one writer warned Governor Benjamin Harrison of Virginia that without "regular administration of civil government . . . everything will be in utter confusion."[37] Another attempt to create a new state came in 1785, when a March advertisement informed settlers of a May election for a constitutional convention. The plan was in open defiance of a 1783 Congressional order forbidding settlement on land claimed by Indians without express Congressional permission. However, the advertiser defied national authority over the issue. "All mankind . . . have an undoubted right to pass into every vacant country, and there to form their constitution," he claimed, and "Congress is not allowed to forbid them, neither is Congress empowered . . . to make any sale of the uninhabited lands to pay the public debts."[38] These attempts at statehood were ignored farther east, but the Confederation Congress was largely inert against the continued incursions of illegal settlers.

From the Atlantic states, the former officers and future Federalists saw this squatter invasion of the Ohio country as evidence of the broader loosening of social ties in Revolutionary-era America. Congress could not reverse the deteriorating situation in the Ohio River valley, frustrating observers who hoped not only for peace with Indians but for orderly white settlement there. The attempt to recreate the Proclamation of 1763 (with just as much enforcement) in autumn 1783 ended in failure, as squatters simply ignored the Congressional edict without legal consequences. Worse, the first seven ranges of townships established by the Ordinance of 1785 were not offered for sale until September 1787 because increasingly hostile Indians constantly interrupted survey crews.[39] Even attempts to control trade with Indians in August 1786 did little. A new law required anyone who wished to trade with Indians to obtain a recommendation from his home state's governor and post a $3,000 bond, a definite attempt to assert national control in the trans-Appalachian West, but few complied and illicit trade continued unabated.[40]

Still more galling, Congress refused to act on Continental veterans' requests for aid or pensions. During the 1780s, many of those veterans went broke during the postwar depression or were forced to depend on government positions for their livelihood. For example, after losing his wealth in the war effort, Arthur St. Clair relied on his salary as a collector of city revenues for Philadelphia. Even toward the end of his tenure as Northwest Territory Governor in 1802, he wrote that he needed his government salary because of debts he accrued while in office. Believing public service involved private sacrifices that should be appreciated, he told President Jefferson his work as Governor "swallowed up much, indeed, nearly all, of my private funds. . . . I may have been sacrificing to vanity, though I have not been sensible of it."[41]

The lack of opportunities in a society apparently turned on its head and crippled by an economic depression represented another major problem to future Federalists. Upon returning home, many former Continentals faced economic difficulties. After he "served with credit" as an officer, Robert Oliver of Massachusetts, who later served in the Northwest Territory legislature, returned to a weak economy that left him "destitute of the means of subsistence, and without an occupation." Meanwhile, veteran Solomon Drowne of Rhode Island and later of Ohio studied and spent "a pretty good estate" to become a doctor, but poor prospects led him to run a pharmacy with his sisters during the 1780s. He found his station in life degrading, grousing that he was "superseded or supplanted in so many instances, or to experience almost every species of slight and neglect" in 1780s America.[42]

Solomon Drowne spoke as a man not only victimized by hard times but insulted by his social inferiors. He believed there was worth in his status as an educated gentleman who served his countrymen during the Revolution. As Gordon Wood has pointed out, men in Revolutionary America became gentlemen by distinguishing themselves in education, occupation, or public service. Drowne had done exactly that. Once he became a gentleman, he had to guard his reputation jealously to save the economic power and psychological advantages of elevated status. According to Craig Bruce Smith, men like Drowne regarded the difficulties Continental officers encountered in receiving back pay as a dishonor to their service and their standing.[43] In the hard times of the 1780s, Drowne found no value in his status, and it upset him deeply. He may have survived years of warfare, but postwar life was apparently too difficult for gentlemen and veterans like Drowne and Oliver to navigate.

The Ohio valley held out promise, but only if they could reestablish an orderly society there. Squatters were too unprincipled and self-interested to be a strong social bedrock, so gentlemen had to cleanse the region of the illegal settlers and their inadequate ideals. To resolve those problems, George Washington revived the Continental officers' plan by prescribing a program of internal improvements and more energetic government in the Ohio valley. In October 1784, he declared, "The Western settlers . . . stand as it were upon a pivot—the touch of a feather, would turn them any way," largely because "they have no other means of coming to us but by a long Land transportation & unimproved roads." They also lacked "excitements to labour," and without improved transportation and reliable markets, the West's potential would go unfulfilled. Canals linking the Potomac and Ohio Rivers, among others, would accelerate communication and invigorate commerce. In turn, Western settlers would work harder, maximize the region's economic potential, and appreciate American authority.[44]

Washington suggesting that squatters needed encouragement to industry and loyalty also implied that they had not yet overcome self-interest and license. Both vices shaded Federalist characterizations of squatters, especially when they were compared to Indians. Eighteenth-century Americans conceived of Indians at the boundaries of civilization and outside of European-style states, defining what was savage against the refinement and civilization of respectable white Americans. Thus, when Indian commissioner and later Northwest Territory Judge Samuel Parsons denounced Western squatters as "our *own* white Indians of no character . . . without Regard to public benefits to Serve," he criticized them on two fronts.[45] He obviously denounced their self-interest, but calling them Indians also connoted that squatters were less than civilized and had transgressed the bounds of respectability.

Others who wrote about the trans-Appalachian West connected squatters and Indians more explicitly. U.S. Army officer William North wrote during his service along the Muskingum River in 1786 that the Westerners were "back woods men, as much savages as those they are to fight against." With their presence, he explained, "Foederal lands will remain unsold & the little measures of the United States be made less, by the Destruction of the frontiers" while they flouted national authority. Writers also used a common term, "banditti," for both Indians and white squatters who ignored national policy. For example, Manasseh Cutler did not hide his hostility in 1787 when saying he wished to see "no vacant land exposed to be seized by such lawless banditti as usually infest the frontiers."[46] That word infestation reveals a conception of squatters and Indians as not simply backward, but also as pests to be eliminated from the Ohio valley.

In this period, the U.S. Army often treated squatters like Indians: they took military action against them as rebels who had ignored the wishes of national officials. Those efforts began as early as autumn 1779, when Colonel Daniel Broadhead reported from Fort Pitt that sixty men "cross[ed] the River . . . to apprehend some of the principal trespassers and destroy the[ir] Hutts."[47] By 1785, the Army escalated its enforcement against the squatters. In March, Josiah Harmar ordered Ensign John Armstrong to "dispossess sundry persons, who had presumed to settle on the lands of the United States on the western side of the Ohio River." Armstrong also posted broadsides warning against further settlement, but squatters were still "moving to the unsettled counties by the forties and fifties." By autumn, the Army built Fort Harmar at the Muskingum and Ohio River confluence to dissuade new squatters and to quell rising Indian-white violence, but the destroyed settlements were already rebuilt. Thus, Captain Hamtramck led another expedition to evict squatter banditti and destroy their homes the next year.[48]

Removing a human "infestation" required an active state response. John Armstrong suggested as much in his spring 1785 report, saying "sensible men" told him, "if the honorable the Congress do not fall on some speedy method to prevent people from settling on the lands of the United States . . . that country will soon be inhabited by a banditti whose actions are a disgrace to human nature." Secretary of War Henry Knox also fretted about the squatters, "If such audacious defiance of the power of the United States be suffered with impunity a precedent will be established, to wrest all the immense property of the western territory out of the hands of the public." Without such an assertion of authority, many other future Federalists worried the Ohio valley could be lost entirely to European rivals or breakaway republics. Worse, with too few soldiers stretched over too long a distance to control the region's residents, Congress could not stop it.[49]

By 1787, national officials and would-be speculators settled on two interlinked solutions to change the tenor of westward expansion and American postwar society, and both reflected Putnam's and Pickering's original plans in 1783. First, a stronger military could quash the growing problems that birthed the Northwest Indian confederacy as well as act against the white squatters who, they believed, were the primary source of tension with the Indians. As Harmar explained from the Ohio country, "a respectable garrison of regular troops established in the heart of the Indian country . . . would keep the Indians in awe, and, in a great measure, secure the frontier inhabitants."[50] Second, New England gentlemen acting as private citizens would replace the Indians and squatters with a more peaceable and law-abiding population. These respectable settlers could then create the political and social institutions needed to build a more virtuous republican society in the Northwest. In short, they wanted to use political means to engineer a new Ohio valley society to ensure squatters never again undermined national prerogatives.

Congress lacked the resources and the inclination to act, so future Federalists from New England took the initiative. As gentlemen who possessed republican virtue and had high hopes for the national government, they formed a land speculation outfit in 1786 to do the work Congress could not and make a handsome profit, too. Organized as the Ohio Company of Associates, this group of New Englanders laid out a plan for "purchasing LANDS in the western territory (belonging to the United States) for the benefit of the company and to promote a settlement in that country." Settlement hardly needed promotion, but it did need firm guidance. Naturally, members of the Society of the Cincinnati who founded the Ohio Company offered that leadership. Respectability and citizenship had an

admission fee: shares cost $1,000 in badly depreciated Continental certifi-
cates or ten dollars in specie, a reasonable price for men of means but pro-
hibitive to squatters seeking free or very cheap land. With a purchase limit
of five shares, they wanted to assure that no man would own too much,
thereby preventing a speculation mania that might poison their enterprise
with self-interest.[51] In essence, they planned to return to a society that
prized the rule of law and the rights of property. These New Englanders
were planning a new errand into the wilderness, but with a secular quest.
Instead of saving Christianity from sin and error as the Puritans imagined
in colonial Massachusetts, these westward voyagers sought to save their
new nation from the excesses of its revolution.

Presenting the company's plan to Congress in Philadelphia while the
Constitutional Convention met in the summer of 1787, Manasseh Cutler
purchased 1.5 million acres for the Ohio Company and opened the Northwest to Federalist-led development. Cutler pitched his company in terms
of their social standing at first, requesting in March 1787 that Congress aid
"men of very considerable property and respectable characters, who in-
tend (for the Company admit no other) to become residents in that country." Cutler was also careful to comport himself as a gentleman, a decision
that marked him as a fine representative of his class and his company, and
it earned him greater access to Congress on the Ohio Company's behalf.[52]
Relying on "many friends in Congress who would make every exertion
in my favor," Cutler won praise from treasury commissioner Samuel Osgood, who called the company plan "the best ever formed in America"
and promised "every exertion" for it. On July 27, Congress offered very
advantageous terms. The Ohio Company could buy 1.5 million acres for
no more than a dollar per acre with a discount on "bad lands." The final
contract in October was even more favorable, with the purchase price of
one million dollars payable in specie or Continental certificates. By accepting the depreciated certificates at full face value, Congress essentially
sold a vast expanse of the Northwest for as little as ten cents per acre.[53]

The sale of land to the Ohio Company led to another, to Judge John
Cleves Symmes of New Jersey. Symmes looked into large-scale speculation in the Wabash valley and then Kentucky, even going so far as to
inform Kentuckians in a circular letter that he would seek a grant there.[54]
However, he turned his attention to the valleys along the Great and Little Miami Rivers in present-day western Ohio after an associate reported
positively on their situation. In August 1787, he asked to buy one million acres from Congress in a deal like the one concluded with the Ohio

Company and "differing only in quantity and place." Symmes had his purchase ready by October and was even mentioned by a third speculation outfit who tried unsuccessfully to buy up to two million acres in present-day southern Illinois.[55] With their purchases in hand by autumn 1787, the Ohio Company and Symmes sought to bring order to white settlement in the Ohio country and, in the process, roll back the radical and destructive social consequences of the American Revolution.

Perhaps the Ohio Company's most important legacy, the Northwest Ordinance, passed that summer as well. Historians have praised the Ordinance, renewed in 1789 and later extended to govern other federal lands, for its extensive legacy in the westward movement, but it is also noteworthy for the influence future Federalists exerted upon it.[56] Congress had been discussing an ordinance since September 1786, but as Nathan Dane of Massachusetts explained, "We found ourselves rather pressed" to action once "the Ohio Company appeared to purchase a large tract . . . and we wanted to abolish the old system, and get a better one." Dane became a Federalist state legislator in the 1790s and attended the Hartford Convention in 1814, but in 1787 he was crucial to writing the ordinance. Its final draft was in his handwriting, and he took credit for the late insertion of the sixth article that prohibited slavery in the new Northwest Territory. Dane even proclaimed himself the father of the ordinance in his commentaries on American law, and Westerners honored him thusly for decades.[57] Well into the nineteenth century, then, the Northwest celebrated an old Federalist as their founder.

Manasseh Cutler influenced the passage of the Northwest Ordinance as well, and he was quite pleased with the results. As its lobbyist, Cutler presented himself to Congress as both a member of the Ohio Company in search of a land grant and a virtuous republican gentleman seeking to extend public interests. He linked the two concepts in his lobbying, wanting not only a purchase but a workable system of government. The Northwest Ordinance, he believed, would establish such an administration by encouraging systematic settlement with the rectangular system established in 1785. Furthermore, he hoped, it would delegitimize squatter claims to the lands they occupied illegally, a primary obstacle to Ohio Company profits.[58] In his diary, Cutler recorded his satisfaction by declaring, "The amendments I proposed have all been made except one" which would have exempted settlers from national taxes until statehood, but he forsook that last wish for the good of a republic that needed revenue.[59] In the end, Cutler achieved his objectives by procuring a contract for the Ohio

Company, helping to bring the national government west with the speculators, and fulfilling the wishes Putnam and other company adventurers harbored for years. Thanks to him, the path westward was staked out for national officials and gentleman speculators.

The Ohio valley presented a monumental challenge that had proven too great for the Confederation Congress. Despite grand ambitions to dispossess Indians and expel foreign influence, the national government accomplished none of its aims. By the late 1780s, the multiracial residents of the Northwest pursued a variety of goals with a variety of loyalties without fear of national intervention. An Indian confederacy had formed, British officials continued to operate with impunity on American soil, and squatters defied the law and refuted national authority as they had under British rule. The Northwest was perhaps the prime example of how the Confederation government had become a failed state.

For many American officials, speculators, and future Federalists, the crisis of the Northwest presented opportunity to remake the region. They remained steadfast in their support for energetic and programmatic solutions in the Northwest, pointing to a stronger military and various innovations to better propel American authority beyond the Appalachians. Continental officers who ultimately joined the Ohio Company and then the Federalist Party were faithful to their desires for a more orderly settlement in the Ohio country, and they formed a private company to advance their policy ends while hoping to make money for themselves. They used the Ohio valley to make the case for a stronger national state through the Constitution as well. By 1787 and 1788, they had received that new government and the ability to take control of the Northwest for the United States. The Federalists were taking power and would have to make the most of their opportunity to govern, and they did so by turning their attention to the United States Army and taking on an expensive and broad-ranging Indian war.

CHAPTER TWO

"To Show All Lawless Adventurers"

The Northwest Indian War, 1789–1795

IN JANUARY 1791, Secretary of War Henry Knox offered President Washington a dire portrait of the Indian war underway in the Ohio River valley. The long-simmering conflict between white settlers and members the Northwest Indian confederacy had only worsened in recent years, and the previous year's campaign under Josiah Harmar had failed to "constrain the said Indians to sue for peace" and only emboldened resistance. Allies soon joined the confederacy in raiding settlers, aided by "certain malignant whites" representing British and Spanish interests. Disaster loomed at this precarious moment. Indians along the Ohio and Wabash Rivers could muster over 2,000 fighters, and by the spring Knox feared they were ready to "spread general desolation on the frontiers." Meanwhile, the region's settlers required and "demand[ed] protection," but little could come in the wake of Harmar's defeat. Thus, Knox worried, "seeds of disgust will be sown" among settlers, and "sentiments of separate interests will arise," no doubt encouraged "by insidious, domestic, or foreign emissaries."[1] As Knox saw it, the stakes never had been higher. The federal experiment in administering the Northwest was on the brink of collapse, and only a swift, decisive federal response would stave off complete ruin for federal prerogatives and American settlers.

Fortunately, the Secretary of War was ready to propose to Washington a U.S. Army campaign and an enhanced American military presence in the Northwest Territory that would achieve two goals at once. First, the Secretary of War targeted the Northwest Indian confederacy to stem frontier violence and make them recognize federal power. Knox believed the new campaign was urgently needed to save the lives of American settlers, but he wanted to build a force against the Indian confederacy substantial enough to "impress them strongly with the power of the United States" and "curb and overawe" resistant Indians. He also called for a new fort among the Miami nation to "afford full security to the territory of the United States, northwest of the Ohio." To carry out that expedition and staff the new fort, he sought more regular troops and federalized militia to prove "superior to all opposition."[2] Using the powers of the new federal government to crush Indian opposition would remove the greatest immediate challenge to American authority in the Northwest, and Knox certainly knew it.

Under the leadership of Knox and Washington, the Northwest Indian War became the linchpin of establishing federal power. As Knox saw it, the war would let federal officials crush Indian resistance, prove federal potency to white settlers, and demonstrate federal legitimacy to all inhabitants of the region. The war would also accomplish a central task for the Washington administration: proving the value and importance that the new government could have for the people of the United States.[3] Further, the military expenditures that the war required also made Hamilton's financial plans all the more necessary in the early 1790s. As a result, the Northwest Indian War was vital to the broader Federalist program of governing the Northwest and the young nation as a whole.

In the Ohio valley, the war had special significance. Defeating the Northwest Indian confederacy would enamor settlers of the federal government, and Knox recognized as much when he later ordered Governor St. Clair to take "frequent opportunities to impress the frontier citizens of the entire good disposition of the General Government." However, Knox wanted to control much more than Indian violence. "It is true economy to regulate events instead of being regulated by them," he observed, and the expedition was a way to take command of events in the Northwest. Further, he claimed federal officials would soon overcome "bold and unprincipled adventurers . . . incessantly machinating against the public peace and prosperity" by showing federal beneficence. Overall, pacifying Indian threats was the foundation of a "wise and rigorous system" that would at once "protect effectually the inhabitants of the frontiers, as to curb the licentious, and prevent the evils of anarchy, and prevent the usurpation of the public lands." Defeating the Northwest Indian confederacy also would send a clear signal "to show all lawless adventurers that, notwithstanding the distance, Government possess the power of preserving peace and good order."[4] In short, Knox wanted to bring federal power to bear on all inhabitants of the Northwest Territory, and winning the Northwest Indian War was the important first step in his broader program to do so.

Requiring three major campaigns in five years, the U.S. Army's victory in the Northwest Indian War established American power and let federal officials take operational control over Indian war-making in the Northwest. In showing its military might as well as its ability to solve the problems of settlers, the new federal government filled a long-standing power vacuum in the region. At the same time, the federal effort directed by Henry Knox and his generals assured that the U.S. government planned, paid for, and carried out nearly all its major operations. Thus, the Northwest Indian War was a truly national effort, and it overturned traditions of Indian warfare dating to the colonial era that largely placed the war effort in local hands. Overall, the war allowed Knox to institutionalize American responses to anti-Indian violence and prove federal power to frontier inhabitants of all races who might question it.

Knox's war plans also had political consequences for Federalists, as the Northwest Indian War became an important issue and a formative experience that helped to solidify Federalist ideology. Federalists in the Washington administration and Congress had to overcome partisan opposition by the early 1790s while Knox and other federal officials dealt with violence along the Ohio River. Thus, while Federalists contended with their Jeffersonian Republican opponents over what sort of a republic Americans had just created, the war was an early and crucial point of departure between the parties. Federalists and Republicans argued in Congress and in the press over the military and tactics needed to prosecute the Northwest Indian War, both during and after the conclusion of the war. For Federalists in Congress and the Washington administration, the Northwest Indian War had to be fought on two fronts. They would not only have to attack Indians in the Ohio valley, but they also would have to overcome partisan opponents and forge a clearer political identity.

Building a State with Indian War
Preparation and Prosecution, 1788–1791

The Constitution offered the Washington administration the powers to carry out all their plans for the Ohio River valley. They needed first to clear Indians out of the way of white settlers, and afterward, victory in the war would allow federal officials to oversee the pace and process of settlement. Thus, once the Ohio valley descended into war, Henry Knox could enact a clear federal program in the region. It was the first step in establishing a fiscal-military state and building a more powerful government capable of creating a commercial empire. This impetus ultimately led the Washington administration to commission an unsuccessful campaign under Josiah Harmar and an unmitigated disaster under Arthur St. Clair. Despite the setbacks, Federalist confidence in their mission remained unshaken.

Even before the new federal government took power, government officials already looked to move on the Indian confederacy. As governor of the Northwest Territory, Arthur St. Clair restarted negotiations in fall 1788, hoping to defuse growing tensions in the Ohio River valley. After asking for a treaty council, St. Clair received hesitant but positive replies in November despite rumors that the Americans poisoned whiskey set aside for the meeting and planned to present smallpox-infested gift blankets.[5] While untrue, the spread and seeming credibility of such rumors attest to the serious disrepair of diplomatic relations in 1788.

Nevertheless, by mid-December some two hundred Indians arrived at Fort Harmar, just outside Marietta. The Indian confederacy members reflected many of their previous concerns during recorded discussions, particularly American designs to take land in the region. Wyandot chief Shandotto complained to St. Clair, "you have gone on from one step to another, so that we don't know when you'll stop." Then, restating the position of his confederacy since 1786, he presented a wampum belt with a black stripe through it to symbolize the Ohio River as the true boundary between white and Indian lands. St. Clair responded by reasserting conquest diplomacy. As he explained, "you took up the hatchet against the United States, and joined the English in the late war. The English, to obtain peace, ceded to the United States all the country south of the great lakes." Refusing American terms meant war, but if the Indians agreed to American terms, the Governor offered "the privilege of hunting any where in the United States' territory." The promise seemed to work. The Indians and St. Clair signed the Treaty of Fort Harmar on January 11, 1789, an event described by observer and Army Lieutenant Ebenezer Denny as "the last act of the farce."[6]

The Treaty of Fort Harmar actually consisted of two separate accords, one with more amicable Iroquois nations and the other with the hostile Northwestern confederacy. While the former established boundaries, the latter attempted to address Indian grievances about horses, trade, and hunting. Indians retained hunting rights on lands ceded north of the Ohio River so long as they would "demean themselves peaceably, and offer no injury or annoyance" to settlers. Further, lands were not directly allotted to the Indian signers, and the United States only quit their claim on lands reserved to the Indians, a subtle but definite distinction. Quitting a claim merely means abandoning contentions of ownership, not an actual recognition of perpetual Indian rights to the soil. Other historians have pointed to St. Clair's agreement to pay roughly $9,000 for the treaty cession (which encompassed hundreds of thousands of acres in present-day southern and eastern Ohio) as proof that Indian policy truly changed.[7] Indeed, the U.S. paid for land for the first time, at literally pennies an acre, but little else changed. St. Clair had refused to treat Indian objections as valid and repeated the conquest diplomacy arguments that the Indians of the Northwest had been hearing since 1783.

St. Clair had great but misguided confidence when he sent the treaties to President Washington on May 2, 1789. He boasted, "their general confederacy is entirely broken; indeed, it would not be very difficult, if circumstances required it, to set them at deadly variance." In reality, the farce at Fort Harmar turned many Indian nations away from treating with the United States altogether. Following the lead of the Shawnee, who boycotted the negotiations, many other nations of the Northwestern confederacy quickly repudiated the treaty and refused to talk further with American officials. Their disgust turned into action against American settlers, too. By December, Virginia legislators representing counties along the Ohio River feared their constituents were "open to the ravages of the Indians" and their homes were vulnerable "until more effective measures are adopted for our defence."[8] The Treaty of Fort Harmar failed to contain violence in the Ohio valley, and Western settlers soon clamored for military protection.

Throughout 1789, the Washington administration was at once conciliatory toward and dismissive of the Northwest confederacy. On June 15, Knox reported to the President that "unless some decisive measures are immediately adopted to terminate these mutual hostilities, they will probably become general" along the Ohio. To defuse the situation, he suggested the U.S. government recognize that Indians "possess the right of the soil," except if gained "by their free consent, or by the right of conquest in a just war." To slow the violence and offer more to the Indians, Knox recommended "a liberal system of justice should be adopted for the various Indian tribes." On September 17, Washington asked Congress to make "national proceedings . . . uniform" in Indian policy to be "directed by fixed and stable principles."[9]

However, the U.S. Army loomed over those promises of a newer, fairer Indian policy. Knox suggested "raising an army, and extirpating the refractory tribes" as an alternative to making peace with the Indians, though "the laws of nature" dictated that the federal government should hear "the cause of the ignorant Indians." If they "persist[ed] in their depredations," though, American soldiers "may with propriety inflict such punishments as they shall think proper."[10] With the Indian confederacy no longer interested in negotiations or restraining their warriors, such a statement merely declared American intentions. War had become a viable, perhaps even preferable option. Thus, by late 1789, Knox had a real opportunity to pursue the plan he wanted for years: to build a powerful new army and smash Indian resistance in the Northwest.

Within mere months of taking power under the Constitution, Knox was already advancing maximalist solutions for the Northwest. He claimed justice slowed him, but he was already looking forward to a military solution in June 1789, when he declared that "the finances of the United States would not at present admit" a punitive expedition against the Northwest confederacy. Even so, dispossessing them remained the goal of his Indian policy. Whether through force, negotiation, or deterrence by a more powerful U.S. Army, he worked to ensure that the United States government would facilitate the nation's expansion. Western settlers—legal or not—could even be useful for his policy ends. As Knox wrote, "As the settlements of the whites shall approach near to the Indian boundaries . . . the game will be diminished, and the lands being valuable to the Indians only as hunting grounds, they will be willing to sell further tracts for small considerations."[11] He may have spoken of justice in Indian policy, but his concern seemed only to serve broader interests in expedience, thrift, and expansion.

Other concerns motivated federal officials, too, particularly interference with American prerogatives in the Northwest by Indians and foreign powers. Indian raids continued to slow the progress of surveyors from the Ohio Company and the federal government, limiting potential federal revenues. In August, raiders fired upon surveyors near the Ohio River, killing a survey crew member and six soldiers escorting them. British traders and soldiers working on American soil also concerned federal officials. British agents and officials were officially neutral in Ohio valley conflicts but continued building friendships with Indians in the region, a fact that worried St. Clair and others. The governor complained about "pernicious Counsels of the English Traders" and their supplies of weapons endangering settlers and soldiers, leading potentially to "the entire alienation of the Affections of the People of the Frontiers." Meanwhile, a U.S. Army officer complained that "nothing can establish a peace with the Indians as long as the British keep possession" of forts on American soil, especially since "they certainly are daily sowing the seed of discord."[12] Thus, quelling Indian threats to American settlers would remove many barriers to federal plans and American expansion into the Northwest Territory.

For all these reasons, Arthur St. Clair was an important ally in Knox's push for war. In June 1789, he requested federal funds to convene a treaty conference with nations along the Wabash River because "the savages should be brought to peace, either by treaty, or by force." By September, force prevailed. St. Clair begged Washington for "the orders you may think proper" to allay the "embarrassing circumstances to the government of the Western Territory" created by the growing Indian-white conflict. He also asked to activate Virginia and Pennsylvania militias temporarily because the mere "handful of troops" in the regular army simply would not suffice. Further, St. Clair said the reinforcements would "justify me in holding a language to the Indians which might obviate the necessity of employing force."[13]

In response, Washington publicly sided with Knox and St. Clair by September 1789. He relayed through St. Clair a warning to recalcitrant Indians that if they rejected "the dispositions of the General Government for the preservation of peace . . . [and] should continue their incursions, the United States will be constrained to punish them with severity." The President also listened to their calls for a larger U.S. Army. St. Clair warned that he did not know if "the Kentucky people will or can submit patiently to the cruelties of those savages" any longer, and he wanted Congress to call out state militias to aid the U.S. Army in controlling the Indians and preserving public order. Washington agreed, asking the Senate on September 17 to allow him to send militiamen from Virginia and Pennsylvania to aid St. Clair and the Western settlers.[14]

Washington saved his strongest call for war until his First Annual Message to Congress on January 8, 1790, in which he placed the Indian war at the center of a Hamiltonian statement of purpose for the Northwest and the United States military. He echoed Hamilton's views that federal power should be used to encourage domestic manufacturing and commerce, seeking to build federal administrative capacities through the post office and public education. First, though, he stressed a stronger military to handle Ohio valley Indians. From a classic Federalist viewpoint, he implored Congress to expand the U.S. Army because "To be prepared for war is one of the most effectual means of preserving peace," and only regular troops "armed, but disciplined" would suffice. That new army was first to "afford protection . . . and if necessary, to punish aggressors."[15] In sum, Washington outlined a new American state that was crucial to the creation of a manufacturing power with a well-educated and well-connected populace, and at the foundation of that American future lay military force against the Ohio Valley's Indians.

On January 11, Congress took up Washington's proposal, and from those debates emerged arguments by budding Federalists for creating a fiscal-military state. As defined by historian Max Edling, the fiscal-military state was primarily designed for financing and waging war. While armies or budgets may grow over time, fiscal-military states grew specifically because states centralized their power over both. These debates upset war opponent Senator William Maclay of Pennsylvania, whose diary reveals the infancy of the fiscal-military state. He saw the bill to increase the U.S. Army as "a spoiled piece of business" inspired by a secretary of war who "wants to labor in his vocation." Administration allies who supported the bill also worried Maclay. He noted that Ralph Izard of South Carolina "wished for a standing army of ten thousand men" and worse, "feared nothing from them." Soon, Maclay feared, "We must have a mass of national debt to employ the treasury," and shortly after would come "an army for fear the Department of War should lack employment." Information from the Ohio valley served their purposes only too perfectly, providing a constant stream of "new phantoms for the day" to make Indian war and the new fiscal-military state unavoidable. "Give Knox his army," he fumed, "and he will soon have a war on hand."[16]

Despite strenuous objections from anti-administration legislators like Maclay, both houses acceded to Washington's request in late April 1790, doubling the U.S. Army to over 1,200 enlisted men, plus officers. Congress also empowered the president to call up state militias at his discretion in order to suppress Indian uprisings and protect Western settlers.[17] While the new U.S. Army was the core of American forces against the Northwest Indian confederacy, Washington essentially could enlarge the military as he pleased, even if only temporarily. Meanwhile, Knox had planned to employ state militias against the Indians but could not do so in the Northwest until the new law was passed. Thus, in 1790, he saw five years of tireless advocacy rewarded with a powerful new U.S. Army and an opportunity to use the militias as he and his commander-in-chief wished.

In May, Knox began to recruit and outfit new soldiers almost immediately while the Washington administration pushed for decisive action.

Hamilton forwarded his sentiments to St. Clair that the U.S government must remove Indian threats to "lay hold of the affections of the settlers and attach them . . . to the Government of the Nation." However, as Knox reported, federal policy was yet to woo skeptical settlers. In his analysis of news about Indian raids along the Ohio River, he noted "the inefficacy of defensive operations against the banditti Shawanese . . . and some of the Wabash Indians." Citing "The bad effect it has on the public mind," Knox recommended "extirpating [them] . . . if any practical measures can be devised."[18]

Two weeks later, Knox authorized Harmar to use the newly enlarged U.S. Army against the recalcitrant Northwest Indian confederacy. With that order, Knox committed the new federal government to a course of action that Knox said would only end with the complete defeat of the Indian menace. Harmar was not to cease until the Indians were clearly defeated, and similarly Knox told St. Clair "no exertions or pains must be spared" for Harmar's campaign. Once defeated, the Indians would be ready to negotiate. Knox wanted the campaign to "produce in the Indians a proper disposition for peace," so St. Clair could conclude a new treaty with the confederacy in "certain circumstances of humiliation." Federalists in the Washington administration clearly had given up on amicable solutions. Peace would only come along the Ohio River after American soldiers vanquished their Indian foes.[19]

To achieve that victory, Knox suggested a small force that could be organized and moved quickly. A mounted army of "one hundred continental, and three hundred militia . . . all picked men" would allow Harmar to strike quickly and "most probably ensure success." Nevertheless, Harmar chose a larger force of mostly infantry and readied it at Fort Washington, near the new town of Cincinnati.[20] After marching north in September, Harmar and his men reached the confederacy's principal town of Kekionga (located at present-day Fort Wayne, Indiana) by October 20. After ordering his troops to burn some three hundred homes and twenty thousand bushels of crops in the fields, Harmar attacked Kekionga on the morning of October 22, but Indian fighters turned back the U.S. Army. The Americans lost 183 men against around forty Indians killed, and the retreat to Fort Washington took twelve days.[21] Despite his troubles, Harmar reported positively that by burning Kekionga the confederacy's "head quarters of iniquity were broken up," and St. Clair relayed with similar confidence that the "savages have got a most terrible stroke." However, their optimism did not convince Washington, who on November 19 expressed his "disappointment" with the defeat that basically meant a large expenditure of federal money "without honor or profit" from any of it.[22]

FIGURE 3. Fort Washington, erected 1790 in Cincinnati, on the ground now occupied as 3d. street, east of Broadway. Print by Ehrgott & Forbriger, c. 1857. Courtesy of Library of Congress, LCCN: 2003656356.

Despite the setback, Washington argued for a strong response in his Second Annual Message to Congress on December 8. Inaction, he feared, would allow continued, frequent raids across the Ohio River, and he asked Congress for the power he needed to end the Indian insurrections once and for all. Washington cited two reasons for his request. First, he wanted to create "sentiments of warm attachment to the Union, and its present Government" from Western settlers, and second, he hoped to preserve "the safety of the Western settlements" while proving to Indians "the Government of the Union is . . . capable of punishing their crimes."[23] Two days later, the Senate promised to comply with whatever Washington required to end the Indian war, and on December 13 the House of Representatives promised to support the president in prosecuting the war to its end. The House wrote, "we sympathise too much with our Western brethren, not to behold with approbation the watchfulness and vigor which have been exerted by the Executive authority, for their protection." Thus, they decided, the U.S. government could not rest until the Indians realized "it is their interest to merit, by a peaceable behavior, the friendship and humanity which the United States are always ready to extend."[24]

Meanwhile, opponents could not agree on how to approach the war after Harmar's defeat. Some committed administration foes like James Jackson of Georgia supported the war effort. In House debates, he was "fully impressed with the importance of an Indian war, and of extending the protection of Government to our defenceless frontiers." Thus, he saw "the necessity of the measures taken to chastise the banditti on the Ohio." On the other hand, William Maclay became a more strident opponent. To him, the war began "without any authority of Congress." After Washington forwarded news about attacks on Western posts to the Senate on January 27, 1791, Maclay seethed in his diary, "The wishes of many people are gratified to involve us in war." War meant growing the fiscal-military state, too, and since "To involve us in expense . . . seems to be the great object of their design," Maclay saw the Federalists using the Northwest Indian War to their advantage. As he concluded, "had a system been needed to involve us in the depth of difficulty with the Indians, none better could have been devised."[25]

Other anti-administration Congressmen also clearly expressed their views of the Federalist program, of which Indian affairs in the Northwest was a primary basis. By 1791, they coalesced from throughout the states around opposition to the standing army Federalists built for the Northwest and the fiscal system that paid for it. In the House, Elbridge Gerry of Massachusetts expressed deep suspicion of Federalists and their standing army like Maclay had, while Jackson and Maclay continued to criticize Hamilton's fiscal system for its reliance on funded debts and its supposed overreach of federal power. Jackson was especially outspoken, declaring Hamilton's national bank a monopoly for Northern mercantile interests that would prove detrimental to the nation's future.[26] While clear on what they did not like, anti-administration Congressmen had not yet developed positive alternatives in early 1791 that could let them gain political momentum.

Despite the opposition, Federalists pressed ahead with a new campaign. Knox reported to Washington on the sad state of affairs for Western settlers in January 1791, and the *Providence Gazette* warned readers that Harmar's campaign made "the Indian War . . . a general one." Various newspapers reported in February and March on Indian raids, including the Big Bottom Massacre in January and a series of other raids along the Ohio River, many of which were republished throughout the Atlantic coast. Because of the renewed war, many Ohio valley settlers abandoned their new homes, but reports remained hopeful that federal action would address their concerns. As the *Providence Gazette* reported, "a force will be sent to Indian country early in the Spring, competent to teach these Barbarians very different Ideas of the Power of the United States."[27]

Moving to demonstrate federal capabilities in the Ohio valley, Henry Knox acted by March to stop the raids through peace offers and war preparations. In doing both at once, he offered what was quickly becoming a pattern in dealing with the Northwest Indian confederacy. Knox clearly believed threats of military force were effective in treaty negotiations, and he often spoke of the U.S. Army as a force capable of bringing peace, even if only after a march of fixed bayonets. Knox's March 11 orders to diplomat Thomas Procter revealed that he wanted to continue dealing with Indians aggressively. He asked Procter to invite Indians to peace negotiations at Fort Washington on the grounds that "[t]he white men and the red men inhabit the same country, and ought to be good friends," but only a treaty would "save them from ruin."[28]

While Knox claimed that the U.S. wanted to make a treaty "unmixed with fear, and dictated by pure principles of humanity," he comingled peace offers with outright threats of violence. He implored belligerent Indians to cease their raids or risk learning "The United States are powerful, and able to send forth such numbers of warriors as would drive you entirely out of the country." According to Knox, Northwestern Indians had little choice but to submit to American terms, too. If they resisted, the Secretary of War predicted "absolute destruction to you, your women, and your children," and even if the confederacy bested American soldiers once, "your doom must be sealed for ever." Predictably, the confederacy was not convinced. Procter reported that the Indians had little interest in the offer, while Mohawk leader Joseph Brant encouraged the confederacy "to pay no attention to what should be said to them."[29] The offer of peace was half-hearted at best and came with serious threats to peoples already inclined to dismiss American diplomatic messages.

That diplomatic effort seems even weaker in light of the two expeditions Knox was planning for 1791 while Procter traveled west to make the oddly belligerent peace offer. On March 9, before Knox even sent Procter westward, he ordered Brigadier General Charles Scott to lead a hand-picked Kentucky cavalry force north "to impress the Indians with a strong conviction of the power of the United States" and to disabuse "deluded" Indians of their opinions of American military power. Along the way, Scott was to "inflict that degree of punishment which justice may require." With cavalry, Scott could also move quickly and take prisoner "as many as possible, especially women and children." Scott struck in late May and early June, sacking villages near the Wabash River with minimal U.S. losses. While destroying the Kickapoo town of Ouiatenon, for example, the Kentuckians killed thirty-two Indians and captured fifty-eight more, while seeing only five militiamen wounded. Elsewhere, his lieutenants captured two other Indian villages without losing any men, and all three villages were burned soon afterward.[30]

The employment of Scott's mounted rangers also represented definitive steps by Henry Knox to federalize Indian warfare. As military historian John Grenier notes, white settlers had established a long tradition of engaging in irregular warfare since the early colonial period. By the 1790s, frontier whites leaned on three general practices to fight Indians: extirpative war, mounted frontier rangers, and scalp bounties. Into the Confederation period, defense against Indian violence fell to locally organized militias. However, Knox's decision to command and compensate Kentucky rangers placed the U.S. government at the center of this style of Indian warfare. He encouraged the tactics that frontier settlers had adopted, indicating a preference "to act offensively against . . . the banditti" through such practices as burning villages and taking Indian captives. By engaging in such tactics with federal troops and federalized militia, Knox endorsed those practices. Ferocious anti-Indian violence became a piece of federal policy and showed sympathy to settler wishes. The move seemingly impressed settlers, with one Kentucky man writing approvingly, "The general government has done, and is about to accomplish great matters, with much attention and no small expence," especially since Knox had assembled "a numerous and well appointed army" led by St. Clair. By taking over this style of war previously led by locals, Knox built legitimacy among western settlers and established a precedent under which the U.S. Army took the lead in dispossessing Indians.[31]

As Scott readied and carried out his expedition, Knox commissioned St. Clair to lead the second major U.S. Army expedition on March 21. St. Clair received funds to build two new forts, one at the old site of Kekionga and another in a forward position to strike at the confederacy once again. While taking "a considerable number of prisoners . . . particularly women and children," St. Clair was also to "humbl[e] the Indians, inducing them to sue for mercy." Knox hoped to prove American military superiority with two successful expeditions, but the lofty goals and great expenses behind St. Clair's expedition were crippled by poor supplies and slow travel.[32] The construction of Fort Hamilton less than twenty-five miles north of Fort Washington and Cincinnati was completed well behind schedule, and in the next month St. Clair managed to travel less than one hundred miles. Meanwhile, his army dwindled from 2,300 soldiers to 1,400. Desertions were so numerous that a full regiment of regulars fell back to deter even more deserters and to protect supply trains. Early on November 4, St. Clair's bedraggled army was ambushed. Soldiers left behind all their cannon, over three hundred horses, and other supplies in such quantities that the Indians could not carry them all away. Meanwhile, 630 U.S. soldiers lay dead and three hundred more were wounded. It was the worst defeat Indians ever handed the U.S. Army, as St. Clair lost three times more men than George Custer did at Little Bighorn.[33]

News of St. Clair's defeat trickled eastward over the next month, but the Washington administration and the Federalist press initially showed confidence in the face of adversity. Washington relayed the news to Congress in a short December 12 message but promised, "Although the national loss is considerable . . . it may be repaired without great difficulty." Knox responded similarly by consoling St. Clair on December 23, "The mind, instead of being depressed, must be braced to prepare an adequate remedy." That remedy was, to Knox, a larger army and a third, even larger campaign. Two weeks later, he remained defiant about Northwestern Indian resistance, telling friendly Seneca chief Cornplanter that the war was "troublesome," but "in the long run, we must conquer." National pride may have been a factor in his decision, but he cited a need to protect settlers and stubbornly declared, "If much evil befall the bad Indians, they will have brought it upon themselves."[34] The administration had decided to stay an unswerving course toward defeating the Northwest confederacy.

The Politics of Conquest
Partisanship and Indian War, 1792–1794

Despite the certitude shown by Washington and Knox, St. Clair's defeat ultimately represented an ordeal for the new Federalist faithful. The war sparked discussion of other questions as well, particularly about what had caused yet another American failure in the Northwest, how to address military shortcomings, and how to win a war that was losing support. Federalists also had to contend with a much more clearly defined opposition on the way to the election of 1792, one of the first truly partisan elections in American history. Federalists eventually emerged from these debates with a clearer idea of who they were, and so the Northwest Indian War represented a powerful formative moment in Federalist Party history. Heading toward the Anthony Wayne campaign, Federalists took ownership of the war, and in the process, they defined themselves by firmly declaring support for a powerful military and national state, no matter the costs.

News of the defeat spread through the press along the Atlantic coast by December 1791, creating uncertainty and fear.[35] As Philadelphia's *Federal Gazette* reported on January 3, 1792, Indian raiding along the Ohio River "continued without intermission to the present." On January 6, the paper reported alarm from Pittsburgh residents over Indian raids because, "Seneca Warriors could, in twenty four hours, come down the river perhaps with not less than 5 or 600, and we in our poor defenceless state . . . could not mass more than 200 raw undisciplined men." Nonetheless, the writer urged the United States to continue fighting and ensure that "the sword of the enlightened citizen banish from our frontiers the tomahawk of the cruel savage." Similarly, a poem on the war appearing later that month predicted an American victory and concluded, "*And when they're ours we'll make them civil,/Or drive them headlong to the devil.*"[36]

Administration opponents, already firming up as the new "republican interest," took umbrage against the Hamilton and Knox plans for war with similar objections about their perceived ambition and British ministerial approaches to government. In fact, in January 1792 the Northwest Indian War became an early point of contention in that year's Philadelphia newspaper war between Philip Freneau's Republican *National Gazette* and John Fenno's Federalist *Gazette of the United States*. It heated up over the Indian war as much as the fiscal policy debates later that year described more fully by other historians. Philadelphia Republicans voiced their opposition to the war in the *National Gazette* and the more neutral *Federal Gazette*, providing multiple reasons for their position. One correspondent hoped the recent campaign "will caution us from prosecuting any longer a war in that country" meant, in a thinly veiled shot at Henry Knox, "to gratify the pride of a few ambitious *overgrown* individuals." The writer hoped Americans would ignore the calls of "a 'war establishment,' urging the necessity of recruiting for a similar expedition," and end the ruinous Indian war.[37]

More pieces questioned the tactics and reasoning for the war. On January 26, the *National Gazette* reprinted an essay from Connecticut that

asked simply, "Why send *large bodies* of men after *Indians*; and let them
know a year before hand what is to be done?" Further, the writer questioned the justice of the American cause: "Is the land where we go in
quest of Indians, ours?" Another piece in the *Federal Gazette* also hoped
to see the war's Indian policy reoriented to an approach consistent with
principles of "Justice and sound Policy." Reflecting concerns about Federalist designs as well, he asked, "Has Government any particular Object
. . . in driving the Indians westward—is there any Point at which we are to
stop?" By November, a writer signing as Many made similar accusations
in *Federal Gazette*. Calling the war "unsuccessful, expensive and tedious,"
he doubted the utility of taking the Northwest by force when lands were
available to the east, and he accused Federalists of using the war as "a pre-
text . . . to establish oppression and slavery."[38] Echoing Maclay two years
before, the burgeoning Republican opposition had come to see something
much darker in Federalist support for the Northwest Indian War by 1792.

Federalists answered by accusing Republicans of political opportunism
in pieces published by the *Gazette of the United States*. On January 14,
"A Friend to Government" attacked Republicans for appealing to natural
(but perhaps distasteful) human urges "to suspect, to fear, and to hate
superior power." Similarly, declaring "Every thing has its season," a February report observed, "the Indian war seems to have beaten the debt"
as a useful campaign issue for 1792, and Republicans would question the
war only until "the public is tired of it." Meanwhile, Federalists defended principles that transcended base electioneering. The correspondent
attacked the patriotism of Republicans as well, declaring flatly of war opponents, "He that is not with us, is against us." As he saw it, their attempts
to "wound the national government" allowed "the tomahawk [to] fall upon
the defenceless women and children." Another accusatory piece argued
war opposition must come by "productions of *foreigners*" since critics
showed "total want of *sympathy* . . . to the prosperity, or the misfortunes of
our country." In the late 1790s, Federalists leveled similar charges of disloyalty, claiming Republicans imported radical foreign democratic ideas
(and newspaper editors) while defining criticism of the Adams administration as dangerous, even treasonous, through the Alien and Sedition Acts.[39]
Federalists may have been accused of trying to recreate British government in the new nation, but they imagined themselves the true defenders
of American republicanism.

To preserve that American future, Federalists decided to create an army
that could not fail again. Knox began the planning quickly, suggesting an

increase of the U.S. Army to 5,168 enlisted men (plus officers) on December 26, 1791, and he wanted to provide the new soldiers higher pay for three-year enlistments. These soldiers would be capable of providing "strong coercive force" to curb Indian aggression. To Knox, St. Clair's army was too quickly recruited, too dependent on militia, and too full of what one Western observer called the "idle and dissipated, picked up along the shores and grog shops."[40] Thus, Knox wanted the new army disciplined, professional, and large enough to crush Indian resistance and maintain order along the frontier. He was nothing if not consistent in his pursuit of a large army in the Northwest, and St. Clair's defeat allowed him finally to convince the president and Congress that one was absolutely necessary.

On January 26, 1792, Congress took up the issue by debating a bill to add three new regiments, as per Knox and Washington's request. Opponents rose immediately to squelch the bill on the grounds that the war and Indian policy overall "was, in its origin . . . unwise and impolitic. The Indians are with difficulty to be reduced by the sword, but may easily be gained by justice and moderation." They saw new regiments as unnecessary. Reflecting their views of how the Revolutionary War was won, and noting the failures of the Harmar and St. Clair campaigns, they thought "frontier militia are not only equal, but infinitely superior to any regular troops . . . against the hostile Indians." Congressmen also reflected arguments in Republican newspapers, concerned the administration would "squander away money by millions" in operations known only to "those who are in the secrets of the Cabinet." Even worse, they worried that these new expenses would require new excises or extend existing ones like on whiskey, which Republicans opposed.[41]

The next day, administration opponent John Mercer of Maryland offered a withering critique of the entire Federalist fiscal-military state that underlay the bill. The new army was too expensive for Mercer, and he feared it would "plac[e] the occupations and productive labor of our citizens under the direction of Government." The estimated annual expense of over a half-million dollars would require new revenues, so "as long as the Indian war continues . . . new taxes must be provided" in separate bills. Worse, in assenting to a larger force, Mercer feared "Representatives [would] surrender up forever the sacred trust of the Constitution, and place in the power and under the control of the Executive and Senate, a perpetual tax."[42] Mercer and other opponents of the new bill staked out their position as one contrary to the themes they identified in Federalist ideology. Their attack on the army bill encompassed wider Republican criticisms about Federalist preferences for standing armies, secrecy, internal taxation, and British-style ministerial government.

Supporters retorted with three arguments. First, they appropriated what Peter Silver has termed the "anti-Indian sublime," imagery of Indian violence against innocent whites meant to promote military actions. As supporters noted, national impotence in the Ohio valley allowed 1,500 Kentucky settlers to be killed or kidnapped, and similar raids into Virginia and Pennsylvania may have claimed another 1,500.[43] Second, supporters used the anti-Indian sublime in hopes of shaming doubters into yes votes. After all, Indians rejected peace offers, insulted diplomats, and mocked American weakness. In one instance, Indians asked why American forces did not take the British posts within American borders, and one Congressman asked simply, "Will it be said that we are unable to do it? Is this language to be used within the United States? No!" Such impotence before Indians and British officials was unacceptable. Thus, to "prove that the boasted efficiency of the General Government is something more than an empty name," Congress should "raise both men and money sufficient to defend the nation." Third, they argued Republican opposition would end quickly with an American victory. They made specious arguments that purchasing Indian lands would lead to the U.S. government "squandering the public money, year after year," preferring instead "vigorous and effectual exertion to bring the matter to a final issue."[44] Whatever their merits, the arguments were persuasive enough. Both houses of Congress passed the bill and Washington signed it into law on March 26, 1792, increasing the U.S. Army to a maximum size of 4,800 enlisted men.

Knox wasted little time planning a third expedition against the Northwest confederacy, worried about securing Western settlers even as expected attacks never came. In mid-April, Knox appointed Anthony Wayne to head this new Legion of the United States, and Wayne almost immediately left for Pittsburgh to assume command and plan the third major expedition against the Northwest Indian confederacy.[45] Meanwhile, Indian leadership was too fractured to capitalize on the success against Harmar and St. Clair. Nations and leaders differed on whether or not to trust British aid, and some chiefs argued for negotiating with the United States in hopes of preserving their victories. Those divisions showed in the lack of raids against settlers and soldiers. At Fort Jefferson, Captain Daniel Bradley reported only one raid on his garrison that year, and otherwise, "Nothing material has happened." In fact, it had fallen so quiet that summer that Bradley cultivated a private garden outside the fort.[46]

While planning the new campaign, Knox sent the confederacy an ill-fated peace envoy. Captain Alexander Trueman was the chosen diplomat, and he carried with him a speech from Knox that paternally informed the Indians, "It will be for your interest to be at peace with the United States." However, the Americans refused to revisit previous treaties, and Knox demanded an immediate end to all raids by the confederacy. Negotiating as if conquest had already been assured was a deadly mistake. By July, Joseph Brant informed Knox that Trueman was "no more," and an October 1792 report from Private William May confirmed that Trueman was one of three men killed and scalped near the site of St. Clair's defeat.[47]

For the next two years, Wayne continued to add new recruits and build a disciplined force, even as moderate Federalist John Steele of North Carolina mounted one last effort against the war. In late December 1792, Steele introduced a bill to reduce the size of the U.S. Army because it placed "extreme burdens . . . on the people." Over the next week, the House engaged in a contentious debate over the bill, but committed Federalists offered the strongest reasons against it. Thomas Hartley of Pennsylvania offered perhaps the most ringing endorsement for the new U.S. Army, declaring it had to remain in place to pacify the Northwest. Echoing Washington's declaration in the First Annual Message, Hartley encouraged the rest of the House to obey "a maxim, that the nation which is prepared for war can most easily obtain peace." Ultimately, the House rejected Steele's bill by a 36–20 vote on January 8, 1793, and maintained the Federalist commitment to a strong military presence in the Northwest.[48]

The year 1793 also brought a last American effort to negotiate, though officials were skeptical and made hardheaded demands. Wayne estimated in August 1792, "from present appearances peace is out of the question . . . nor shall we ever have a permanent peace with those Indians until they experience our superiority in the field." Knox believed similarly in November, expressing of Indian negotiators, "I am apprehensive they will be extravagant in their demands." Those supposedly extravagant demands were essentially the same ones they had been making since 1789, that the only acceptable boundary between Indians and white settlers was the Ohio River. Meanwhile, the United States was willing to revisit only annuity amounts, not land cessions previously made north of the Ohio River.[49]

In the negotiations of 1793, American treaty commissioners made the same demands they always had, and Indian negotiators realized quickly that American policy remained unchanged. British Lieutenant Governor John Graves Simcoe welcomed the diplomats in June, inviting them to a ball and offering them official protections as they traveled to meet with the confederacy in July.[50] In response, the American commissioners made demands. They wanted Simcoe not to attend the ensuing negotiations, since in their words, "The views of the United States being thus fair and liberal, the commissioners wish to embrace every means of making them so appear to the Indians, against any contrary suggestions." In short, the British need not interfere in the fairness of American Indian policy. The negotiations proved fruitless, though. In the opening speech, the Northwest confederacy maintained its stance that the Ohio River was the boundary between white and Indian lands and demanded of the U.S., "If you seriously design to make a firm and lasting peace, you will immediately remove all your people from our side of the river." Their final outright rejection of American offers came in August. "Because you have at last acknowledged our independence," they said, Americans seemed to think that "we should for such a favor surrender to you our country."[51]

Once peace talks had broken down, Knox refocused on Wayne's campaign, while Wayne had maintained his efforts throughout the failed peace process. By the autumn, Wayne marched his soldiers north to establish Fort Greenville to stave off Indian attacks, and in January 1794, he proudly reported his army had built Fort Recovery on the site of St. Clair's defeat. Such a move, he said, would "afford an additional security to the Western Frontiers." At this point, the Legion had retaken the site of the great American defeat in the war, and the symbolism behind it was surely not lost on nearby Indians who attacked it in late June 1794. However, the American victory vindicated Wayne's methodical and disciplined style as well as the Federalist approach to the Northwest. Where a poorly assembled army fell nearly three years earlier, a smaller but more professional force won the day through discipline and careful preparation. The battle produced one of two major fractures between the British and many Indian warriors, too, as they found British promises of aid had been empty in their time of need.[52]

Four weeks later, Wayne led his full army of 3,500 men away from Greenville to the north and east.[53] Throughout the ensuing campaign he insisted on moving "rapid & as secret as the Nature of the case will admit," to prevent another Indian ambush. By August 8, they reached the confederacy's new principal town along the Glaize River, where the Legion built Fort Defiance and tarried until August 15.[54] As Wayne and his men approached the trading post of British agent Alexander McKee on August

18 and readied for combat, the Indian army followed its custom of fasting the night before battle. However, Wayne's choice to camp two nights instead of one led many warriors to leave to hunt or forage for food by the morning of August 20. Thus, as Wayne's Legion marched to battle, the Indian army had shrunk from 1,400 to roughly 900.

In the Battle of Fallen Timbers on August 20, Wayne's men implemented the maneuvers in which they had been drilled since autumn 1792. Rather than frenzied retreats like under Harmar and St. Clair, Wayne oversaw a rout in favor of the U.S. Army. In full flight, the Native Americans ran to nearby British Fort Miamis, where they expected aid but instead discovered the garrison under full alert and the doors of the fort closed to them. In a moment soaked with symbolism the British, who had refused to supply direct support to the Northwest confederacy, literally shut the fort's doors in the faces of desperate Indians. In the aftermath, Wayne marched within pistol shot of Fort Miamis without incident, and the Legion burned Indian fields and villages during their return to Fort Defiance. Soon after, the Legion built Fort Wayne where Kekionga had stood and Harmar had been defeated. Meanwhile, the Northwest Indian confederacy was left homeless and beaten, while some warriors believed the Covenant Chain with the British had been permanently severed. By the end of September, a Wyandot chief asked the U.S. government "to bring forth, from the bottom of your hearts, your sentiments respecting to making a definitive treaty of peace," and another unsigned request hoped, "We should take our rest, and enjoy, the remainder of our lives, the blessings of peace."[55] Finally, the Washington administration had struck a decisive blow against the Northwest Indian confederacy, and peace would come solely on federal terms.

Legacies of Conquest
The Outcomes of Fallen Timbers

The Battle of Fallen Timbers led to three diplomatic triumphs for the United States that solidified its hold over the Ohio River valley by the end of 1795. The first, Jay's Treaty with Great Britain, underscored American power in the Northwest Territory. Second, the Treaty of San Lorenzo (or Pinckney's Treaty) with Spain opened trade opportunities and made the Ohio valley more attractive to American settlers. Finally, the Treaty of Greenville reaffirmed Wayne's victory and proved to prospective settlers that it was safe to settle in present-day Ohio. In sum, the victory at Fallen

Timbers accomplished two objectives: not only did it prove federal power by defeating Indians, it laid a claim in the region that pushed away European rivals.

Jay's Treaty aroused deep resentment from merchants and proud nationalists farther east, but it was an untrammeled victory for Ohio valley settlers. While many Americans saw the treaty's trade restrictions and lingering issues from the Revolutionary War as injurious to national pride, the article governing military matters made settlement in the Northwest much more attractive. In article two, Britain promised to evacuate its posts on American soil before June 1, 1796, leaving the U.S. unrivaled control over the Northwest for the rest of the 1790s. The treaty also successfully drove a wedge in British-Indian relations that further weakened Indian resistance.[56] The resolution of lingering issues concerning the Northwest also proved one of the more convincing points in its favor during the bitterly divided House of Representatives debates over Jay's Treaty in April 1796. For example, arch-Federalist Fisher Ames of Massachusetts took to the floor on April 28 to defend the treaty, and he was most dramatic when discussing the Ohio valley. While the rest of the speech was full of Federalist red meat—especially in rebuking Republicans for their attachments to France—he argued forcefully that rejecting the treaty would throw the Northwest back into open warfare.

Ames's reasoning was clear, simple, and powerful. He first suggested that voting against Jay's Treaty was an implicit vote to resume the Northwest Indian War so recently concluded. Meanwhile, rejecting the treaty meant for Westerners, "It will not be peace, but a sword; it will be no better than a lure to draw victims within the reach of the tomahawk." Strengthening his case with the anti-Indian sublime, Ames continued with a wish that he could bellow to "every log-house beyond the mountains. . . . Wake from your false security! Your cruel dangers—your more cruel apprehensions—are soon to be renewed; the wounds, yet unhealed, are to be torn open again" by Republicans killing the treaty. He even appealed to the gallery when discussing the plight of those innocent Westerners, telling the full room in an emotional appeal that renewing the war would be a terrible message to deliver. As he explained, the government would basically be telling every Westerner, "You are a father: the blood of your sons shall fatten the corn-field! You are a mother: the war-whoop shall wake the sleep of the cradle!" The Northwest without Jay's Treaty and the British retreating from the frontier posts was, quite simply, "a spectacle of horror which cannot be overdrawn." Ames also leaned on a basic Federalist tenet of Western administration by claiming settlers deserved and demanded energetic government to look after them. "Protection is the right of the frontier: it is our duty to give it," he said.[57] Speeches from Ames and other Federalists proved convincing enough that the House recommended ratifying the treaty and the Senate did so in 1796.

Jay's Treaty offered protection and the promise of lessened conflict in the Northwest, and the Treaty of San Lorenzo protected their commercial prospects. The latter agreement was born of fading Spanish military prowess in the Americas, and rising American power was an important factor in Spain's decision to accommodate rather than resist American commerce.[58] Concluded in October 1795 by Federalist Thomas Pinckney of South Carolina, the treaty opened the Mississippi River to American trade and allowed Americans the right of deposit at New Orleans. The Mississippi River was the lone realistic outlet for exports from most of the trans-Appalachian West, and the fact that it remained in foreign hands had long caused worry for Ohio valley residents and would-be settlers. However, the Treaty of San Lorenzo suddenly guaranteed settlers on both sides of the Ohio River the right to travel to the Gulf of Mexico and then the Atlantic Ocean without interference from foreign powers. It was also popular enough that allies of the Washington administration linked it to Jay's Treaty to attract votes for both.[59] Taken together, the treaties provided the region an immediate and dramatic boost, with many Americans convinced to finally head to Kentucky and the Northwest Territory.

Both treaties also led residents in Kentucky and western Pennsylvania toward greater loyalty to the young nation by 1795. In Kentucky, federal judge Harry Innes had inquired into what the Spanish could offer the people of his state while other Kentuckians protested the whiskey excise in 1794, but the next year Innes abandoned his interest in Spain. Meanwhile many western Pennsylvanians shifted from hardline Republicanism and vociferous protests against federal action to demanding that their representatives accept the Federalist-negotiated treaties. Guaranteeing safety and opening commercial markets had bred satisfaction and helped to increase property values. As the *Pittsburgh Gazette* proclaimed proudly of western Pennsylvania in the wake of the two treaties, "land that two or three years since was sold for ten shillings per acre, will now bring upwards of three pounds."[60] Federalist victories in the Northwest again opened the way to further gains by the United States and its citizens.

The final victory also came at a bargaining table, as Anthony Wayne negotiated, or more correctly extracted, a large land cession from humbled

Indians at the Treaty of Greenville. Many scholars have praised the treaty, claiming it showed the U.S. had given up conquest diplomacy in favor of voluntary purchases and fairer dealing.[61] Clauses for laying out Indian lands and purchasing the land cession make such a conclusion understandable, even somewhat convincing. However, negotiations were hardly fair, and Wayne treated them as little more than empty theater. While opening negotiations on July 15, 1795, Wayne told the Indians, "Should you have any well grounded objections . . . come forward and speak your minds freely." Many Indian negotiators did object to certain provisions, but Wayne rejected nearly all of their claims and largely dictated the treaty to them. In fact, Wayne had already drafted a version before negotiations began, and he based the final treaty on it.[62] By refusing to genuinely revisit nearly all the treaty's provisions, Wayne reasserted the old belief that the Indians had little right to object to American demands. The treaty was signed August 3, securing much of present-day Ohio for white settlement and quelling any concerted Indian resistance until the rise of Tecumseh's confederacy.

Patrick Griffin described the Treaty of Greenville as the moment when "Jefferson's famous 'empire of liberty' . . . took shape," but events leading to the Treaty of Greenville were hardly a Jeffersonian achievement. Rather, it was the culmination of a war that Federalists carried out. Over the course of the war, Federalists claimed ownership of its successes and failures, and they discovered and articulated their own partisan identity through it. They also left a clear legacy in U.S. Indian policy. William Henry Harrison received an education in fighting Indians and negotiating with them while serving under Anthony Wayne.[63]

The war was also a primary engine in developing the new American state from the formation of the Constitution through the 1790s. To paraphrase Charles Tilly, Indian war made the early American state, and the early American state made war on Indians. From the Confederation army of less than six hundred to an army authorized to be as large as 5,000 in 1795, the Northwest Indian War keyed the growth of the American military and with it, American power in the Northwest. Outlays by the U.S. government for that army grew exponentially as well. St. Clair received a paltry $14,000 in October 1787 to govern the Northwest Territory for two years, and only five years later a three-year commission for Wayne's Legion expended a total of over $1,000,000.[64] Those two statistics show that the new federal government was capable of much more than its predecessor, and Federalists in the Washington administration were responsible for increasing that power so dramatically.

As the war ended, the Federalists needed new outlets for the energies of their government. Knox had a recommendation ready in his final report as Secretary of War on December 29, 1794; government had to control "desires of too many frontier white people, to seize, by force or fraud, upon the neighboring Indian lands" to secure a lasting peace in the Northwest. In other words, federal order had to come to the whites who resettled the lands that the Northwest confederacy would cede and vacate. Washington foretold a similar turn in his Seventh Annual Message to Congress on December 8, 1795. While he reported that "our affairs with regard to the foreign powers . . . and with regard also to those of our Indian neighbors with whom we have been in a state of enmity or misunderstanding, opens a wide field for consoling and gratifying reflections," directing white settlers would ensure the tranquility that the U.S. Army had brought. Better administration of white settlers was needed because provisions made to protect Indians from "the lawless part of our frontier inhabitants are insufficient."[65] With the Indian threat removed and the U.S. Army at the head of settlement, Federalists had to approach their next task of administering their conquest.

CHAPTER THREE

The Speculator's Republic

Federalists in Territorial Ohio

Upon his arrival at Marietta as territorial governor, Arthur St. Clair hoped to make July 15, 1788, an important day for the inhabitants of the Northwest Territory. He had copies of the Northwest Ordinance printed in Marietta and declared it would help to usher in a new era for the territory and for the young nation's westward expansion overall. As St. Clair said, the Ordinance and his implementation of it would prove that the U.S government could preserve "the welfare of the citizens of the United States, how remote so ever their situation may be." After all, "good government, well administered, is the first of blessings to a people" and would assure "passions of men are restrained within due bounds; their actions receive a proper direction . . . and the beautiful fabric of civilized life is reared and brought to perfection." In time, he imagined settlers and U.S. officials would observe "vast forests converted into arable fields, and cities rising in places which were lately the habitations of wild beasts" through their mutual work.[1]

St. Clair's audience that day was not the ragtag band of hardy frontiersmen and rugged individualists commonly imagined, but rather corporate stockholders in the Ohio Company of Associates. Their leader Rufus Putnam replied on behalf of the residents, "our efforts can succeed only under a wise government," and he promised a partnership with St. Clair. "Whatever difficulties may oppose the progress of your noble and beneficent designs," Putnam said, "we will, as far as in our power, share in the burdens, alleviate your cares, and, upon all occasions, render a full obedience to the government and the laws."[2] The partnership became tangible by late 1789, as the Ohio Company appointed a five-member committee to welcome St. Clair back to Marietta after a leave of absence and show him "the House prepared for him, & request his Acceptance thereof." By the end of 1790, St. Clair lived in the two-story house provided by the company and held nearly 1,200 acres of company lands. Other national officials purchased Ohio Company stock as well, including Josiah Harmar, Henry Knox, and Alexander Hamilton. Also, company executives gained federal offices. Rufus Putnam was appointed territorial judge in 1790 and U.S. surveyor-general in autumn 1796, and the company's unofficial lobbyist, Manasseh Cutler, joined Congress from Massachusetts in 1800.[3]

While historians have often judged the Ohio Company of Associates for its business failures, the company was a prime example of a public-private partnership between speculators and territorial officials. Such partnerships in early America encouraged, according to William J. Novak, "the development of a national infrastructure through the delegation of special powers."[4] In Ohio, this partnership helped oversee settlement and enhance federal power. Speculators took over the distribution and settlement of land while federal officials secured the region militarily, combining to establish a Western society that relied on federal security and guarantees of private land claims. Thus, when Manasseh Cutler wrote of the "design of Congress and of the settlers," it was in frank recognition that private profit and public prerogatives dovetailed quite nicely for these settlers of the Northwest Territory.[5]

Further, this partnership in supervised settlement was distinctly Federalist. Speculators and officials (and some acting as both simultaneously) sought to realize their vision for the new American republic in the West, a clear political battleground over the American Revolution's social implications.[6] While squatters sought to extend equality to land ownership and access in the West, the Federalists populating the Ohio Company and new federal government tried to rein in the Revolution with careful westward expansion. Remaking the Northwest Territory meant creating institutions to resolve conflicts and reorient Western societies, and these institutions existed to protect speculator interests and enhance American state power. This partnership did not create a profitable corporation or a reliable Federalist majority in Ohio, but frontier Federalists still left clear legacies in Ohio politics and society. Meanwhile, the institutions they created were the foundation for continued American expansion into the rest of the Northwest Territory.

Land Speculation Outfits & Government
Partners in the Federalist Frontier

The new settlers and speculators who began heading west in the late 1780s were shock troops for a new Federalist vision and represented a cardinal shift in westward expansion. Corporate adventurers took a four-part plan with them to the Northwest, and their goals both reflected Federalist ideals and included government institutions. First, they believed strong central authority would make the Northwest part of a healthy and virtuous republic. Second, they planned to create a rational society, and the U.S. government would be crucial in creating it. Third, speculators pursued commercial development vigorously in order to help the Northwest realize its economic potential. Through that development, they hoped to mold respectable and industrious Westerners who could surpass their counterparts farther east. Finally, the Ohio Company encouraged social order by strictly enforcing national law, hewing closely to company policies, and encouraging education and religion. They hoped social order would ultimately provide economic benefits and help to redeem American society from the post-Revolutionary problems that Federalists often decried.

Manasseh Cutler explained the logic behind the Ohio Company's plans and the role of government power in their efforts very well. Once the national government cleared Indians and squatters, company adventurers would proceed into a deserted wilderness. "In order to begin *right*, there will be no *wrong* habits to combat," Cutler explained in his promotional tract, and even better, "there is no rubbish to remove, before you can lay the foundation." That foundation would also bring government west with the settlers, minimizing the evils of "distance from the old States" that he believed left the people of Kentucky and the Illinois country "in danger of losing all their habits of government, and allegiance to the United States." The U.S. government was a stabilizing force in settlement as well because sound administration would strengthen settler loyalties. Thus, "every act of Congress under the new constitution" would have to be "looking forward to this object" of engraining new understandings and expectations of federal control in the Ohio valley.[7] Cutler clearly saw in the new federal government under the Constitution an essential partner to the success of the Ohio Company. Meanwhile, the Ohio Company would be a powerful ally for federal aims; in Cutler's view, westward expansion was a symbiotic public-private partnership.

Similarly, John Cleves Symmes laid out plans in the promotional literature for his Miami Purchase, setting strict guidelines enforced by centralized control. Symmes wrote openly of preventing speculators from "engrossing large tracts of land," and therefore he outlined rules requiring purchasers to forfeit up to one-sixth of their claims if they did not arrive in the territory within two years. Rather than allow lands to lay dormant and prove "very prejudicial to the population" of the region, he wanted to use those forfeited lands to place eager settlers who would gain full deed after seven years of continuous occupation. Symmes was more populist than the Ohio Company in his approach, offering purchases starting at 160 acres and even proposing to give settlers six months of food supplies that could be repaid within two years—with interest, of course.[8] Despite the differences, both speculator groups expected to direct settlement from above and offer settlers the salutary benefits of authoritative supervision.

Both the Ohio Company and Symmes bowed quietly but significantly to American authority by choosing town sites near U.S. Army forts. Richard C. Wade argued decades ago that towns led frontier settlement, but the military often came first in the early Northwest.[9] Marietta was built across the Muskingum from Fort Harmar and included a blockhouse for the first settlers to defend themselves. Symmes laid out a fort next to his planned town of Columbia, founded Cincinnati near Fort Washington, and even used the promise of military garrisons providing protection from Indians to sell land.[10] Partly out of necessity, the earliest and most prominent settlements in Ohio sat near military installations, making the U.S. Army the true spearhead of the Federalist frontier. White settlers then began filling in Ohio near army forts, placing national power at the fore of the new Northwest.

Speculators also looked to government and central planning to aid their goals of engineering a rational society in the Northwest, beginning with the ways speculators planned to occupy their new purchases. Cutler noted, "the *Ohio Company* are about to commence the settlement . . . in so regular and judicious a manner" that settlements would leave "no vacant lands exposed." Systematic settlement was also a selling point with Congress in 1787. According to Cutler, Samuel Osgood seemed overtaken with the concept, saying "much on the advantages of System in a new Settlement." Osgood further hoped "it would prove one of the greatest undertakings ever yet attempted in America." With the U.S. government behind them and allies like Osgood, the speculators hoped their new regular system would be the catalyst for a better, more logical American West.[11]

Perhaps the most prominent feature of their plans for rational settlement was their redefinition of property ownership. Legitimate ownership would come only by titles from the speculation outfits with authority flowing directly from the U.S. government. Symmes advertised federally-backed titles compared to "titles . . . not easily ascertained, frequently very doubtful, and too often not well founded" in Kentucky. Ironically, Symmes's malfeasance in land sales eventually created similar problems in the portions on lands for which he failed to pay, but his initial claim was valid: those who bought from Symmes or the Ohio Company enjoyed unmolested claim to their small piece of the Northwest Territory. New property definitions also marginalized alternative ideals about land ownership held by squatters and Indians, and Manasseh Cutler's descendants noted that the new property regime helped to transform the Northwest. They noted "a transition from 'tomahawk' to systematic, permanent improvement," that ushered in new concepts of property creation and ownership, all depending on American state power.[12]

Ohio Company investors also saw themselves as exemplars of a new order in which settlers embraced Enlightenment logic. Their attempts to alter the environment presented the clearest example of reorienting the Northwest. Believing people were products of their environment, they made reforming the environment the first step to reform society with the rectangular grid and the surveyor's chain replacing the hatchet in marking Western boundaries. Rectangular townships brought a scientific regularity to rural space that appealed to Enlightenment ideals, and they led Cutler to enthuse that systematic settlement would "inbosom many men of the most liberal minds" while offering "examples of government, science, and regular industry . . . and revive the ideas of order, citizenship, and the useful sciences."[13] In short, they thought careful oversight and scientific principles could transform the vulgar masses of settlers into orderly and respectable citizens.

Speculators also wished to serve the new Western public by promoting commercial prosperity, another Federalist goal. The Ohio Company created a fund of two thousand dollars to lend for "Business[es] that Shall be of Public Utility." Requiring loan applicants to work for the greater good is telling, and they also restricted loans to "Worthy industrious Persons." Meanwhile, Cutler advertised commercial opportunities in Ohio, hoping to bring "companies of manufacturers . . . under the superintendence of men of property."[14] Federalists were wary of overt self-interest and acquisitive spirits since both smacked of license, so they pursued alternatives that emphasized public good and deference to the "better sort" of the new Northwest.

Nonetheless, the Ohio Company was founded to turn a profit, and economic opportunity in the Northwest Territory was a source of optimism about the company. The postwar depression of the 1780s meant "almost every kind of business is stagnated," Cutler observed, and he thought New Englanders of greater means "would become adventurers in our company."[15] Cutler had success with that pitch as well, shown particularly by Dudley Woodbridge of Connecticut. In several queries to eventual business partner James Backus about Marietta in late 1788, his first question concerned "the prospects of Business," largely because business farther east grew "more gloomy and dull" and he was seeking to start an operation in "the Merchantile Line." Impatience for news showed in a letter three weeks later that declared his "intentions of becoming an inhabitant of your new world and requesting a particular description of the Country and the prospects of Doing Business."[16] For migrants like Woodbridge, profit was a powerful recruiting tool.

In their search for private wealth and the public good, speculators promoted commerce and new industries to encourage a robust, diversified economy. In a single February 1790 meeting, the Ohio Company gave Dudley Woodbridge 120 acres to build a grain mill, and members voted to "give sufficient encouragement to any Person or Persons who will Erect Iron Works" and invited applications for that purpose. Symmes also looked to aid commercial growth with internal improvements. As settler Jacob Burnet recalled, Miami Purchase lands were initially priced at one dollar per acre, but Symmes planned to invest any money paid above that price for "opening roads, and erecting bridges, for the benefit of the settlement." He also proposed taxing purchasers who did not settle on their lands within two years for transportation projects. "The difficulty of opening and making roads in the country," he reasoned, made it necessary to make them finance road constructions, "thereby rendering . . . their land more valuable" while benefitting the settlers already on Symmes's lands, too.[17]

Speculators seemed to find the greatest public utility not in commercialism but in seeking social order through political and cultural institutions, with the Ohio Company planning for supervised settlement to inculcate a love for order and the company's objectives. As the Reverend James Varnum reminded Marietta settlers during the 1788 Independence Day celebration there, they had gone west to save Americans from themselves, especially since they were "sullied and dishonored by the control of un-governable passions." However, with the aid of the Ohio Company and firm guidance from government, "Reason and philosophy are gradually resuming their empire in the human mind," and eventually "the assaults of passion will be subdued by the gentle sway of virtuous affection."[18] For Varnum and so many other company adventurers, obedience to the law was a paramount concern for speculators in the territory, and it was a clear signal of a new social order.

Promoting social order also extended to encouraging religion as a cor-rective against the problems they believed plagued the Northwest and American society overall. Symmes trumpeted section 29 of each town-ship being reserved for churches as per the Northwest Ordinance, and he invited "Ministers of gospel of every denomination of Christians" to use the land set aside for them. Varnum also said the Ohio Company's fortunes "depend upon the Supreme will," so they prized "the great prin-ciples and institutions of religion" among them. Similarly, St. Clair praised Ohio Company settlers for recognizing "the importance to society of a strict attention to the duties of religion and morality," and by month's end, Marietta had its first church fully built. For these Federalists, religion was a necessary social institution that would increase property values and en-courage settlers to follow the strictures of their new society. After all, as St. Clair noted in his praise, such men found that "love of liberty and of order is a master passion."[19] In their minds, the laws of God and of territorial officials were linked. The spiritual would aid the temporal in creating the orderly society speculators wanted so badly to replace the chaos they saw everywhere else they looked.

While religion aided their mission, speculators saw education as the linchpin in their plans to remake the Northwest. Symmes advertised that he saved one township to fund a new academy or college, and like with ministers he invited teachers to take section 16 of each township to build schools. Ohio Company investors were also quick to point out their com-mitment to education. On July 4, 1788, in the same sentence that he spoke of promoting religion, James Varnum proudly declared that the company "made provision, among our first institutions, for scholastic and liberal education" by offering two full townships—more than 46,000 acres—for a public university. Company members agreed to place it "as near the cen-tre as may be, so that the same shall be of good land."[20] Of course, good land meant better prices, so the company hoped to endow their university as much as possible to make Westerners proud of their new institution.

The Ohio Company moved quickly on education, too. Even before the first settlers headed to Marietta in 1788, a company committee recommended they "pay as early attention as possible to the Education of Youth and the Promotion of public Worship" and find "an Instructor eminent for literary accomplishments and the Virtue of his Character." In July, Marietta settlers built a school. Their commitment to education continued over the years, shown by their April 1791 resolution to offer company funds to pay for public teachers in three towns.[21] Company members hoped those schools would have two clear effects. First, they would cast, according to Manasseh Cutler, "a most favorable aspect upon the settlement" by encouraging "the acquisition of useful knowledge" among Westerners, especially its youngest inhabitants. Second, education was an important component of their state-building plan. Cutler explained it well, writing in promotional literature that settlers in Kentucky and the Illinois country were isolated from finer schools and good administration. Losing access to education was an early step in those settlers "losing all their habits of government." To remedy the problem, he made the company's university into his hobby and expended so much energy on it that his grandchildren claimed the university was likely his favorite pursuit while with the Ohio Company.[22]

While speculators implemented their social and political vision in the Northwest, other Federalists supported them through federal policies. With regular public land sales, a stronger transportation network, strengthened regulations, and an enhanced military presence, Federalist policies aided the objectives of speculators and demonstrated a shared partisan vision for the trans-Appalachian West.[23] Their efforts to create a system for surveying and disposing of public lands reflected speculator aims to entrench central authority and a rational order to society in the Northwest. Meanwhile, Federalist officials used diplomacy and internal improvements to aid commercial development, and they took great pains to inculcate public order by using the military for law enforcement and in passing and enforcing laws meant to alter the behavior, daily life, and political orientation of Westerners.

Federalists saw the disposal of public lands as a way to realign Western political sensibilities toward federal power. Thomas Scott of southwest Pennsylvania was the leading proponent of an energetic land policy in Congress, arguing that it would establish an effective federal presence in the trans-Appalachian West. As he said on the floor in May 1789, land offices would "increase the public income" while responding to and accommodating "a great number of people on the ground, who are willing to acquire by purchase a right to the soil they are seated upon." As he reasoned, settlers merely wanted "well grounded hope that the lands they cultivate may become their own," and federal land offices obliged those wishes. Careful not to roil speculator interests, though, he clarified that the new land office would still allow "your million acre purchasers" while selling smaller plots for the greater good, especially to "people who stand in need of land."[24] By his reasoning, the land office could build legitimacy by sating the demands of all Westerners, thus encouraging them to be loyal citizens and look to the new federal government as a legitimate authority among them.

The land office also increased the infrastructural power of the federal government. Scott saw offices planting "a government among them" that would give settlers secure title to prime lands, an important priority since "Much will depend upon the energy and force of the Government established in that country." After all, land offices would show how federal officials can "furnish sufficient power for its own internal purposes" even to settlers far beyond the Appalachians. By defining property, marking boundaries between neighbors, and tying land titles to the federal government, American officials could set the limits of lawful land ownership and respectability in the Northwest Territory while embedding federal power into civil society. Theodore Sedgwick of Massachusetts added that the land officers could "check the enterprising spirit which might grow up" to harm settlement plans in the trans-Appalachian West, and the offices would facilitate sales both to speculators and to "that class who had little money or property . . . [to] enable Congress to get the best market and highest price for their lands."[25] In short, Scott and Sedgwick saw in the land office an agent of change and a source of revenue, and they wanted to maximize both roles for it.

Alexander Hamilton also planned for the land office to project state power into the trans-Appalachian West. By his reasoning, the office would both facilitate "advantageous sales" to speculators and accommodate "individuals now inhabiting the western country, or who may hereafter emigrate." In raising revenues—some of which undoubtedly would be spent in the Northwest—Hamilton could include Western lands in his fiscal-military state structure while satisfying new settlers. Territorial land offices would also make government more flexible, he claimed, by aiding settlers through a proposed credit system, while speculators could negotiate large purchases at the national capital.[26] For Federalists back east, a land office system was a prime opportunity to extend American central authority into the Northwest.

Like the Ohio speculators, Hamilton and Washington hoped to use state power to promote commercial growth. Washington first looked to canals and improvements to the Potomac River as a method for projecting American influence and easing commercial access to the Ohio valley, and he believed the federal government was empowered to conduct such projects by the Constitution. Similarly, Hamilton believed strongly in the helping hand of government to develop the capital-poor national economy, telling Congress that federal power should be used to drive market growth and national improvement.[27] For example, he sounded like other Ohio Company stockholders, believing it important to "diversify the industrious pursuits" of the people. However, ventures like the Ohio Company needed protection and aid: "The existence or assurance of aid from the government of the country," he wrote, "may be essential to fortify adventurers" against negative market forces, Indian attacks, or European interventions.[28] In Marietta and in Philadelphia, Federalist leaders had decided upon a course of government-driven commercialism by 1791, and any national program the Federalists developed would surely help new Westerners.

Federalist officials at the federal level looking to implant the new American state into the Northwest also formed partnerships with speculators to promote a common vision of social order. As governor, Arthur St. Clair served as a liaison between national and Ohio Company Federalists. St. Clair approached his administration with three important attitudes linked with Federalist policy aims. First, St. Clair was undoubtedly an elitist and imagined himself an ambassador of gentility and intelligent government to the inhabitants of the Northwest. A believer in wise administration and federal benevolence, he saw many benefits to the arrival of respectable settlers provided by the Ohio Company and often praised the company's efforts at Marietta. On the other hand, he clearly held low opinions of the French and American settlers who had occupied the region before 1788, castigating them in a May 1790 letter as "the most ignorant People in the World" and lamenting to Hamilton that he often felt like "a poor devil banished to another planet."[29]

Second, St. Clair shared with other Federalists an enthusiasm for energetic government. To support that energy, he approved of Hamilton's system of taxation and decried Jefferson's plan of "abolishing the internal taxes" in 1802, fearing that "public credit [would] be destroyed" and worse, "a new revolution . . . where that might land us no man could possibly tell." He supported other means of raising revenue as well, advocating to Washington in August 1789 plans to sell lands through a land office "in small Quantities, and . . . payment of the purchase Money, which should run upon Interest." Overall, he argued, the land office and a system of credit would allow the federal government to "derive nearly the same Advantage as if the Lands had been paid for in the first Instance; for an Interest would accrue."[30] Raising public money and spreading government power through the Northwest was clearly a priority to him, and his policy prescriptions supported those goals.

Finally, St. Clair used government power to create an orderly and obedient population. As he told Washington of the new federal presence, Westerners "would learn to reverence the Government; and the Countless multitudes which will be produced in that vast Region would become the Nerves and Sinews of the Union." He also rewarded settlers from Europe who declared their loyalty to the United States, appointing them to local offices in order to further entrench federal authority among established settlements.[31] Conversely, disobedience required stern correction. He tried (even if spectacularly unsuccessfully) to punish Indians for their perfidy in 1791, and he believed unruly whites could deserve similar treatment. He praised Hamilton for his handling of the whiskey excise protests, believing protesters should be made "to comply with the Excise Law" and offered whatever aid he could, including a law disallowing "all ardent spirits into the Territory, the duties upon which have not been either paid or secured."[32] His comments reveal his commitment to what can only be characterized as an orderly republic. It was orderly because obedience to federal law would be absolute, but to him, obedience was also best for republican virtue. If opponents did not realize the excise was in the best interests of the republic, then federal officials would demonstrate why they should obey.

St. Clair's attitudes toward alcohol also fit a larger pattern among Federalist leaders, as controlling the importation and sale of alcohol in the Northwest Territory showed their commitment to social order. Indian alcohol consumption earned the greatest scrutiny. In Congress, Thomas Scott of Pennsylvania was once again a leading voice of frontier Federalist interests, emphasizing the need for "competent regulations to secure the peace of the frontiers" during debates for the Trade and Intercourse Act of 1791. In his estimation, prohibiting unlicensed trading as part of comprehensive trade regulations would also curtail the flow of alcohol into

Indian country. Other Federalists in the House even argued unsuccessfully for using the U.S. Army to enforce the new regulations since they would "probably have the greatest influence with the Indians." Territorial officials concurred. St. Clair complained that "desire for spirituous liquors" motivated Indian raids, and their violence was rewarded because of so many boats on the Ohio River "carrying more or less of that commodity." Rufus Putnam also blamed alcohol for Indian troubles, lecturing Vincennes settlers in 1792 that "none of you are Ignorent . . . of the law that prohibits the Selling any Spiritous liquors to Indians," and the Indian war demanded that officials enforce the law "in an especial maner."[33]

Other Northwestern officials tried to control the alcohol market among white settlers. Judge Symmes praised the whiskey excise in a letter to friend and New Jersey Congressman Jonathan Dayton in 1791, but he hoped for more. "I wish that congress had . . . made it felony," he said, for anyone other than clergy to "transport even the smallest quantity of any kind of wine over the Alleghany mountains." In Marietta, Thomas Wallcut argued for and secured a February 1790 town ordinance to regulate the establishment of taverns in the name of the public peace.[34] For both men, alcohol was simply too corrosive to society and required careful regulation. However, their advocacy had a clear tenor. Only strong measures would reform the ways of white Westerners, and the success of their new society required firm guidance by strict authorities.

Wallcut even linked his efforts to control alcohol with Federalist notions of republican virtue. He complained of an unruly inn "destructive of peace, good order, and exemplary morals," and he wanted regulations for taverns because society needed "sufficient checks . . . to restrain and punish the inordinate passions of oppressive, cruel, and avaricious men." Alcohol unleashed those terrible passions and undermined the morality "upon which not only the well-being but the very existence of society so much depends."[35] This talk of restraining passions mirrored other Federalists who thought only strong leadership would enable the evils of license among white squatters to become virtuous republican liberty among the new, more respectable white settlers. Thus, he saw government in the Northwest needing not only to be energetic but also to use that energy to steer American society.

Despite their clear vision and the cooperation of national and territorial authorities, the Northwest Indian War interfered with speculation in Ohio. "Our Settlement does not encrease," Marietta resident Return J.

Meigs, Jr. complained in 1792, since settlers were "circumscribed within narrow Limits . . . [by] the Indian War." Population statistics kept by Rufus Putnam attested to the same problem, as Marietta slipped in size from 312 people in 1790 to 226 at war's end.[36] Without new settlers making new land purchases, the Ohio Company simply could not raise new revenues. Defending its settlements also harmed company prospects. In July 1790, the company passed resolutions to dig a well and repair the defenses at Campus Martius, and later the company agreed to raise a thirty-man militia for company settlers and erect stronger defenses against Indian attacks. To help staff those defenses, the company offered 100 acres of free land to "All Persons . . . who now reside, or may during the present troubles," the resolution read, "and who shall continue, with us to defend the purchase through the present Indian War."[37] Their situation was obviously desperate, as the company was willing to mortgage its future to shore up its lowly defenses.

Clearly, the expenses of defending against Indians threatened the future of speculators in the Northwest Territory. In 1791, the Ohio Company petitioned the federal government for help covering defense expenses. Meanwhile, Rufus Putnam lobbied for aid by appealing to other Federalists' sense of duty to their fellow citizens. In 1790, he begged arch-Federalist Congressman Fisher Ames for aid to prevent "an infinite mischief to the United States." The company made its purchase "in full confidence that Such protection would be afforded," he claimed, and their success depended on that protection because *of what value are lands without inhabitants, and who will wish to inhabit a country where no reasonable protection is aforded.*"[38]

The war also gave reason to fret over the future of westward expansion. Putnam warned Washington in early 1791 that without effective protection, their vision for the Northwest would give way to "privit adventurers who will pay little or no reguard to the laws of the United States." After all, only "federal Troops at the point of the Bayonet" could evict squatters who "flood & Seize the country to them Selves," and making them recognize federal authority would require "a much greater expence then the chastizeing the Indians in a proper manner." Knox agreed that administering justice and teaching Westerners "proper habits of submission to the laws" required settlers to "be effectually protected against indian depredations . . . and on this point it behoves government to be inflexible."[39] To preserve a public-private partnership in frontier Federalism, government had to protect the interests and investments of speculators.

As it continued, the war forced speculators and settlers into deeper desperation. The Ohio Company was in financial straits after investors forfeited 150 shares in 1790, and by 1792, Congress had reduced the purchases of both the Ohio Company and Judge Symmes to only lands for which they had already paid. Meanwhile, Ohio settlers had to alter daily activities to remain secure. In autumn 1792, Territorial Secretary Winthrop Sargent ordered Cincinnatians under penalty of law to attend church services while armed or face "most serious and melancholy circumstances" from Indians. Meanwhile, Symmes complained to Congressman Jonathan Dayton, "Instead of favor, to which we are fully entitled," settlers who had served "at an early day in aid of Government and pushing forward to . . . extend the empire of the United States" were abandoned. As a result, their project to "reclaim from savage men and beasts a country that may one day prove the brightest jewel in the regalia of the nation" was near ruin. In righteous indignation, he asked Dayton, "Is this what you call fair, sir?"[40]

By the war's end in 1795, the Ohio Company and Symmes's speculations were effectively finished. The Ohio Company made its last grants in February 1796 and Symmes saw his land sales challenged more often as the 1790s progressed, and for those failures, historians have often discussed Symmes as an impractical dreamer at best and a criminal at worst.[41] However, Symmes and the Ohio Company failed partly because the Northwest Territory was unsafe for white settlement and incredibly difficult for economic development before 1795. In the end, speculators simply could not pay off their large purchases without enough settlers buying land. In a way, Symmes's speculation and the Ohio Company were the last casualties of the Northwest Indian War, but their social and political ideals were very much alive in the Northwest.

Settlement and the Aftermath of the Speculator's Republic

Even after their speculation outfits ended, John Cleves Symmes, Rufus Putnam, and others continued to affect the direction of settlement through their political service.[42] Under the guidance of the original speculators and Arthur St. Clair, the rest of Ohio's territorial period saw Federalists continue to implant the early American state. Settlers arriving in ensuing years tended to vote for Jeffersonian Republicans, but Federalists ultimately won their war on a disorderly West by making government integral to westward expansion and engineering a society in which gentlemen led. They failed to make Ohio a Federalist bastion, but they turned back the radical implications of the American Revolution and oversaw the transformation of the Northwest from a region where loyalties were fragile into one fully supportive of the Union.

Partisan fractures were first evident during the Northwest Indian War, especially over alcohol regulations. In hopes of controlling the trade in alcohol and the character of drinking establishments in the territory, laws required would-be tavern owners to license their businesses and pay a fee of sixteen dollars. In Cincinnati, opponents of the measure published their concerns in the first editions of Cincinnati's Jeffersonian organ, *Centinel of the North-Western Territory*, in 1793. Essays by "Manlius" railed against the tavern licensing law and its supposition that tavern owners and patrons were "less virtuous than their fellow citizens."[43] By implying the opposite, Manlius took the implications of the Revolution into the social sphere of Cincinnati: all men's virtues were created equal. Federalists in the Northwest, however, believed settlers needed strict guidance to attain respectability.

Opponents quickly became more courageous. Within weeks, Manlius claimed "the American revolution fully prove[d]" Americans would not tolerate "taking away their money without their consent." In early Cincinnati, Republicans opposed new taxes as part of extending Revolutionary promises of equality and fairness to all aspects of their lives, while Federalists wanted a more stratified and harmonious social order. Some even sought to reenact the Revolution in their efforts to topple Federalist rule. In October 1794, an opponent compared St. Clair unfavorably to King George III, claiming that while the governor held the same control over the military and the civil administration, at least King George required his appointees to be "under good behavior."[44] In the Northwest, Jeffersonian opponents would continue the Revolution, at least in their own minds, and push for a more egalitarian social vision.

The explosive growth of the white population in the Northwest Territory after 1795 only exacerbated partisanship. With security guaranteed more firmly, the white population of Ohio grew exponentially from a few thousand in 1793 until statehood (which required 60,000 people) ten years later.[45] That influx only made the extension of state power more important to Governor St. Clair, who worried in 1796 that without sufficient federal action to extend land sales and update policies for the public lands, "such numbers of people will take possession of them as may not easily be removed."[46] Those migrants included Federalists like Jacob Burnet, who moved from New Jersey to the Miami Purchase in 1796, but many more settlers came from Virginia and Kentucky and were more likely to be Republicans. Many of them settled in the river valleys between the Ohio Company lands and the Miami Purchase, giving them a clear base of political strength from which to assail the Federalist establishment. Ironically, the guarantee of security that came from defeating the Indians in Ohio even worked against Federalists. As Donald Ratcliffe has pointed out, the lack of an Indian threat likely emboldened some of St. Clair's opponents who had other priorities—namely, staying alive—during the war. Quite simply, safety allowed settlers to worry about battling partisan enemies instead of Indians.[47]

Despite resistance, Federalists pressed ahead with their state-building plans in 1795 and 1796 by seeking to maintain the U.S. military presence in the West. Shortly after the Battle of Fallen Timbers, territorial judge Rufus Putnam asked for a fort along the Scioto River to guarantee regular mail service and security for settlers. He argued that mail was essential because "the knowledge diffused among the people by Newspapers, by corrispondence between frinds and other communic[a]tions with these remote parts of the American Empire may be of infinite consequence to the goverment." In order to offer that protection and occupy new and existing forts in the Northwest, Secretary of State Timothy Pickering argued in 1796 that the military should be maintained "even in time of peace, in order to preserve peace with the Indians, and to protect theirs and the public lands."[48]

Federalists also looked to provide a system of public land sales and orderly settlement to accommodate settlers arriving quickly. Urged by worrisome comments from Western officials like St. Clair, who suggested opening offices "where any person might locate, [and] purchase land in small quantities," Federalists in Congress moved to answer those concerns. Speaker of the House Jonathan Dayton, also a close friend of John Cleves Symmes, spearheaded support in debates on a new land bill in February 1796. While Republicans proposed shrinking minimum land purchases and opening more offices, Dayton stood for carefully supervised, systematic settlement maintained by higher prices and larger purchase requirements, hallmarks of the speculators' original plans. He attacked Republican plans for their "loose manner" of westward expansion and suggested contiguous settlement and sales to regulate settlement and enhance land values. Further, he said, compact settlement would allow surveyors to better keep pace with demand and provide "a fresh quantity of land" whenever previous townships had filled.[49]

In the end, Dayton and the Federalists won. The 1796 land act mandated land auctions at federal land offices in Cincinnati and Pittsburgh and regular sales afterward, with purchases beginning at 640 acres and only as the newly created office of Surveyor General completed surveys. Further, it offered sales on credit; settlers could make a five percent down payment on the total price and settle the balance within a year. Federalists also left out any preemption rights for squatters on the principle that "illegal settlements on the lands of the United States ought not to be encouraged," said William Smith of South Carolina. After all, "yielding to the said claims would interfere with the general provisions for the sale of the said lands." Upon its passage, Treasury Secretary Oliver Wolcott, Jr. and President Washington placed the new offices in the hands of Federalists and distinguished Western gentlemen. John Neville, a tax collector attacked during the Whiskey Rebellion, became receiver of public money in the Pittsburgh office. Meanwhile, Rufus Putnam became surveyor general, a clear signal that the speculator's republic was still alive even if his company was withering away. The new system also paid quick dividends, as the new Pittsburgh land office sold over $110,000 worth of land by January 1797; credit worked well, too, with over one-third of that sum already collected.[50]

While Federalists planned a benign state distributing lands to settlers, force also had a role in maintaining public order. Pickering listed saving "lands of the United States, from intrusions, and to remove the actual intruders" among his reasons to maintain a standing army, and he proposed a rudimentary intelligence service in which commanding officers wrote regular reports to give him and the president a comprehensive picture of frontier developments. Meanwhile, when settlers sent by Putnam to found Athens in 1797 discovered squatters at the site and many of them "disposed to practice the principle that, might makes right," Putnam's men took "forcible possession of the land and improvements." Soon, Athens authorities gained a reputation for treating criminals strictly, leaving unruly locals "frightened" according to one description, while local judges threatened to send disorderly citizens to the Marietta court known "for firmness and strict justice." Such threats "filled them with terror."[51]

Other officials agreed with treating squatters roughly, and they often defended the use of force by pointing to squatters' lawlessness and lack of republican virtue. St. Clair railed against squatters as threats to his power and castigated them for being "little tinctured with Justice or humanity" and having a "pretty strong sympathy with their Pockets." Meanwhile, Territorial Secretary Winthrop Sargent fell back upon another trope, declaring that squatters wished *"to be as free as the Natives."*[52] Desires of those squatters for preemption offended frontier Federalists. Officials believed squatter hopes of gaining free or cheap land epitomized the lawlessness and self-interest that they deplored in American society of the 1780s. They disrupted Federalist plans for orderly settlement and sought preemption that would harm public land revenues. In a sense, the new round of squatters represented everything Federalists had attempted to turn back in Ohio.

Federalists in Ohio pivoted their political attacks on squatters toward the Republicans who poured into Ohio, especially as the territory moved into the second stage of government laid out by the Northwest Ordinance in 1798. The second stage meant a territorial legislature and elections for it, and Federalists described their electoral opponents as self-interested and less virtuous. Jacob Burnet of Cincinnati, elected as a Federalist in 1798, derided Jeffersonian representatives from Ross County because they had "not excelled in talent and energy." Voters there had merely chosen the "strongest men as guardians of her interest." He also found Republicans in the territorial legislature "influenced by motives of ambition," the great enemy of republicanism, "and were more anxious to gain power, than to reform abuses." Worse, their slander that "Federalists were *aristocrats*" led may voters to see the "framers and fathers of the Constitution . . . as its worst enemies."[53] In Burnet's view, Ohio's Republicans were usurpers of rightful and deserving Federalist leadership.

St. Clair also went on the partisan offensive whenever he could. He accused political rivals Thomas Worthington and Edward Tiffin, both of whom migrated into the Miami valley in 1798 and settled at Chillicothe, of trying to locate the territorial capital at their adopted home in order to augment their property values. As the center of political power in the territory, the location of the capital was a legitimate issue that animated the imaginations of town boosters throughout Ohio, but to St. Clair it was a simple question of self-interest that disgusted him and affected the voting habits of many citizens. The new citizens were "indigent and ignorant," he complained in 1799, and "ill qualified to form a constitution and government for themselves." However, of greater concern were their lack of political principles and their economic ties to the wealthiest landowners of the area. If Miami valley voters controlled the political future, he worried that government would become "democratic in its form and oligarchic in its execution," with creditors supporting their political careers by dictating votes to debtors.[54]

Meanwhile, St. Clair, Burnet, and other Federalists imagined themselves paragons of republican virtue and gentlemanly leadership in the Northwest. St. Clair saw himself as the final defense against self-interest and license, leading him to veto bills quite frequently to preserve the Federalist mission in the territory. In 1798, he rejected a petition from settlers living in unincorporated lands they bought from John Cleves Symmes, pointing out the proper methods to obtain land in the territory. As he explained, the petitioners did not have valid title because they occupied their homes contrary to acts of Congress. Without government-backed titles, he told them, "You stand . . . on the same ground as those who have sat down on the public lands that are not claimed." He also continued Federalist patterns of carefully regulating the alcohol trade. On the last day of the first territorial legislature's meetings in December 1799, he informed lawmakers that he vetoed an "act to regulate taverns and other public-houses, especially in country places" because they have "the worst effects upon the industry and the morals of the people." Further, he explained, the required nine recommendations on their character were *too few*, and the law failed to regulate where taverns could operate.[55] St. Clair rejected petitions and bills not because he was a tyrant (as his opponents claimed), but because he would not cave to his opponents and risk all the work Federalists had done to implant state power and encourage settlers to respect the law.

St. Clair's efforts to preserve public order are especially clear in his Indian policies. He allowed Moravian missionaries to work with Indians in the territory, swayed by promises to spread Christianity among the Indians, establish schools on their lands, and "inculcate habits of industry and sobriety, and instruct them to live a quiet and peaceable life in all godliness and honesty." He also advocated for and signed the bill to outlaw the alcohol trade in Indian towns, believing it would preserve the "considerable progress in agriculture, and the arts" by Indians who interacted with the missionaries.[56] His hopes for the Indian population mirrored the hopes he expressed during his landing at Marietta in 1788. With the Indians, he wished again to see good government allow the better angels of human nature to prevail. With an active government presence among the Indians and another public-private partnership, this time with Moravian missionaries, he could do just that.

However, St. Clair's hopes to control the direction of settlement faced two major problems by 1800. Republicans threatened Federalist control of the territorial legislature as well as the federal government in the fall election, and he faced a population growing too quickly for him to control effectively. By 1800, the population topped 45,000 with the required figure of 60,000 inhabitants to apply for statehood approaching quickly, and St. Clair pushed to partition the territory through the Miami valley and present-day central Ohio to slow the march to statehood. Doing so, he explained to Ohioan James Ross, would allow more time "for the cultivation of a disposition favorable to the General Government" and stymie the designs of Republican elites in the Miami valley. As a result, he said, the westernmost territory would remain a "colonial state for a good many years to come" while the state formed from the eastern section would be "surely Federal."[57]

Republicans in the territorial legislature defeated the plan and, while looking to oust St. Clair in their own Revolution of 1800, offered a two-pronged response to the Federalist plan for settlement and government. First, they called for universal white male suffrage, prospectively to boost their influence in the territory. Territorial law required men to own fifty acres of land to vote, but in its place, Republicans wanted to extend voting rights to all men who paid taxes to their county or the territory. Second, they wanted to reform public land policies to make land ownership more accessible to existing residents and encourage new settlers. The plan reflected the worries of settlers like those along the Scioto River who petitioned Congress for a new system in 1798, complaining of "enormous prices" for land that must be purchased in large tracts. It left them, they said, "Disappointed in getting lands on easy and equitable terms in hopes of which we adventured *our lives*."[58]

Republicans saw their wishes realized by Northwest Territory Delegate William Henry Harrison, who engineered a new land law in 1800 to reorganize land offices and better accommodate small purchases by reducing purchase requirements to 320 acres and opening more land offices. The law enabled a new era for prospective landowners in the Northwest. As Jacob Burnet recalled, it allowed "men of limited means . . . to purchase," and so they "flocked . . . from every part of the Union" and made statehood possible all the more quickly. The land law of 1800 did not live up to all

of its promises, especially since one bad harvest could undo many farmers, and the need to profit quickly or forfeit their payments gave many
purchasers illusory control over their futures.[59] Furthermore, Congress
agreed to partition the territory in 1800 along the state lines of present-
day Ohio, enhancing the political position of Republicans there.

Gaining strength and with a friendly territorial partition, Republicans
saw statehood as their escape from Federalist rule after Adams renewed
St. Clair's appointment as territorial governor in 1800. Casting themselves
as a new generation of the Revolution, they campaigned against the tyranny of "King Arthur" or "Arthur the First." The move to statehood especially added momentum after one of St. Clair's leading opponents, Thomas
Worthington of Chillicothe, lobbied in Washington, D.C. unsuccessfully
for a new governor during the winter of 1801–1802.[60] Meanwhile, Federalists had recommitted to their paternalistic style of politics in the Northwest. One clear signal of that commitment came from the old Federalist
stronghold at Marietta, where a town meeting passed a resolution against
statehood as too chaotic for the territory's settlers. Statehood would expose
Ohioans to "the storms of party and the agitations of intrigue," a terrible
combination while settlers remained "a mixed mass of people, scattered
over an immense wilderness."[61] In essence, they suggested, society in the
Northwest simply needed to mature, and until then, the citizens of the
territory required the guiding hand of federally appointed gentlemen like
St. Clair.

Undeterred by Federalist resistance, Ohio Republicans proposed a
state constitutional convention and forced Federalists into a curious, strict
constructionist position. During early debates on a statehood bill in late
March 1802, Northwest Territorial Delegate Paul Fearing, a loyal Federalist who practiced law in Marietta since settling there since 1788, claimed
the bill was unconstitutional and violated the Northwest Ordinance. As
he pointed out, "Congress had nothing to do with the arrangements for
calling a convention." Further, he claimed, proponents of statehood did
not speak for the entire territory, and he suggested once again that Jeffersonians in the territory were merely self-interested and ambitious. Roger
Griswold of Connecticut added that Congressional action in the statehood
process began a slippery slope of federal interference with the states, saying, "If we interfere with the first, we may interfere with the last."[62]

Federalist settlers and former speculators in the Northwest Territory
agreed that the enabling act was unconstitutional. The Ohio Company's
former lobbyist, Manasseh Cutler, serving in 1802 as a Congressman from

Massachusetts, fumed about unconstitutional interference from Congress via the statehood bill. "Never was a bill passed so opposed to so many constitutional, just and equitable principles," he told his diary, declaring that "It tyrannizes over every principle of liberty and freedom." Meanwhile, territorial legislator Jacob Burnet claimed it was "unauthorized . . . by any legitimate authority," and worse, "prescribed the boundaries of the State, fixed the number of members of which the Convention could consist, and apportioned the number to be chosen by each county." Overall, he thought Congress made "assumptions of power, not warranted by the Constitution, or the Ordinance." Nonetheless, the bill passed and was signed into law April 30, 1802.[63]

Once the Enabling Act passed, St. Clair tried to shape the convention to favor Federalists. Speaking in Cincinnati, he described his ideal convention delegate. "A Constitution fitted to the habits, the manners, and the genius of the people . . . requires strong minds, improved by a thorough acquaintance with the faults as well as the excellencies of all the Constitutions that exist, not only in the United States, but in the whole world," he said. In essence, education and gentlemanly sophistication made a candidate worthy to St. Clair, and he added that good candidates "should be well informed" on matters of "rational liberty" and "true republicanism." Showing old Federalist worries, he noted that liberty "is not an unbounded license to do what every one sees good in his own eyes. It requires direct study and deep reflection, with a facility of speaking readily and convincingly."[64]

However, by the convention's opening on November 1, 1802, St. Clair was flailing helplessly at the political currents soon to sweep him out of power. Twenty-six of the thirty-five delegates were committed Republicans, with many Federalist hopefuls handed humiliating electoral defeats. In his remarks to open the convention, St. Clair proudly noted the progress since the start of his tenure, "when the affairs of this country were committed to me; when your numbers were only about thirty men; a wilderness before them to subdue, and surrounded by numerous tribes of savages." He also declared that he had succeeded in teaching Ohioans "morals and . . . the institutions of religion" and the importance of social order, "without which civil society can not exist." On the other hand, the Republican-dominated constitutional convention was evidence of "party rage . . . stalking with destructive strides over the whole continent" and threatening all his achievements. Further, he complained about the conditions placed upon Ohio's statehood, especially that the road funds

promised by Congress would not be given easily and that the rush to statehood had cost Ohio an opportunity to lay taxes on recently sold lands to
cover state and local needs. Following his remarks, he left the convention, and the convention voted 32–1 to begin writing a constitution. Only
Manasseh's son Ephraim Cutler voted no.[65]

Despite Republican dominance of the convention, the new state constitution reflected Federalist influence. For example, Federalists succeeded
in altering the third article, outlining the state judiciary, to their ends with
Ephraim Cutler proving pivotal. He believed it "the duty of the convention, and a wise policy, to provide a mode of administering justice that
would bring it as near every man's door as was practicable." He spoke of
making courts accessible to all citizens, a form of state penetration in Ohio
that would continue Federalist goals of an orderly Northwest. As a result
of his work, the new article required each county to carry at least two associate judges and the state supreme court to meet in each county once
per year. Cutler reflected proudly on the fact that his influence earned
the Federalist delegates "respectful attention by those who had before
manifested something bordering upon contempt" throughout the rest of
the convention.[66]

In the final article, the bill of rights, Federalist influence is clear in
two key instances. Section two affirmed the Northwest Ordinance ban
on slavery, for which Cutler assumed much of the credit in his records.
Abolishing slavery in Ohio hinged on the vote of John Milligan, who had
voted against allowing slavery while a territorial legislator, so Cutler aimed
his speech specifically at Milligan. "It cost me every effort I was capable
of making," Cutler claimed, but Milligan voted against introducing slavery
in a one-vote majority. Cutler also claimed credit for section three, which
in hallmark Federalist language declared "religion, morality and knowledge . . . necessary to good government and the happiness of mankind."
To assure those qualities and good government, the constitution required
that "schools and the means of instructions shall forever be encouraged by
legislative provision." Because of these victories, Cutler said, "I very much
doubt whether any of the members of the convention were, at the conclusion, better, if so well, pleased with the result of our labors, as General
Putnam" and other Federalists at the convention's outcome.[67]

Soon after the convention concluded on November 29, St. Clair received news that President Jefferson had removed him as territorial governor, and on December 8 he offered his farewell address defending his
legacy. He had presided over "a period that necessarily required your

Governor should be vested with a considerable portion of power, and that power was applied to your benefit only." During his tenure, he reminded citizens, "You have been protected from dangers from abroad, and made happy at home . . . your liberties and your property were guarded by wholesome laws, executed with exactness and at the same time with mildness."[68] At its unceremonious final moment, St. Clair reviewed his governorship as steering Ohioans through trying times, while statehood left them in an uncertain new era. Similarly, Manasseh Cutler took little pride in Ohio's statehood even as a member of the House of Representatives. As Congress approved Ohio's constitution and it officially became a state on March 1, 1803, his diary was silent about the matter. Apparently, he found moving trunks and barrels to be of greater importance that day.[69]

Federalists no longer led Ohio in 1803, but their rule left important legacies. They secured the Northwest for the United States, as decisive actions in the Northwest Indian War and in establishing a territorial government quieted worries about the region's attachment to the Union. Additionally, Federalists constructed a state in which gentlemen ruled. Delegates to the 1802 constitutional convention owned an average of 1,537 acres in 1810, more than five times the state average and worth ten times the average landholder's estate in the 1810 Census. Even Jeffersonian leaders were major landowners. For example, the first Speaker of the Ohio Senate, Nathaniel Massie, held over 78,000 acres in the Miami valley, and future Ohio Governor and Senator Thomas Worthington owned 18,000 acres. As historian Lee Soltow has observed, the land barons in Ohio—twelve of whom controlled 7.5 percent of the state's resident acreage in 1810—also controlled state politics for the next decade.[70] State legislators were growing less wealthy in the 1780s, when Ohio Company settlers first arrived. By 1810, Ohioans saw that trend reversed in their General Assembly.

Federalist administration also left two important political legacies in the former Northwest Territory. First, Federalists continued in Ohio politics and worked with the next generation of Federalists who would continue the partisan fight well after St. Clair headed back to Pennsylvania. Second, Federalists had built a series of institutions that their Jeffersonian successors would enlarge and refine during the succeeding decades. In a sense, the Jeffersonians who followed Federalist administration in the Northwest only extended the state power Federalists established there.[71] Ultimately, both legacies intertwined as Jeffersonian Republicans in the

Northwest moved toward state-building and as aging Federalists sought new political allies. The new American state in the Northwest did not die with Federalist administration in Ohio. It merely assumed new management under a series of enterprising Western Jeffersonians who saw the value in government guidance of westward expansion. Their leadership would usher in a new era for the early American state in the nineteenth-century Northwest, as Jeffersonians offered a new articulation of Federalist institutions and visions for future of the Northwest.

CHAPTER FOUR

Energy and Republicanism

Jeffersonian Administration in Indiana and Illinois

In 1787, as the Ohio Company was laying out its plans and the Philadelphia convention ironed out the Constitution, residents of present-day Indiana and Illinois were clamoring for more energetic government. In July, residents of Vincennes along the Wabash River asked Congress for help because they were "addicted to the Indian trade," and wanted the United States to provide land grants for adult male inhabitants as well as common lands to aid new industries, build "Court houses, Jails, churches, bridges, repairing roads—&c.," and raise funds for them. Meanwhile, the people of Kaskaskia, on the east bank of the Mississippi, hoped for similar aid. As they informed U.S. Army commanding officer Josiah Harmar, "The people of this district Sir do not refuse to be under the Administration of a salutary police, and a good government."[1] In advocating for stronger government, the people of these Western towns reflected a paradigm shift in American politics. Even in the wake of the American Revolution, Western settlers hoped for energetic government to aid them in their pursuits.

After 1800, more attentive government came under William Henry Harrison and the new Indiana Territory. Conventional wisdom presents this period of Jeffersonian Republican triumph as a marked retreat from Federalist leadership and ideals. In this telling, 1800 represented a sea change, offering victories in turns for Jefferson, democracy, libertarianism, egalitarianism, small government, the American people, and even the American Revolution. The maximalist style of Federalist governance was replaced by a new Republican ethic that sought to make the United States government as cheap, simple, and unobtrusive as possible. With Federalists out of the way, American democracy reigned. Taxes and spending fell, government institutions shrank, and Americans everywhere sighed in relief after groaning under twelve years of Federalist control. Meanwhile,

westward expansion was a primary path to redeeming the republic, allowing Jefferson and his party to prolong the lifespan of agrarian America
before industry and urbanism swept across the Atlantic states.[2]

In Indiana and Illinois, however, federal and territorial leaders worked
within Republican politics to maintain and even enhance an energetic
government presence over American westward expansion. By emphasizing cost-effective policies, egalitarian ends, and accessibility, these energetic Republicans pursued four policy objectives. First, they believed
government should be active in westward expansion, so they remained
committed to improving education, transportation, and other government
institutions to spread state power in Indiana and Illinois. Second, they
chose to make government more available to Westerners and a helpmeet
for their needs, setting them apart from Federalist administrators in Ohio.
Third, they continued hardline Indian policies, supporting a strong U.S.
Army and aggressive negotiations with Indians that enhanced federal
power. If successful, they looked to secure land for settlers while driving
away European influences. Finally, they tried to attain their goals relatively cheaply, thereby minimizing the tax burden on the American people.
William Henry Harrison summarized their hopes well, telling the Indiana Territory legislature in summer 1805 that he wanted a "system which
would unite simplicity with energy."[3] As a result, energetic Republicans in
Indiana and Illinois enlarged, not shrank, the American state.

To achieve their policy goals, energetic Republicans often repurposed
Federalist institutions as well. Some of them even supported those Federalist creations before 1800. For example, William Henry Harrison, veteran of Anthony Wayne's campaign and a signer of the Treaty of Greenville,
aligned with some Federalists as Congressional Delegate for the Northwest Territory, especially in maintaining the standing army. Speaking in
the House of Representatives, he claimed to speak for the entire territory
since "nine-tenths of his constituents . . . would with much more readiness
bear the proportion of the expense which would be necessary to maintain
these forces" and hold back Indian threats.[4]

As a result, energetic Republican officials ensured a strong state remained to oversee American expansion in the Northwest. Republican
administrators spread Federalist policies and institutions in education,
public lands, and Indian trade into Indiana and Illinois after 1800.[5] Led
by Republicans like Albert Gallatin and William Henry Harrison, federal appointees like John Johnston in the Indian trade factories and John

Badollet in the land offices were the foot soldiers of the American state, executing grand designs for extending it westward. At Fort Wayne, Johnston was a successful trader but was so much more to Indians and the U.S. government, gaining power as the payer of Indian annuities, a confidant of Governor Harrison and Indian leaders, and ultimately an Indian agent and negotiator. Meanwhile, land officers like Badollet were direct outlets of federal power who were simultaneously government auctioneers, real estate agents, mortgage brokers, and on a voluntary basis after 1817, even meteorological record keepers.[6] Through these men, white and Indian inhabitants of Indiana and Illinois had personal experience with government power, and they came to appreciate the benefits federal power provided them.

Energetic Republicans Harrison, Illinois Territory Governor Ninian Edwards, and others followed Federalist examples in Indian policy. Aggressive negotiations once again were the rule, provoking Indian resistance and ultimately a war that forced Native Americans away from white settlements in the Northwest. Also, after the War of 1812 cleared Indian challenges to white settlement, the state articulated by energetic Republicans was ready to oversee and aid the new settlers. Rather than a period of drawing down the state in the West, the Revolution of 1800 brought a new era of state growth and a new life for the institutions that lay beneath the Federalist frontier. In turn, settlers continued to lend those institutions legitimacy through their widening participation in the new regime.

The State in the Territory
Energetic Republican Government in Indiana

Government institutions in Indiana and Illinois filled vital spaces for both white and Indian inhabitants. Army forts projected American power that Indian peoples respected, and forts offered a sense of security for newly arrived settlers. In addition, the presence of the U.S. Army was an incredible economic stimulus to local settlers. Andrew Cayton claimed that soldiers provided "the best market on the frontier," paying cash for food, alcohol, and a variety of services, while William Bergmann pointed out the importance of federal contractors to local markets. Farmers found the contractors, who preferred local sources for supplies, to be ready and reliable customers paying good prices for their produce.[7] The security and economic stimulus provided by these military garrisons often assisted the development of towns nearby. For example, the town of Fort Wayne grew up around its namesake, and Chicago was founded in the shadow of Fort Dearborn. Forts also offered other services like medical care often hard to find elsewhere, too.

Outside of the new towns, the institutions Republicans prized also extended American influence to the edge of white settlement and deeper into Indian country. The Indian trade factories, usually built as adjuncts to existing forts, gave Indians, soldiers, and white settlers alike a place to buy American-made goods at good prices. Eventually, white people could only pay cash for goods; predatory debt practices were reserved solely for Indians. Schools, colleges, and libraries that energetic Republicans supported were investments in future economic opportunities while offering yet more services to the new Western inhabitants.[8] Meanwhile, the land office offered security in land ownership and delineated a path to respectability. As the sole source of legitimate land titles, these federal offices provided settlers with financing, secure land titles, and much more. In all these ventures, energetic Republicans were sure to provide government services on a broader scale that helped make the early American state much more effective.

Republican administrators often built these institutions upon Federalist creations from the 1790s. As discussed in the previous chapter, Federalists like western Pennsylvanian Thomas Scott argued in Congress for creating a federal land office, even if Federalists differed on where to locate the offices. Federalists also created institutions to oversee the Indian trade. George Washington wanted to open government-run trading posts as early as the 1780s to alleviate fraud, attach Indians to the new republic, and boost American influence in the fur trade. He continued to make his case as President in his Annual Messages of 1791, 1793, and 1794, and Congress agreed on the final day of the Third Congress, March 3, 1795, creating Indian trading houses and appropriating $50,000 for the task.[9]

In early 1796, a bipartisan multiregional coalition emerged in the House of Representatives to expand trade factories. Federalists Josiah Parker of Virginia and William Vans Murray of Maryland rose quickly to favor expansion, with Parker extolling the "humanity and benevolence" of the plan and Murray claiming in Hamiltonian tones that only the federal government possessed the necessary capital and influence to compete directly with British influence.[10] Meanwhile, Republicans emphasized economy and expedience while supporting factories and, more broadly, energetic government. John Swanwick of Pennsylvania said they would allow "the fruits of commerce, that beneficent power which cements and civilizes," to pacify Indians until American influence and private traders grew stronger. Jefferson's future Secretary of the Treasury Albert Gallatin also saw factories as a means to reduce military spending, while future Secretary of War Henry Dearborn declared himself "in favor of the general principle of the bill" on the grounds that it was "economical," and he supported it along with "a reduction of the Military Establishment." The bill passed the Federalist-led Senate as well, making the factories a new outlet for energetic government in Western economic activities. It also, as William Bergmann recently has shown, stretched federal power beyond the frontiers of white settlement.[11]

Similarly, Western Republicans made the land office system more accessible. House members from western Pennsylvania made that case by 1796, with William Findley seeking to cut 640-acre minimum purchases to give all "an opportunity of purchasing fifty or one hundred acres" from a land office that was "not only . . . a wholesale but a retail store." Gallatin agreed, wanting policies to enhance federal revenues and favor actual settlers over speculators.[12] To those ends, William Henry Harrison shepherded the Land Law of 1800 through the House of Representatives. The bill cut minimum purchases to 320 acres, created a four-year credit system for purchasers, and opened four new offices in Ohio. The law cemented for Harrison a reputation as an advocate for federal energy in the Northwest willing to reach across the aisle. Though a declared Republican, Federalists liked Harrison enough that Adams appointed him Governor of the new Indiana Territory on May 13, 1800, a choice that only fueled rumors he might secretly be a Federalist.[13]

The next year, Henry Dearborn and Albert Gallatin joined Jefferson's cabinet as Secretaries of War and the Treasury, respectively, and found themselves in prime positions to advance the state projects they had supported. The War Department supervised the Indian trade factories Dearborn liked in the House in 1796, and as Secretary of War he pressed for reviving factories in the Southwest and expanding them in the Northwest. His advocacy was only supported by the system turning a slight profit, despite neglect of it during the Adams administration. Dearborn reported that trade factories "had a very salutary effect on the minds of the Indians," and therefore he wanted "a much more extensive distribution of the fund, among the several Indian nations . . . attended with all the good effects." Meanwhile, Gallatin frequently took his Treasury work home in the evening to effectively manage 1,285 employees in customs offices, internal revenue, financial capacities, and other offices, but he especially cared about public land sales. Overall, he hoped to glean half a million dollars of revenue annually from land and post offices.[14]

In the Indiana Territory, Governor Harrison found a very different situation in Vincennes when his administration began on January 10, 1801. Left to build a territorial government from scratch, he began by adopting Pennsylvania laws on taxable property, adding a territorial treasurer's office, and issuing a proclamation on May 9 that forbade "all persons from setleing, hunting, and surveying on any of the Indian lands" and required "all officers Civil and Military to remove any that should have setled, and prevent . . . any such attempt in future."[15] While Dearborn and Gallatin expanded their respective operations into Indiana, Harrison oversaw their implementation by fellow Republicans like John Badollet in the Vincennes land office and John Johnston at the Fort Wayne factory. In sum, Jeffersonian administrators continued Federalist efforts to build a state in the Northwest but under new management.

In his first year in the Indiana Territory, Harrison followed the Ohio Company's example in securing education for Vincennes. Signed by Harrison, the town's French leaders, and the territory's Federalist Attorney General John Rice Jones, an 1801 petition asked Congress to alleviate "Inconveniences arising from the total want of an Institution for the Education of Youth." In the small, isolated river town, "a sufficient fund cannot be raised for a permanent Establishment, without the benevolent Aid of the United States," so they requested a township of land "made for a similar Institution in the Ohio purchase."[16] Using the Ohio Company as a precedent was partly pragmatic. Referencing the company helped make their case, but they also wanted to stress education. Schools were central to Harrison's vision for Indiana, and he hoped federal action would help him establish educational institutions there. Congress went further than the petitioners hoped on March 26, 1804; Vincennes received a federal land office and a full township to fund higher education, as did the other new land office districts based in Detroit and Kaskaskia. In 1806, the territorial legislature established Vincennes University supported by the township, and Harrison saw five years of effort rewarded by becoming its first president. They continued to seek additional funding as well, asking Congress unsuccessfully in November 1807 for new taxes on salt works and Indian trade licenses to augment university coffers.[17]

Harrison was resourceful about encouraging education. He was an important part of a Vincennes library company created in 1806, which boasted nearly 250 volumes within three years. Members dedicated the library to educating the public, too, with a collection focused on informative and scientific works. In addition, Harrison served as president of the Vincennes Society for the Encouragement of Agriculture and the Useful Arts, positions that historian Robert M. Owens said the governor took in pursuit of sociopolitical status.[18] However, Harrison was also driven by a broader social vision. Good societies required learned populations and ready access to education, so Harrison lent his political and social prestige to enhance the territory's educational institutions.

Harrison worked in Vincennes as Dearborn, Gallatin, and the Republicans in Congress looked to promote Jeffersonian ends and extend federal control in the Indiana Territory. As the direct supervisor of Indian affairs, Dearborn saw three immediate benefits to trade factories: greater opportunities for peace, honest trade with U.S. factors, and a method to provide Indians goods that promoted civilization policies. Further, trade helped to internalize Indian affairs. Federalists used the army to force out European competition, but as Dearborn wrote in 1801, trade factories could aid in "detaching [Indians] more and more from the influence of neighboring Governments" much more cheaply than warfare.[19] By February 1802, Dearborn reported progress on Indian trade to Harrison. Congress was soon to ban liquor sales to Indians—welcome news for settlers worried about Indian attacks—and, more importantly, Congress was ready to open new trading houses in the Northwest. The new factories, he detailed further, would quarterly "make correct returns of the state of the factory, of the sales and receipts, etc. to the governor of the territory." When Congress extended the Indian factory system in April 1802 and February 1803, it spread the Federalist creation to Fort Wayne and Detroit (later moved to Chicago) under the advice of Dearborn and Jefferson.[20]

From the Treasury Department, Albert Gallatin pursued a new law to sell public lands in the Indiana Territory. After Harrison secured new Indian land cessions in 1803, Gallatin noted in January 1804 that "No provision has yet been made by law for the sale . . . of the tracts lying below the mouth of the Kentucky river, and lately purchased from the Indians." Gallatin suggested Congress act quickly to allow land sales at the same two dollars per acre minimum and the same terms of credit that applied in Ohio. Only two months later, Jefferson signed a new law to extend the Land Law of 1800 into the Indiana Territory and created three new offices at Vincennes, Detroit, and Kaskaskia, with $20,000 appropriated to enact the new measures.[21]

Dearborn and Gallatin filled the new offices in Indiana with two immigrants they trusted well. Dearborn chose Irish immigrant and War Department clerk John Johnston for the Fort Wayne factory. Once there, Johnston quickly gained power and prestige because he became a prominent trader in the region and controlled the payment of treaty-mandated annuities. He also held his influential position atop the former Native political and trading center of Kekionga, between the Maumee and Wabash Rivers, which placed him in the midst of older trading networks.[22] For the Vincennes land office, Gallatin tapped his old friend John Badollet from Switzerland to serve as register in 1804 after previously appointing him to lay out roads northwest of the Ohio River. Badollet also served other important purposes as a loyal Republican and a supporter of education, joining Harrison among the founders of the library and university in Vincennes.[23]

Johnston and other trade factors were the nerve endings for the Jefferson administration's sinews of federal power. Johnston took on many other responsibilities to improve government services, such as learning surgery because Fort Wayne lacked doctors and the fort's surgeon was descending into alcoholism. Ultimately, he became assistant surgeon as well as trade factor and, after 1809, federal Indian agent. He also kept an orchard for himself and local Indians, with twenty-five peach trees by autumn 1804 and with plans "next spring to procure from the State of Ohio or Detroit a quantity of young Trees to consist of as many kinds as can be had."[24] Johnston also furthered Jefferson's Indian policies. In a January 1803 message to Congress, Jefferson promoted his civilization policy goals through his plans "to multiply trading houses among them, and place within their reach those things which will contribute more to their domestic comfort than the possession of extensive, but uncultivated wilds." Jefferson also saw factories offering Indians "the benefits of our Government" as the linchpin of his Indian policy. Furthermore, the factories provided goods and markets for white settlers, and they were popular enough that Dearborn could later order 10–25 percent markups on goods for non-Indian customers. Johnston worked to oblige his President's prerogatives, too, carrying carpentry tools and spinning wheels in his store as early as 1803 and keeping his orchard as a model for local Indians.[25]

Jefferson and Dearborn planned on Indian trade factories forcing Indians into new cessions, and thus the factory partnered with other institutions in spearheading white westward expansion. Jefferson told Dearborn in August 1802 that trade factories were "the cheapest & most effectual instrument we can use for preserving the friendship of the Indians," and he hoped to use their consumerism against them. "There is perhaps no method more irresistible of obtaining lands," he explained, "than by letting them get in debt, which when too heavy to be paid, they are always willing to lop off by a cession of land." Jefferson similarly told Harrison that with trade factories "good & influential individuals among [the Indians] run in debt," which would lead to "cession of lands." However, factories like Fort Wayne succeeded not because of the snare of debt they laid, but rather because of their proximity to regular army posts. As Francis Paul Prucha noted, the presence of the U.S. Army so close to the factories lent protection, prestige, and sometimes critically important labor to factors and their operations.[26]

Similarly, Badollet was at Vincennes an agent of federal power and Republican ideals as he implemented the land policies of the Jefferson administration. Land officers like him had two primary purposes. First, Secretary of the Treasury Albert Gallatin wanted them to run a consistent, efficient, and above all profitable system to reap the financial windfall he believed lay in the public lands. Land revenues were an important component of Gallatin's plan to pay off the national debt, leading to Badollet and other land officers facing regular audits of the register and receiver's records as per the Land Law of 1804.[27] Second, land officers set out to achieve Gallatin and Jefferson's goal to make land ownership accessible to all Americans. Gallatin wanted to make owning a farm in the Indiana Territory a realistic possibility for most Americans, arguing for and getting in 1804 a reduction of the minimum purchase to 160 acres. Buyers who paid cash or made their credit payments on time also received a discount to $1.64 per acre. The overall goal, said Ninian Edwards in 1806, was "that every man might have an opportunity of procuring a freehold of his own."[28]

Consequent to their interest in aiding freeholding farmers, Jeffersonian leaders tried to minimize the baleful effects of land speculation. For example, Gallatin advised Badollet to reject claims by the Illinois and Wabash Company, which claimed two million acres in southern Illinois based on a 1770 agreement with local Indians. Gallatin noted that the purchase was illegal under the Proclamation of 1763 and never recognized by other governments, so it lacked "the shadow of a title to support their claim, which has been repeatedly before Congress" and thus was wasting everyone's time. Even worse, Western Republicans like Edwards suggested, speculators were a danger to the republic, as large-scale landlords not only gobbled up good land but also abridged the independence of Western small farmers. Thus, to "ameliorate the situation of the citizens of the district, and to promote the general prosperity of the State," the good of the republic required federal power to be deployed to thwart speculators and would-be landlords.[29]

Johnston and Badollet proved themselves strong and effective agents for the Jeffersonian state in the Northwest by operating their offices well. Johnston managed the Fort Wayne factory in exemplary fashion, dutifully recording his business from the first shipments of goods he received in May 1803. After taking his first inventory of goods in 1805, he complied with regulations requiring annual inventories and turned in multiple reports in some years. Meanwhile, Johnston turned a profit—as did the entire factory system—inspiring Dearborn to seek from Congress another $100,000 to open new factories in Chicago and St. Louis. In April 1806, Congress empowered the administration to create any new factories it deemed necessary along the Mississippi River and created the Office of Indian Trade to oversee the factory system. Thus, Jefferson and Congressional Republicans opened the first government agency devoted solely to Indian policy.[30]

The factory system also exerted a great deal of influence among the Indians of the territory, and some Indians welcomed this form of federal power. Very quickly, trade factories became parts of treaties and negotiations. As Jefferson boasted of the system in January 1803, "Indians, perceiving the advantage of purchasing from us, are soliciting, generally, our establishment of trading houses among them." For example, the Sac and Fox had a promised factory written into the treaty they concluded with William Henry Harrison in November 1804. The United States agreed to stem "abuses and impositions which are practised upon the said tribes, by the private traders" by building a new factory in their country "at a convenient time . . . where the individuals of the said tribes can be supplied with goods at a more reasonable rate than they have been accustomed." West of the Mississippi, the Osage nation asked for and received promises of a trade factory, too.[31] With the economy of scale offered by government enterprise and without demands to profit from Indians, factories meant more equitable trading and cheaper goods for many Indian nations. These successes spoke well to trade factories as an institution, too, as Indians essentially came to request a greater state presence among them through new factories.

The benefits of the trade factory system became clearer while British-American relations deteriorated. Johnston wrote to Superintendent of Indian Trade John Mason in early 1808 asking for more goods if war was declared, deducing that war meant "British Traders will of Course be prevented from entering our Territory with Goods." Still needing many European goods, "the Indians would have to rely on the public store." In requesting greater quantities of rifles and ammunition, Johnston also hinted that his factory could dissuade many Indians from fighting the United States. Even as war loomed in April 1812, Indians in the Illinois country wanted greater government involvement. Potawatomi chief Gomo said in negotiations with Ninian Edwards, governor of the Illinois Territory, "I thought of asking you to place a factory in our town of Peoria." However, with war brewing and the neighboring Winnebago "roving about, should any be killed, we might be blamed; therefore I will not."[32] Only threats of war and death could interrupt the flow of federally-backed commerce, a testimony to the depth of influence held by trade factories.

Meanwhile, John Badollet oversaw the Vincennes branch as the land office grew in size before the War of 1812. The office at Vincennes was part of the its first expansion into the Indiana Territory, and Congress added offices at Jeffersonville across the Ohio River from Louisville in 1807 and Shawneetown in the Illinois Territory in 1812. Even before opening the Shawneetown office, the offices at Kaskaskia, Vincennes, and Jeffersonville were but the farthest west of the nearly dozen offices that sold almost 2.5 million acres of land from 1804 to 1812.[33] The offices also grew in complexity after 1800, especially because of the credit system. The hallmark Jeffersonian change to the land office, the credit system made work demanding for officers like register Badollet and receiver Nathaniel Ewing in Vincennes. Settlers came first to the register to buy sections, half-sections, or quarter-sections, and registers marked the claims as taken on township plats. Next, the receiver collected a down payment of at least five percent and created an account in his ledger, where he would mark subsequent payments and calculate either interest on late payments or discounts for punctual payments.[34] Regular audits after 1805 also forced Badollet and Ewing to check and recheck their records for accuracy, all while paying attention to currency exchange rates and authentication for paper notes. After all, settlers visiting the Vincennes and Jeffersonville land offices often brought paper money from the Bank of the United States, Bank of North America, and other banks in Kentucky and Ohio. Notes came from as far away as South Carolina, and they saw insurance and commercial enterprise notes from across the nation, too.[35]

While Ewing oversaw the complex system of exchanges and credit, Badollet worked to standardize land office practices on frequently shifting orders from Albert Gallatin. To maximize revenues, Gallatin looked to develop an auction system when public lands entered the market, and his correspondence to Badollet about spring 1807 land auctions is a prime example. After Jefferson announced the auction at Vincennes in October 1806, Gallatin gave Badollet minutely detailed instructions for carrying out the sale. Before sale day on the last Monday of April 1807, Badollet was to publish advertisements about the new lands for sale in newspapers throughout the Indiana Territory and in Cincinnati, Chillicothe, Louisville, Frankfort, and Lexington once per month until May 1807. In addition, Badollet was to hire a crier to announce the lots for sale and, as Gallatin said, "fix on their plan . . . all its details, so as to proceed regularly & without interruption" to make his auction more professional.[36]

At the sale, Gallatin wanted bureaucratic precision. He recommended uniformity by informing Badollet in March 1807 of the "mode adopted in other Offices," which included "call[ing] aloud for each quarter section successively in each Township; and if no person bids for such quarter section during half a minute to pass to the next." If no bids came, Gallatin's guidelines allowed land officers to offer a full township in about seventy-five minutes. With a five-minute break for purchasers to make their initial payments, Gallatin noted officers could offer up to seven townships in a single day. When attendees wished to bid on quarter-sections, he recommended keeping bidding to five minutes. Even if the full five minutes were needed for each quarter-section, they would be able to offer 160,000 acres in just ten days. Gallatin's efforts to standardize practices and grow the land office made it even more important in westward expansion. As Malcolm Rohrbough observed in his study of the land office system, settlers often knew the processes behind auctions, retail sales, and federal credit for the public lands, and a trip to the local land office became a significant event in the life of white settlers, ranking with marriage as a passage into adulthood and independence.[37]

In sum, Johnston and Badollet were vital to growing federal administrative capacities in the Indiana Territory at Fort Wayne and Vincennes, respectively. By 1812, energetic Republicans like Gallatin and Badollet made the land office an institution ready to advance west along with white settlers. The office expanded into the Illinois Territory after Congress created it in 1809, beginning with Shawneetown in 1812. Meanwhile, land offices stretching from Ohio to Kaskaskia in the Northwest and along the edge of white settlement in the Old Southwest sold more than 575,000 acres in 1811, with their records contained in 173 different ledgers. By then, the job of administering the land office had simply become too enormous for Gallatin, so that year Congress created the General Land Office to oversee operations.[38] Afterward, the GLO led a very long life. It remained an independent agency until it became the backbone of the new Bureau of Land Management after World War II, and the BLM remains a powerful federal agency in the Great West today. However, its roots lie in the work of Rufus Putnam, Alexander Hamilton, and other Federalists, developed by the energetic Republicans who expanded and reshaped it to make federal power more accessible throughout America's westward movement.

At Fort Wayne, Johnston made his factory into the crown jewel of a system that extended federal influence among the Indians. After a rocky start that saw Indians burn the factory in 1803 and that delayed his first purchases of furs until 1804, Johnston built up a successful enterprise. Ultimately, Johnston sold the factory's high-quality furs (mostly "hatter's furs" making excellent insulation for coats and hats) for more than double what he paid.[39] By 1808, Johnston's shipment receipts showed the Fort Wayne factory was doing brisk business. In March and April, he sent 111 packs of furs weighing around ninety pounds apiece, containing a total of 20,800 raccoon skins, 624 deerskins, some 450 skins of "Cats & Foxes" and nearly sixty bearskins in two shipments to Detroit and on to market.[40] Such business along with Johnston's methods made the Fort Wayne factory lucrative, as it made $10,502.77 in profit from late 1807 to September 1811. In fact, the profits from Fort Wayne and Chicago were higher than the profits of the whole factory system during that period.[41] In other words, effective administration and profitable trade in Indiana and Illinois made the trade factories a financial success before the War of 1812. The factories at Fort Wayne and Chicago might have been unbridled successes in finance and administration, but they did not guarantee peace. In continuing Federalist policies, William Henry Harrison's aggressive approach to Indian policy sowed the seeds of discord even while Johnston was securing Indian goods.

Civilization and Confederacy
Jeffersonian Indian Policy in Indiana and Illinois

As the administrative state spread in Indiana and Illinois, the Jefferson administration also had to manage relations with Indian communities undergoing turbulent change. As the face of federal power to Indians, Governor Harrison followed his Federalist forebears by pressing relentlessly for both land cessions and American policy goals of "civilizing" Indians, but after early success, a burgeoning religious and political movement emerged to strongly critique American policy. From this point, relations followed the same pattern as in Ohio during the 1780s and 1790s: American aggression at the treaty table provoked a fierce reaction from Indians, Indians united to defend themselves, American officials both feared and dismissed the new confederacy, and tensions continued to escalate. Throughout this period that roughly corresponded to Jefferson's presidency, Harrison relied on a hardline negotiating style he learned from Federalist leaders. He single-mindedly pressed American interests forward but, like the Federalists did, blamed British influence for the shortcomings of his approach.

Settlers arrived steadily in the Indiana Territory from 1800 to 1810, creating a host of problems for Indians. The white population grew from around 5,000 in 1800, largely scattered along the Ohio, Wabash, and Illinois River valleys and small French enclaves at Green Bay and Peoria, to 28,000 when the territories split in 1809.[42] Competition for land tested Indians' patience with both invading settlers and land-hungry American treaty commissioners, all while their populations shrank during influenza and smallpox epidemics. Settlers also upset environmental relationships for Indians by competing for game critical to Indian commerce. They were more aggressive hunters, too, with Harrison estimating whites killed five times as many animals as did Indians. The Governor complained of "persons who make a practice of Hunting on the lands of the Indians in violation of law and our Treaty," which he termed "a monstrous abuse," but claimed he could do nothing about it without a fuller survey of treaty boundaries.[43] Thus, Harrison could not—and perhaps would not—offer much aid to Indians.

This competition sharpened an already epic decline in fur harvests by Indians. When French settlers established Vincennes in 1732, leader François-Marie Bissot Vincennes estimated that the new post could bring in 30,000 furs per year from local Indians. However, by 1800 Indian sales of valuable beaver skins declined sharply, and in turn they hunted less profitable animals like deer, raccoons, and bears, whose skins Johnston and other factors purchased. The new furs reduced the purchasing power of Indian men, making it difficult to provide sufficient meat and imported products for their families.[44] Thus, when trade factories arrived with offers of fair dealing and stable prices, many Indian nations had good reason to welcome the federal system and ask for greater access to it in negotiations.

Indians also suffered from the malignant effects of the liquor trade and injustices caused by settlers, both of which led Indian chiefs to seek federal relief. Shawnee chief Little Turtle, the military leader at St. Clair's defeat and the Battle of Fallen Timbers, asked Jefferson to ban liquor sales to Indians, and Jefferson and Congress complied with a new law in 1802. Dearborn informed Harrison in September that traders were not to sell liquor to Indians and "disturb the peace and harmony, which has subsisted between the white people and the Indians," leading Harrison to issue a proclamation that licensed traders who sold liquor could lose their bonds paid to the U.S. government.[45] However, those laws did little to alleviate the problems Indians had with white trespassers. Laws theoretically treated whites and Indians equally, but Harrison observed, "There is a wide difference in the execution of those laws. The Indian always suffers." Meanwhile, whites stole from and murdered Indians with impunity because territorial juries invariably acquitted them.[46]

With life growing more precarious, Indians in the Ohio valley became restless enough to frighten officials. In August 1800, Arthur St. Clair worried new depredations and horse thievery signaled new hostilities, and by early 1802, Dearborn heard Delaware and Shawnee Indians visiting the new capital at Washington "complain loudly of the white peoples hunting and killing game on their lands." In turn, he related Jefferson's wishes that Harrison "take every means in your power to prevent such abuses and to punish the offenders."[47] However, Harrison was already moving on the issue. In May 1801, he forbade settlement on land claimed by Indians and threatened to use the military to remove trespassers, and that summer, he issued two other proclamations that banned liquor sales to Indians near Vincennes and warned against unlicensed trade. As he noted, "in the future the said regulation would be strictly Enforced," and territorial citizens should "govern themselves accordingly."[48]

Hampered by these problems, Indians in the region fell into patterns of dependency that posed new challenges with Americans. The politics of intercultural interactions shifted in the Northwest as annuities became more important, as arguments over dates, locations, and even the worth of goods used in federal payments figured more prominently in Indian relations and treaty discussions. In turn, controlling annuity payments lent new prestige to officials like Harrison and John Johnston, and Republican officials promoted civilization programs among the region's Indians even more ardently. Even from Washington, Jefferson noticed the growing problems. As he observed in February 1803, "the decrease of game [is] rendering their subsistence by hunting insufficient," but that meant an opportunity for Americans to "draw them [Indians] to agriculture, to spinning & weaving." To that end, John Johnston used his orchards to teach new forms of agriculture and "took much pains to instruct them in the manner of . . . saving the seeds themselves in future." His primary motivation was simply "that they might not have to depend on us."[49]

These policies also sent Indians mixed messages that encompassed the difficult conflicts always simmering beneath U.S. Indian policy. On one side, civilization sounded enlightened with talk of Indians plowing fields and joining American society. For example, Henry Dearborn explained in glowing terms that federal officials would "instruct the Indian women in the arts of spinning and weaving, to introduce among the men a taste for agriculture and raising of stock, and to infuse into the nations generally a spirit of emulation in industry." Plows and spinning wheels were the new weapons of conquest, but in this version, Indians could live quietly in farmhouses rather than flee from the fixed bayonets of the U.S. Army. To secure their happiness and prosperity, Jefferson suggested, Indians would sell their lands for necessities of farm and home, and the trade factories held an important place in that mission by selling those tools in their stores. The President painted a harmonious picture of an interracial society, too, telling a gathering of Indian chiefs at the end of his second term, "In time you will be as we are." Soon, Indian and white farmers might live peacefully and side by side all over the continent.[50]

Civilization sounded peaceful, but it arrogated American victory in the trans-Appalachian West, as had conquest diplomacy in the 1780s. Harrison told Indians at Vincennes that whites and Indians should "live in peace with each other," and Jefferson passed along an "ardent wish to see you prosperous and happy" in August 1802. However, peace and happiness required Indians to cede their lands and alter their lives radically. After all, Jefferson explained, "It requires an immense extent of country to supply a very few hunters," but farming on family plots needed much less land. When those goals conflicted, American officials like Harrison urged land cessions first, even at the cost of the civilization program. The reasoning was clear to all: government officials simply prized the needs of settlers above those of Indians.[51] No matter the exact message, though, federal officials consistently told Indians that they could only adapt to the onrush of white settlers and give up most of their lands.

Those new demands bore fruit for the U.S. in treaties signed during Jefferson's first term. In June 1803, nine nations relinquished over a million acres around Vincennes, and two months later, Harrison concluded another treaty with the Kaskaskia nation that included an eight-million-acre cession in southern Illinois. In November 1804, the same treaty in which they received promises of a trade factory, the Sac and Fox gave up claim to a massive tract along the Mississippi River ranging as far north as the Wisconsin River. Also contained within those treaties was language that encouraged civilization policies. For example, Article 4 in both the 1803 treaty with the Kaskaskia and an 1804 treaty with the Piankeshaw allowed the United States to split annuities among individual families. In promoting civilization but more so in securing land cessions, Harrison was a successful negotiator. By the end of 1804, he had secured Indian cessions for most of present-day Illinois.[52]

Harrison preferred to negotiate aggressively through a combination of bullying and bribery that showed especially well in treaties from 1805. Quite often, just as he saw Anthony Wayne do in 1795, Harrison ignored or dismissed Indian objections. Reginald Horsman observed a similar pattern, writing that Harrison often "rode roughshod over Indian resistance" to new cessions and treaties. That pattern showed in negotiations from August 1805. He tossed aside Indian complaints about "a fair bargain with the Delawares and Piankeshaws, who were the owners of the land," made in June 1803, and he refused to spend "a six pence . . . in consideration of that purchase." Any increase in annuities also would require "further cession of land." Harrison also leaned on friendly chiefs and bribed others to get his desired cession. In the negotiations, he offered Little Turtle a black slave and a personal annuity of fifty dollars, and he gave the Delaware and Potawatomi annuities for lands they did not actually occupy. The methods got results. On August 21, the assembled Indians agreed to cede two million acres and confirmed American title to land between Vincennes and the Greenville treaty line that ran through eastern Indiana.[53] Harrison signed another treaty with the Piankeshaw on December 30, affirming earlier cessions for an increased annuity in a deal "highly advantageous to the United States." Further, the Indians gained with the new annuities "a certain resource to them, when they shall be no longer able to procure subsistence from the chase."[54]

Harrison acted as if Indians acquiesced to his demands happily, but he signed no Indian treaties for four years because of Indian discontent. It showed during the December 1805 negotiations, as voiced by Kickapoo chief Oulaqua. "Since we have known our father the Long Knife," he said, settlers "arrive every day . . . [and] we know nothing of it." Using the language of Indian revivalism, Oulaqua noted that the "master of Life gave us this land" on which settlers trespassed, and yet it was "the Long Knives who complains."[55] The speech was especially prescient because it expressed two major developments at once. First, even the chiefs negotiating for treaties were tiring of continual American demands for land, and the barely hidden hostility suggested Indians would not remain submissive to American prerogatives. Second, Oulaqua's reference to the Master of Life suggested at least some Indians already sought divine help for solace and, if necessary, redress from their problems.

As Olaqua expressed his frustrations, spiritual messages of personal renewal and political change were emanating from Shawnee country. Earlier that year, Lalawethika passed out an alcoholic, insignificant man but awoke as Tenskwatawa, the prophet of Indian renaissance in the Northwest. In the midst of various revivals in the region, Tenskwatawa began as just one of many Indians and frontier whites who had powerful religious visions and experiences. Soon known simply as the Prophet when his movement took off, he built on teachings of earlier Indian revivalists Neolin and Handsome Lake while adding elements of Catholic theology. This formulation resonated widely, as Tenskwatawa crafted a movement that emphatically rejected American demands for land and cultural adaptation. By 1806, Tenskwatawa rounded out a compelling three-part message that stressed revitalizing Indian cultures, cleansing communities and politics of corruption, and building a pan-Indian alliance to halt white intruders.[56]

In practical terms, the Prophet radically challenged Indians' daily lives and political leaders. Cultural renewal meant rejecting alcohol as well as European-style clothing, tools, and even guns (at least when hunting). Furthermore, Tenskwatawa said the Master of Life required confession of past sins, a nod to Catholicism but also a continual reminder for followers to remain diligent in their ways.[57] His anti-corruption stance and support for pan-Indianism also threatened Indians who agreed to further land cessions or worse, were pro-American. In 1806, that political challenge escalated. The Prophet led a group of Indians who burned to death unfriendly chiefs and a Christian Indian, and he erected his first spiritual center only a few miles from the old fort at Greenville, Ohio.[58]

Harrison and other officials reacted by attacking the Prophet's character and threatening his followers and potential converts. Early in 1806, Harrison told the Delaware of the Prophet, "Drive him from your town, and let peace and harmony once more prevail," especially since following the Prophet could mean war with the United States. The next year, he called Tenskwatawa "your deceiver" in talks with Shawnee chiefs, warning the new teachings would bring them to ruin. Fort Wayne Indian agent William Wells used similar language in 1807, referring to Tenskwatawa as "the Shawnese Impostor" and warning that "if He is not Interrupted He will Bring a bout a war between the Indians—if he cannot git them to go to war against the whites."[59] Federal officials in the Indiana Territory swiftly and decisively identified Tenskwatawa as a threat to white settlers and American prerogatives, which by extension meant American soldiers would threaten Indian homes and lives.

Harrison also saw British intrigue in the rise of Tenskwatawa. During his governorship, Harrison followed many American officials, particularly Jeffersonian Republicans, in constantly imagining Indian opponents as British agents. That pattern continued with the Prophet. Harrison called the Prophet "a fool, who speaks not the words of the Great Spirit but those of the devil, and of the British agents" in August 1807. Even after the Prophet assured him that he was not a British spy, Harrison still warned him against being "seduced by the British agents." Curiously, British officer William Claus believed the Prophet to be a French agent, and he did not enter a British fort until the War of 1812 had already begun. Looking to prove his independence, Tenskwatawa responded to rising tensions with American officials and growing alarm from settlers in Indiana and western Ohio by moving his principal town, Prophetstown, west to the confluence of the Tippecanoe and Wabash Rivers.[60]

The move coincided with a shift in a secular, more clearly political direction. When growing numbers and dwindling food stores forced the Prophet's followers to seek aid, Tenskwatawa's brother Tecumseh traveled to Fort Malden in Canada to visit British officials. Meeting in June and July 1808, Tecumseh declared he would fight the Americans if necessary, but it was not the right moment. Nonetheless, Tecumseh's declarations of friendship satisfied the British, who sent him away with food and other gifts to sustain Prophetstown and show friendly intentions. While he was gone, too, Tenskwatawa's new followers continued to stream in from all around the region. After returning to the growing settlement, Tecumseh commenced in sending lieutenants or traveling personally among surrounding nations in search of political and military allies while spreading his brother's religious messages. By 1809, the brothers had won over many Kickapoo, Potawatomi, Wyandot, and Winnebago Indians.[61]

Jeffersonian Indian policy had clearly failed to bring lasting peace and stability between the cultures in Indiana. Amid rising tensions in many directions, the Prophet continued to grow his movement and Tecumseh kept attracting new converts and political allies throughout the trans-Appalachian West. Meanwhile, William Henry Harrison railed against the Prophet to little effect, and complicating factors would soon make affairs even worse. War with Britain was brewing, and American expansion into Indiana was at stake.

Assuring the Jeffersonian State
Britain, Indians, and the Northwest War of 1811

As with Harmar and St. Clair in Ohio, resolving concerns with Indians once again demanded crushing national military force to provide security and to enable more robust white settlement. Matters became complicated very quickly, as simmering Indian conflicts joined growing problems with Great Britain into a broader conflict for supremacy in the Northwest. While Harrison's methods helped to provoke Indian resistance, the war ultimately allowed him to subdue it. His victory meant that federal officials would continue to lead American westward expansion. In essence, a second major Indian war in the Northwest helped to enhance federal power. By the end of the War of 1812, American troops had radically altered the dynamics of intercultural diplomacy and smashed large-scale resistance to white settlement in Indiana and Illinois.

As Tenskwatawa and Tecumseh saw their movement rising in the midst of tensions between the U.S. and Britain, Harrison and Jeffersonian officials ripped away the benevolent mask of civilization policy to reveal an American state that demanded Indians submit or face destruction. In June 1808, Harrison wrote to Tenskwatawa that he hoped rumors of the Prophet becoming a British agent were false and added a warning. He also forwarded Jefferson's decision that "Tribes who became his children at The Treaty of Greenville should lift up the Tomahawk against him that he will never again make peace as long as there is one of that Tribe on this side of the Lakes." Further resistance, he concluded, "would conduct you to certain misery and ruin."[62] Whether by the arts of civilization or the rights of conquest, thinking about Indians and their rights had changed

little. Like the Federalists of the 1790s, Harrison offered Indians no right
to resist the American advance across the Northwest.

As his concerns mounted, Harrison sought to prepare the Indiana Territory for war. First came improving the militia. Opening the territorial
legislature in 1807, he urged "perfection of the militia system . . . [as]
an object of the first importance" in order to offer "efficient and competent protection to our country in time of war." He recommended a law
to either provide a stronger, more organized militia or require settlers
who could afford it to supply their own guns for militia duty. After all,
he observed, Indiana was "peculiarly interested in the contest which is
likely to ensue," and mingling his worries over Indian relations with his
Anglophobia, he noted that legislators should "know that the tomahawk
and scalping knife of the savage are always employed as the instruments
of British vengeance." His concerns remained prominent in September
1808, when he told Henry Dearborn that he wanted to improve the militia
further by enforcing more military obligations.[63]

Hoping to repair relations and entice new settlers, Harrison began
seeking a new treaty and land cession in spring 1809. As he told the new
Secretary of War William Eustis, serving under the new president, James
Madison, "Our settlements here are much cramped by the vicinity of the
Indian lands" and would remain so "unless a further extinguishment of
title is effected." Once he received permission, Harrison called a treaty conference that began at Fort Wayne on September 15. He told the
gathered Indians that they were only being asked to sell "land which was
exhausted of game and which was no longer useful to them." He also
offered increased annuities so the Indians—nearly all of whom were
pro-American—could "procure the Domestic Animals necessary to commence raising them on a large scale."[64] By month's end, both sides signed
the Treaty of Fort Wayne, and Americans passed out gifts and annuities.
In the end, the United States acquired title to at least 2.5 million acres
in the southern portions of the Indiana and Illinois Territories from the
Miami, Delaware, and Potawatomi in exchange for $5,200 in goods and a
total increased annuity of $1,750.[65]

While Harrison bragged to Eustis that the treaty was "a better one for
the United States than any that has been made by me," the Treaty of Fort
Wayne tore apart Indian communities and brought the U.S. closer to war
with the rising Indian confederacy. Harrison told the territorial legislature that the cession "laid the foundation for a great increase of wealth
and population," but Tecumseh and Tenskwatawa saw it differently. News

of the treaty and its cession prompted Tecumseh to threaten the signing chiefs and travel farther afield for new allies, north to the Great Lakes and south to the shores of the Gulf of Mexico. French trader and American spy Michel Brouillette also explained that after the treaty, the Prophet "was very much exasperated at the cession of lands," and war was on the horizon. As Brouillette reported, "the Prophet certainly intended to make a stroke on the white people and when asked where he intended to strike he pointed toward Vincennes." Unsettled by the threats, Harrison began speaking of military solutions, and Eustis recommended arresting the Shawnee brothers to maintain peace.[66]

After a council between Harrison and Tecumseh in August 1810 resolved nothing, the governor planned a military strike against Prophetstown. As early as October, he called for a new post north of Vincennes to hold back the Indians, and in June 1811 he warned Eustis that intelligence from Prophetstown proved Tenskwatawa's "determination to commence hostilities as soon as he thinks himself sufficiently strong." Thus, he begged for a commission to attack Prophetstown because as he reasoned, "If our government will submit to this insolence, it will be the means of making all the tribes treat us with contempt." Eustis agreed, commissioning Harrison on July 17, 1811, to call out regular troops and the militia "to attack the prophet and his followers, the force should be such as to ensure the most complete success."[67] In a sense, they did the Federalists one better. While Knox and St. Clair pressed for war in response to Indian raids on white settlements, Harrison and Eustis raised an army to crush Indian resistance based upon only threats, real or perceived, from Tenskwatawa and Tecumseh.

Harrison wasted little time. During a last attempt to restore peace in July and August, Harrison met with Tecumseh at Vincennes but called in eight hundred militiamen in order to show as much force as possible. Much as Wayne did at Greenville and St. Clair at Fort Harmar in 1788, Harrison found it good policy to negotiate with an army behind him. If there remained any mystery among the Indians about the American approach, the militarization of Vincennes removed it. Tecumseh was not swayed, and if anything, he knew afterward the cause was more urgent to maintain his new confederacy. After the conference produced no agreement, he set out to find allies among the Creek and other nations in the South.[68]

Tecumseh's absence offered Harrison an advantage, and he seized it by marching from Vincennes with 1,225 troops on September 26. On October

1, they stopped near the present site of Terre Haute to build Fort Harrison, their base of operations. Four weeks later, Harrison headed north, stopping within a mile of Prophetstown on the afternoon of November 6. At about 4:30 the next morning, Indians fired on the camp under orders from Tenskwatawa. They inflicted real losses, killing 62 American soldiers and wounding 126, but Harrison's counterattack dispersed the Indian force and gave the town to the American army by 7 a.m. The rest of the day was spent burying the dead, burning the town and much of its surrounding fields, and preparing for a counterattack that never materialized. Two days later, they returned to Vincennes victorious.[69]

The Battle of Tippecanoe won fame for William Henry Harrison and was hailed initially as a decisive stroke against the confederacy, but it was only the opening battle of a Northwest War of 1811. Harrison declared his win over Tenskwatawa "a complete and decisive victory," but it was nothing of the sort. As Robert Owens wrote so well of the battle's effects, "In cleaving the hornet's nest with his sword, Harrison had simply loosed enraged hornets." In the months after Tippecanoe, angry Indians raided settlers throughout the Indiana and Illinois Territories and turned to the British for trade and continued aid.[70] Tippecanoe might have been an American victory against the Prophet's religious community, but it only signaled the start of a major conflict between the new Indian confederacy and the United States.

Decaying U.S.-British relations soon led Britain to enter the war officially. By the start of 1812, some Americans spoke of war with Britain as inevitable, and Governor Edwards of the Illinois Territory was no exception. In peace conferences in March, he told a Potawatomi chief that in the coming war, "We do not want you to fight for us" since he claimed, "We can whip the English ourselves." However, Edwards warned that if they fought the Americans, "We will never suffer a British trader to go among you again." In April, he repeated his warning in Cahokia, promising that "if you join them in the war against us . . . British traders and English goods will never be suffered to go among you again" and the U.S. "will strike such a blow as will be sufficient to prevent the red people from ever going to war with us again."[71] Thus, territorial leaders were prepared for war with Britain, but they saw that war within the Northwest War of 1811 already aflame when Congress declared war against Britain on June 18, 1812.

While war with Britain widened the conflict, the War of 1812 in the Northwest involved Indians more than British regulars. Early on,

American losses at Fort Mackinac on July 17, Fort Dearborn on August 15, and Detroit on August 16 came to British-led but mostly Indian forces, and settlers and officials feared Indians more. When Edwards fretted in early August that "The combination of indians appears to be universal, thousands that belong to it could attack the settlements of this territory and Missouri," he did not mention the British at all. Neither did Major Martin D. Hardin of Kentucky when describing war aims in the Northwest in May 1813. As he saw it, Americans planned "to strike a blow, take an imposing attitude, and awe the Indians into respect and neutrality." However, after defeats at Forts Mackinac, Dearborn, and Detroit that came before the United States could mobilize and reinforce the posts, he lamented, "These objects are now lost—perhaps entirely beyond our reach."[72]

To salvage the war effort and preserve their safety, Westerners looked to Congress and the Secretary of War for enhanced protections and to Harrison for leadership. As the British and Indians took forts in the Northwest in August 1812, Harrison analyzed the course of the war in a letter to William Eustis. As he saw it, "Two species of Warfare have been used by the United States in their Contests with the Tribes upon the North Western frontier." The first was "rapid and dessultory expeditions by mounted men" to destroy villages, the old model in which mounted frontier rangers protected their homes with offensive strikes. The second, which he called "more tardy but more effectual," involved a large trained infantry "penetrating the Country of the Enemy and securing the possession by a chain of Posts." Noting that the Northwest Indian War terminated because of the latter approach, he advocated similar methods and requested U.S. Army forts on the Illinois River from the Mississippi to Chicago as well as "to march immediately a Considerable body of Troops to Fort Wayne." Such energetic defenses would serve as "a Considerable check upon the tribes" of the region.[73] Simply, Harrison saw the unequivocal embrace of military force in the Northwest Indian War as a blueprint for success.

In the Illinois Territory, Governor Edwards and Delegate to Congress Shadrach Bond also pushed for a powerful army to crush Indian resistance and provide security for their constituents. Until that army came, Edwards implored the territorial legislature in late 1812 to reform the territorial militia system "to render it better adapted to the present conjecture" and to assure "prompt obedience to . . . emergencies." He also suggested adding mounted rangers as a rapid response corps for Indian

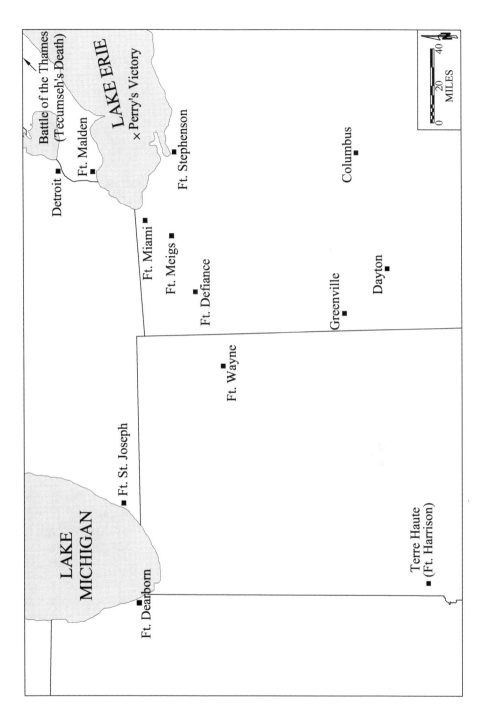

FIGURE 4. The Northwest Theater, War of 1812. Map created by the author.

attacks. By February 1813, he began recruiting a naval militia to patrol the Mississippi and Illinois Rivers. Meanwhile, the legislature sent resolutions to Congress asking for more cavalry, and Bond insisted on "the necessity of a strong force on our frontiers." In February 1813, he secured ten new cavalry companies for Western defenses, seven of them for Indiana and Illinois.[74]

Harrison led Western defenses as well, as Kentucky named him their militia general and Madison commissioned him as a major general in the U.S. Army. With his new position, Harrison resigned as territorial governor in December 1812 and proceeded on his military expedition. He began by breaking up a British and Indian siege at Fort Wayne, the last major American post between Canada and white settlers in the Northwest. Then, on April 28, 1813, he successfully defended Fort Meigs in northwest Ohio against a force of over 2,000 British and Indian troops with a much smaller force of roughly half regulars and half Ohio and Kentucky militia.[75] Throughout the summer of 1813, he led a methodical march north, gaining reinforcements from Kentucky and dispatching British and Indian resistance along the way. After Oliver Hazard Perry defeated the British on Lake Erie on September 10, Harrison's men chased the Indian forces under Tecumseh and the retreating British troops into Canada, occupying Detroit and Fort Malden on the way. By October 5, Harrison's army of 3,500 men caught up to them, and in the Battle of the Thames that followed, the Americans surrounded the British troops and forced them to surrender after a short fight. Far more significantly, Tecumseh died during an Indian charge on the Kentucky militia. The Indians broke rank quickly as word of his death spread, and with Tenskwatawa already in Canada, the new Northwestern confederacy was leaderless and broken.[76]

The victory allowed American officials in Indiana and Illinois to pivot toward the postwar future. Only twenty days after Tecumseh's death, Harrison told John Johnston that Indians were already begging for an armistice. In turn, Harrison ordered Johnston to provide conciliation through supplies of food and even "a sufficiency of ammunition to support their families." Nine months later, Harrison and Johnston were among the American treaty commissioners who signed a new Treaty of Greenville on July 22, 1814. The simple treaty of four articles declared hostilities over and guaranteed Indian signatories the lands they held before the war in return for their support against a new British invasion that never came. Once again, a defeated Indian confederacy submitted to American power by signing a treaty at Greenville with the general who had overrun them.

Harrison commemorated the significance, too, requesting a "flagstaff erected . . . on the spot where Gen. Wayne's quarters were in 1795" while making "all the details . . . conform as near as could be to the one which had preceded it nineteen years before." As Johnston recounted, "our flag waved over the spot on which General Wayne's quarters stood" during the treaty negotiations.[77] In nineteen years, Indian relations had come full circle. In the same place, signers from many of the same Indian nations accepted American control. After this new treaty, however, Indian nations of the Northwest never again seriously threatened the future of American settlers and federal control over the region.[78]

New States under the American State
Statehood for Indiana and Illinois

After the conclusion of the war, territorial government in Indiana and Illinois for the next few years before statehood involved reimplementing the state that energetic Republicans had built up before the war. The Indian factory system spread farther to the north and west ahead of white settlers, and the land offices did much brisker business after the Battle of the Thames. By the late 1810s, settlers in Indiana and Illinois depended on the federal government to provide orderly expansion through guaranteed land titles, improved transportation, and other services Hoosiers and Illinoisans came to expect and support. In the end, energetic Republicanism helped to spawn a generation of politicians and voters in the two states who relied upon and later advocated for state involvement in shaping economic development and civil society.

The United States government was not done with the Indian trade, nor did it abandon assuring a clear military presence ahead of white settlement among the Indians. By 1816, the War Department had ordered U.S. Army troops to reoccupy Fort Dearborn and to build Fort Howard at Green Bay and Fort Crawford at Prairie du Chien in present-day southwest Wisconsin. The forts solidified American power over the region against British competition, and each one also received a trade factory. After assuming office in October 1817, Secretary of War John C. Calhoun wanted to expand the American military presence even further into the Michigan Territory, on the Minnesota River, and even up the Missouri River to keep away British traders and influence. With military aid and effective policing against British traders, the system showed real promise. After all, despite being essentially shut down during the War of 1812, the factory system turned an overall profit of $12,500 from 1811 until 1815.

Soon after the war Thomas L. McKenney, director of the Office of Indian Trade, lobbied for more trade factories and new government-supervised schools for Indians that would, he hoped, someday be run by Indians.[79] The end of the war allowed federal officials to revive the factory system and even offer new wrinkles to the civilization program.

Business was brisk at Prairie du Chien, but otherwise, optimism never translated to profitability for the Northwestern factories. The factory at Chicago made over $3,000 in profits from 1807 to 1811, but it lost $2,000 from 1816 to 1818. The Green Bay factory fared even worse, with trade factor Matthew Irwin, Jr. complaining often about its poor prospects. He told McKenney, "so little business has been done at the Factory during the winter" of 1816–1817, and by summer 1818, he slashed prices in hopes of attracting business. Even Prairie du Chien's prosperity was short-lived, as its 1816–1819 boom fell off dramatically after 1820. In part, the factories began to fail as private traders like the American Fur Company were spreading quickly. Old issues arose, too. Irwin blamed his need to cut prices on British traders who "under sell the goods in the Factory," and elsewhere he accused them of illegally selling the Indians whiskey.[80]

Government officials and poorly enforced trade regulations also harmed the factory system. Because Indian testimony could not be accepted in American courts, private traders who broke federal and territorial law by selling alcohol to Indians could not be prosecuted without the aid of another American fur trader (and many of them were allied under Astor's American Fur Company). From Green Bay, Irwin especially deplored selling alcohol to the Native populations, telling McKenney "the Indian trade is confined to the British traders, who, from selling whisky privately, and from the ties of relationship, etc. with the Indians, will continue to enjoy it" without determined federal intervention. Jedidiah Morse also agreed after his tour of the West, telling McKenney that for whiskey, "Indians sell their kettles, guns, clothing, horses, etc., for that article, the excessive use of which sometimes leading to the destruction of property, and the loss of lives." Such a strong demand for a product the factories would not and could not sell undermined consumer interest from Indians. Further, licenses issued by Indian agents worked against the factory system by increasing competition for the Indian trade. The conflicts in administration and problems in execution of the factory system undermined it to the point that some Western officials like Ninian Edwards came to oppose the factories remaining in business.[81]

Frustration with the system boiled over and spelled doom for a factory system that had already served its purpose. Irwin vented to McKenney in 1817 that after the problems he encountered, "I can promise nothing from this Factory" and thus he declined "any more merchandise here, unless the Secretary of War can correct" administrative issues that tested his patience. In July 1821, he recommended closing the factories at Chicago and Green Bay because they were "useless to the Indians, and . . . to the Government also." Combined with the efforts of Missouri Senator Thomas Hart Benton working on behalf of private trading interests, Congress decided to close the factory system completely in 1822. With it came the end of the federal experiment in controlling the Indian trade. However, the factory system had gained Americans a foothold in the fur trade upon which private traders like John Jacob Astor could capitalize, and it even provided aid to white settlers and American officials serving other functions. As Jedidiah Morse reported of the factory at Green Bay, for example, goods sold to Indians totaled only about $1,600 annually, but it also sold $3,500 worth of goods to whites and mixed-blood Indians, $500 to Indian agents, and $2,450 to the military detachment at nearby Fort Howard.[82]

While the factory system withered away, the land office flourished in the wake of the War of 1812. The war had essentially halted new settlement, as public land sales diminished quickly in the face of British and Indian threats. Citizens of the Indiana Territory complained to Congress that the same threats made them unable to pay for lands because of lost planting or because they had to "erect forts to save their women & children from that ruin and distruction which has for some time past threatened our frontier." Land sales in Indiana showed a slow market for land since the embargo and the rise of the Prophet and Tecumseh. Sales at Vincennes had been slow since 1807, and the period from 1811 to 1813 saw only 27,000 acres sold. Meanwhile, sales at Jeffersonville were slow but steady after 1807 until the war led them to drop by more than ten percent in 1812–1813.[83]

Settlements grew quickly after the war for two reasons after the British and Indians were defeated at the Battle of the Thames. The first, an 1813 order from Congress that gave preemption rights to settlers, led many settlers to visit federal land offices to legitimize their previously illicit homesteads. Preemption kept business so brisk through late 1814 that the Kaskaskia land office "could do little more than make the Entries of Lands applied for and Journalize the Accompts." Also, more importantly, clearing Indian threats jumpstarted the pace of settlement, as the Battle of the Thames seemed to affect settlement almost immediately. Benjamin Parke of Vincennes reported in November 1813 scarcely six weeks after the American victory, "Emigration to the Territory is recommencing—I suppose it to be the supposed favourable aspect of our Indian affairs." Sales statistics certify Parke's assessment. Settlers in Indiana bought 45,000 acres in 1812 but 166,000 acres in 1814, and the Vincennes office saw its sales quadruple from the fiscal year of 1812–1813 to 1814–15, rising from 13,366 acres to 53,236 acres. By war's end, the head of the General Land Office, Edward Tiffin of Ohio, oversaw further standardization of practices to increase operational efficiency as well.[84] As after the Northwest Indian War in Ohio, decisive federal action to clear Indian opposition led directly to a rapid growth in the pace of white settlement.

That sudden growth intensified during the second half of the 1810s. With the war finished and American control over the Northwest and its Indians secured, settlers purchased over 2.2 million acres from the General Land Office in Indiana and Illinois between 1814 and 1819, and land officers complained of still more settlers intruding on unsurveyed public lands. To hold them back and maximize eventual revenues, they demanded energetic federal measures to ensure a survey of the land or a removal of squatters. Meanwhile, squatters or not, federal land revenues from the former Northwest Territory more than doubled from 1814 to 1819. Indiana was the epicenter of that growth. Its land offices sold nearly 1.3 million acres during the period, with over half a million acres sold for more than a million dollars in 1817 alone.[85]

The influx of new residents quickly allowed statehood for Indiana and Illinois. Indiana's population rose 150 percent from 1810 to 1815 (from 24,520 to 63,897 inhabitants) and to 147,178 in 1820, another nearly 150 percent gain. With only 60,000 residents required by the Northwest Ordinance and petitions presented for statehood by Delegate Jonathan Jennings, Congress passed an enabling act for a state constitution in April 1816. Jennings led the convention held June 10–29 and attended by forty-three men, including John Badollet, and Congress officially accepted Indiana as a state on December 11, 1816. Illinois required more careful manipulation. The then-new territory contained 12,282 white citizens in 1810, grew very slowly to 1815, and then saw explosive growth over the next three years. It still lacked the 60,000 residents required for statehood and, gaining an enabling act in 1818, required careful maneuvering by

House Delegate Daniel Pope Cook. He persuaded Congress to lower the statehood threshold to 40,000 residents and to let Illinois conduct its own census. The massaged numbers revealed a population of 40,258, and Illinois won an enabling act in April 1818. In August, an elected convention wrote a constitution, and Congress accepted Illinois into the Union on December 3, 1818.[86]

The new state constitutions embraced two primary pieces of the energetic Republican program. First, the Indiana constitution included support for a system of public education. Article IX considered "Knowledge and learning generally diffused . . . essential to the preservation of a free Government," so the constitution required "as soon as circumstances will permit . . . a general system of education, ascending in a regular gradation, from township schools to a state university, wherein tuition shall be gratis, and equally open to all." To that end, the constitution established a fund for education based on proceeds from the sixteenth section of each township, while another fund drawn from sales of town lots sponsored public libraries in every new county created by the state legislature.[87] Second, both state constitutions allowed for central state banks, an idea originating with Albert Gallatin and reflecting state-level versions of Hamilton's banking plans. Article X of the Indiana constitution explicitly allowed for "a State Bank, and branches," while the Illinois constitution allowed "a state bank and its branches, which may be established and regulated by the general assembly of the state as they may think proper."[88] State banking became contentious later, but in the conventions of 1816 and 1818, central banking was hardly controversial.

Federal institutions also continued to influence life in the new states, perhaps best seen in two purchases from land offices in Indiana and Illinois. The first involved Kentucky farmer Thomas Lincoln, whose experiences with land ownership in Kentucky and Indiana highlight the contrast that federal supervision provided in the Northwest. Kentucky lacked a coherent system to survey and sell its public domain, instead developing a convoluted four-part process for land ownership that caused land claims and patents to overlap so often that one observer quipped that land purchasers in Kentucky also bought a lawsuit. Kentucky's federal court dockets testify to that comment, as nearly half of all federal cases filed in Kentucky (712 of 1,515) revolved around land disputes. Thomas Lincoln felt the sting of that system, being ejected from two farms he bought and holding clear title for less than one-fourth of the land he purchased during his life in Kentucky.[89]

Federally-backed land titles in Indiana offered security to Thomas Lincoln. After settling in the southwest corner of Indiana in late 1816, he planted and harvested one crop before he traveled to the Vincennes land office to purchase 160 acres, located plainly and marked on the maps as the southwest quarter of Section 32 in Township 4 South, Range 5 West of the Second Principal Meridian. Whether he brought along his eight-year-old son Abraham is unknown, but on October 15, 1817, Thomas Lincoln registered his claim with John Badollet. By bureaucratic routines already set, Badollet marked the claim as taken on his plats before sending Lincoln to receiver Nathaniel Ewing, to whom he paid the required minimum of $16, one-twentieth of his $320 purchase price. Thomas traveled again to pay another $64 in late December. Overall, the Lincoln family benefitted from a clear, unimpeachable title to his 160 acres. Although he reduced his holding to 100 acres through subsequent private sales, he never again had to worry about losing a lawsuit based on an overlapping survey or some claim from a forgotten speculator.[90]

Another purchase, made in Illinois by Englishmen turned Western settlers Morris Birkbeck and George Flower, showed customers quite pleased with the maturity of the American state. After registering at the Shawneetown land office a claim to thousands of acres around their eventual settlement of Albion, Birkbeck encouraged other immigrant settlers to make a pilgrimage to the land office as soon as they arrived in the West. As he explained, buying a quarter-section of federal land on credit allowed settlers an unmolested right to their land. As a result, he argued, new arrivals to Illinois and elsewhere could look "to the land to reward your pains" because the fruits of earnest labor would pay off the balance of financed lands.[91]

George Flower found the experience almost sublime. He rhapsodized in his diary that land offices formed "a valuable Institution" for not only his interests but for the nation as a whole. While laying out the various terms of land purchases and credit, he noted the land office prevented conflicting claims and resultant legal disputes. Overall, he wrote of it, "The whole territory to the pacific Ocean may be considered as belonging to it. The savage Tribes cannot maintain themselves against the intelligence of civilization."[92] Birkbeck, Flower, and Lincoln all found in the American state a helpmeet for them to attain the lands they wanted and to assure an orderly expansion of American society across the continent. The American state had clearly matured by the time the new states of Illinois and Indiana joined the Union in the late 1810s, and that development was spurred by Federalist institutions and ideals that helped to make many Westerners into advocates for education, industrial growth, transportation, and orderly expansion.

By statehood in Indiana and Illinois, Westerners saw a much different state than existed in 1800. The United States government and its territorial representatives had overseen Indian policy, the conquest and removal of hostile Indians from land white settlers coveted, the settlement of that land through land offices, and even the development of a political culture that prized state involvement and wished to see it infiltrate American society even more deeply. The General Land Office had come a long way from Rufus Putnam's log cabin, forming as an agency under the Department of the Treasury and operating some twenty locations throughout the trans-Appalachian West that sold more than four million acres of land during the twelve months preceding September 30, 1819.[93] Further, as the locus of legitimate land purchases and titles, land offices became the distributors of proper ownership and thus respectability and potential economic independence for Western settlers.

Reflecting on those changes in the Northwest, Indiana resident John Dumont found much to celebrate in his 1817 Independence Day speech in the town of Vevay. As he told the assembled crowd, "The sons & daughters of Columbia are all equal partakers in the blessings of our Government." After offering plenty of praise to the Declaration of Independence, he also noted that Americans had "witnessed the growth of the arts & the progress of the sciences, more than thirty years expereance has tought them that ours is a good practical Government established on the Solid foundation of Union & Equality."[94] Energetic Republicans oversaw the expansion of white settlement and the early American state, and they dispersed their ideas and institutions throughout the Northwest to a generation of Westerners and officials who expected more of their government by the end of the 1810s. Those raised expectations of state activity led to a new Western style of politics after 1820 in which those Republicans found surprising allies from Ohio: old Federalists who survived the partisan battles that raged there until the War of 1812. How those Ohio Federalists first survived and then united with the proponents of their institutional creations will be considered in each of the final chapters.

CHAPTER FIVE

"Our Strength Is Our Union"

Federalists in Ohio, 1803–1815

AFTER TAKING THE oath of office on December 8, 1810, Governor Return J. Meigs, Jr. offered a message of pride and unity in his inaugural address to the Ohio General Assembly. Despite a "world-convulsing contest for power" in Europe, he said Americans were at peace, "governed by institutions, emanating from our own choice." To maintain that freedom and the republic, he asked legislators to remember one principle, that "our strength is our union: to cultivate sentiments of union is then a duty, and worthy of being cherished with a holy zeal."[1] In other words, Ohioans would get the good, fair government they deserved if legislators trusted federal leadership and worked together for the best interests of Ohio. While timely with the War of 1812 approaching, Meigs was giving an alternate version of Jefferson's inaugural message. In the General Assembly, Meigs saw that they were all Republicans and they were all Federalists.

Meigs had multiple reasons to seek unity, including overcoming Jeffersonian divisions to govern effectively. In that fall's election, Meigs defeated Thomas Worthington, a leading figure in the opposition against Arthur St. Clair who became leader of Ohio's most powerful wing of Jeffersonian Republicans. However, the first few years of statehood saw a divide between Worthington's wing and a more working-class Republican faction led by Michael Baldwin of Chillicothe. By 1810, Meigs led a group of conservative Republicans who opposed Worthington and his allies in another party schism. Thus, as governor, unity meant power for Meigs. His faction would gain power if the General Assembly acceded to his prerogatives, so his statement in the inaugural address against "Fluctuations of design, and changes of legislative construction" had real implications for fellow Republicans.[2]

Meigs had another reason to push for unity: he was the son of an Ohio Company adventurer and left the Federalist Party after 1800, but he remained popular among Federalists. In 1807, Meigs won election as Governor under the Republican banner, especially where Federalists remained strong. Cincinnati voted for him by a three-to-one margin, Dayton favored him by a tally of 161–6, Athens County gave him over 95 percent of the vote, and his hometown Marietta chose him unanimously. However, the Ohio House of Representatives declared him ineligible because he lived outside Ohio too recently while serving as a federal judge.[3] He would not be deterred in 1810, and Federalists continued to prefer him then, too. In a sense, Meigs forsook the Federalists, but they did not leave him.

Federalists could find a number of Meigs's policy positions appealing, though he remained a good Republican. For example, he supported a public school system in Ohio like many Federalists did, and in his inaugural, he even quoted Ephraim Cutler's passage in the state constitution that schools reflected the "Religion, morality and knowledge . . . necessary to a good government." Meigs also expanded upon it. He saw public schools "the auxiliar of virtue" that promoted "respect for religion, purity of morals, and love of country." Meigs also wanted to build federal roads in Ohio, following up on positions first advocated by Rufus Putnam in the early 1790s. Finally, Meigs spoke in 1811 of expanding the state inspections of Ohio's exports first established under St. Clair and the Federalist-leaning territorial legislature ten years earlier.[4] Overall, strength in union seemed to mean incorporating Federalist ideas that prized an obedient populace and commercial development into Republican politics.

Meigs also stood before the Ohio General Assembly as a living, breathing anomaly that complicates current historiographic understandings of Ohio politics in early statehood. To Andrew Cayton, Meigs represented the end of Federalism because he had changed parties when the political winds shifted, while Donald Ratcliffe has observed that after statehood Ohio's Federalists almost immediately ceased as an organized party running slates of candidates. Ohio also never cast an electoral vote for a Federalist Presidential candidate. To these interpretations, the accusation of being a Federalist was sufficient to silence political opponents.[5] However, parties were less and more than lists of candidates in newspapers. As Ronald Formisano has argued, political parties in this period functioned more as interests of limited durability than the modern parties that scholars have often imagined. Taking this more protean view of parties reveals that parties functioned as organizing identities in a decentralized political landscape. Rather than a distinct structure observed later, these early parties engaged voters through culture: newspapers, civic activism, and public celebrations.[6] Ohio's Federalists had all of these avenues available to them, and at many times in many places, they had Federalist candidates to support for local offices and the state assembly.

Though often outnumbered, Federalist voters and a handful of successful Federalist politicians exerted outsized influence through skillful politics, local public service, and pro-commercial policies. Meanwhile, these Federalists saw programmatic approaches continue to gain traction in Ohio, as both Federalists and Jeffersonian Republicans enthusiastically supported internal improvements and other policies meant to stimulate economic development. As office seekers and public servants, Federalists continued to influence statewide politics through the War of 1812, especially after Jefferson's embargo enlivened Federalist politics in Ohio and enabled new successes for Federalist politicians. The war also brought Federalists like Jacob Burnet, Ephraim Cutler, and Charles Hammond into public service, and they developed clear differences from their counterparts to the east that let them remain in the public sphere afterward.

A Controlled West
Education, Inspection, and Louisiana

The first few years of statehood were the political times that tried the souls of Ohio Federalists. With their political fortunes waning, Federalists in Ohio took two primary courses of action. On one side, younger and more ambitious politicians continued to seek office and otherwise advance their political careers with limited success. However, losses in the legislature and at the polls mounted quickly. As Donald Ratcliffe has noted, Federalists no longer ran a formal partisan opposition to Republican rule after 1804, and the state legislature never boasted more than a few Federalists at a time after 1805.[7] Thus, many Federalists left politics for many years, if not permanently. Immediately after statehood, Ohio Federalists wielded little influence in elected offices but remained committed to refining Western society through education and other institutions outside of political office. Furthermore, they differed from other Federalists to the east by remaining friendly to national westward expansion.

Voters greeted Federalist candidates coldly in the first statewide contests, and perhaps the clearest signal came in the gubernatorial election of 1803. Arthur St. Clair received 234 votes (mostly from the Ohio Company home of Washington County), while Benjamin Ives Gilman of Marietta picked up 246 votes around Cincinnati. However, Republican winner Edward Tiffin of Chillicothe received nearly ten times as many votes as St.

Clair, Gilman, and all other Federalists combined.[8] The legislative election was also discouraging. Jefferson and Belmont Counties, both in the eastern part of the state and populated heavily by Quakers who tended to side with Federalists, sent the bulk of the Federalist contingent to the legislature. A few other Federalists throughout the state, chief among them Philemon Beecher of Lancaster, won seats in the Ohio General Assembly over the next few years but were badly outnumbered.[9]

Federalists in Ohio had to choose their moments. The Louisiana Purchase, for example, offered Philemon Beecher a moment of political stardom and other Federalists in Ohio an opportunity to develop a separate political identity. When France retook New Orleans and revoked American rights of deposit, thereby threatening Western commerce in October 1802, Ohio lacked a vote in Congress. They still lacked representation during Congressional discussions in February 1803, but Federalists to the east tried to take up their cause through an attack on New Orleans. In the *New York Evening Post*, Alexander Hamilton wrote as "Pericles" that French control of Louisiana "threatens the early dismemberment of a large portion of our country." Assuming Napoleon would ignore diplomatic offers, Hamilton argued that Congress should enlarge the U.S. Army to ten thousand men and let President Jefferson activate forty thousand militiamen to conquer New Orleans. Such a force "would astonish and disconcert Bonaparte himself," Hamilton suggested.[10] Overall, the Revolution of 1800 seemed not to chasten Hamilton's approach to the military. As with the Whiskey Rebellion and the Northwest Indian War, Hamilton continued to believe that enemies needed to learn the dire consequences of resisting American expansion in the trans-Appalachian West.

In the Senate, Federalist James Ross of western Pennsylvania also demanded force to resolve the Louisiana controversy. Seeing Western commerce as essential to American prosperity and federal revenues, he offered a resolution on February 16 that declared Americans "have an indisputable right to the free navigation of the river Mississippi, and to a convenient place of deposit" at New Orleans. If the French interrupted that right, "it materially concerns such of the American citizens as well on the western waters, and is essential to the union" to the point Congress should authorize the president to call up fifty thousand militia and "obtain complete security for the full and peaceable enjoyment of such their absolute right." In debates a week later, Federalist Samuel White of Delaware warned that Westerners could detach themselves from the Union if the situation was not resolved in favor of the United States.[11]

Even as James Monroe and Robert Livingston were negotiating the Louisiana Purchase in March 1803, the *New York Evening Post* printed news to agitate for military intervention. A correspondent complained that Americans would soon be "obliged to submit peaceably to any halter which [France] may impose." He also blamed perceived weakness on Jefferson, noting, "If the government of the United States had authorised a descent on this place, as a pledge for negociation . . . they would have been joined and applauded by the principal part of the inhabitants." Thus, he suggested, Federalists were the true guardians of Western interests. Five days later, the paper ran a piece from Kentucky stating American interests required "every exertion" from the federal government "to obtain one entire side of the river Mississippi." Hoping for swift and decisive action, the New York editor's remarks about the latter declared that if Jefferson sent troops, "we stand ready to give him all the credit such an act would deserve; but . . . we cannot join his democratic friends, and bestow it in advance."[12]

Federalists hardly trampled one another to congratulate Jefferson once news broke about the Louisiana Purchase, finding it by turns too large, too expensive, and negotiated too secretly. New England Federalists were the harshest critics, fretting over the waning influence their party and region held over the rest of the nation.[13] The Federalist *Columbian Centinel* from Boston attacked the Louisiana Purchase in July because of its supposed low quality of land, calling it "an aukward and heavy trouble" and "a great waste, a wilderness unpeopled with any beings except wolves and wandering Indians."[14] Whether they thought the purchase too much, too broad, or simply of a Great American Desert, Federalists in New England seemed convinced that the Louisiana Purchase was foolhardy and the latest example of irrational exuberance from Jefferson.

Further, the *Columbian Centinel* argued, the purchase violated Federalist ideals of careful, well-supervised westward expansion. As "Fabricus" observed on July 16, Louisiana offered "empire that is boundless, or whose bounds are yet unexplored," which might bring pride to European monarchs but was a curse to the Federalist writer. "So vast a machine as the government of the whole empire" would escape the Republicans, he wrote, and if they kept Louisiana "an untrodden waste. . . . they have not the vigor, and they dare not use the means to prevent the 'squatting' of hosts of renegadoes, and outlaws, and fugitives" until those disreputable characters formed a breakaway republic.[15] Overall, Federalists thought Louisiana could undermine energetic government and social order, especially since Republicans lacked the political will to curb the base desires of squatters or contravene the wishes of voters for the public good. Ultimately, the Louisiana Purchase might even destroy the United States, and thus Federalists must oppose it to save the Union.

However, unified resistance broke down as some Federalists, especially the *New York Evening Post* and its sponsor Alexander Hamilton, saw commercial advantages and economic opportunities in the Louisiana Purchase. On July 5, it declared the diplomatic situation "terminated favourably to this country," with New Orleans "essential to the peace and prosperity of our Western country, and as opening a free and valuable market to our commercial states." Therefore, the writer argued, "there is all the reason for exultation which the friends of the administration display, and which all Americans may be allowed to feel."[16] The Louisiana Purchase was essential to overseeing mercantile growth throughout the nation, and backing the purchase held consistent with Hamiltonian ideals of using state power to stimulate economic growth.

The Louisiana Purchase was quite popular in Ohio because residents believed, much like Hamilton, in its great economic promise. They celebrated the news of the purchase as it spread throughout the state in autumn, with Lancaster residents having a candlelit parade featuring a four-foot lantern inscribed "THOMAS JEFFERSON, THE MAN OF THE PEOPLE." In Chillicothe, the *Scioto Gazette* heralded American control of the Mississippi River as an end to "ruinous fluctuations in commerce" for the state, while citizens held public bonfires to celebrate and offered toasts to Jefferson and the Louisiana Purchase. The purchase was so popular among Ohioans that Republican leader Samuel Huntington thought Federalists would "not presume to oppose it" even if they wanted to do so.[17]

The purchase was indeed popular, but Philemon Beecher voiced Federalist objections to congratulating and supporting Jefferson via an Ohio House resolution. On December 17, 1803, Beecher argued against it and rallied fourteen votes to his side from a Jeffersonian supermajority, but the resolution carried by a single vote. Promising a message of protest against the resolution, Beecher presented the opposition case on December 19. Above all else, he was careful to note that they supported Jefferson's efforts "to acquire and secure to the people of the United States, the free and uninterrupted navigation of the river and waters of the Mississippi, and to procure . . . the province of Louisiana." However, he offered two objections. First, he found it "inconvenient, useless and absurd" to give the Jefferson administration "faint and unavailing encomiums . . . for performing that which they were required to do." Second, he was concerned the resolution implied that "state governments to be silent . . . is an evidence of their disapprobation."[18] For Federalists like Beecher, obedience was simply expected, so by offering support, the General Assembly was being redundant at best and sycophantic at worst.

While Beecher enjoyed momentary importance, other Federalists noticed mounting electoral defeats by 1804. In turn, many formerly prominent figures in the territorial period left politics for years, while some never returned. Former territorial governor Arthur St. Clair was already moving to Pennsylvania by the time of the first gubernatorial election, and the first Federalist candidate for governor, Benjamin Ives Gilman, focused more on managing his business concerns at Marietta than seeking office until he moved to Philadelphia in 1813. He did not abandon Federalism, though, shown by his choice in 1807 to name a 300-ton ship built in his shipyard the *Rufus King* after the New York Federalist. In Cincinnati, Jacob Burnet temporarily quit politics to focus on his law practice after he could not organize an effective Cincinnati Federalist ticket for the state legislature in 1803, and he did not return until the War of 1812. Even Rufus Putnam, the administrator of the old Ohio Company land office, pursued his work as a trustee of Ohio University and retired from active political life.[19]

Those Federalists faced a dilemma after 1803 because they wanted to remain in control of Western development but felt real antagonism toward the people they wished to lead. Ephraim Cutler was a fine example of the problems such an attitude posed. Beginning his political career in the territorial legislature in 1801, he won a seat at the Ohio constitutional convention but changes in Marietta soon distressed him. In his view, poorer voters held too much sway locally and favored Republicans too much.[20] In rejecting the leadership of gentlemen like Cutler, Marietta voters were an affront to the goals of the Federalist frontier and its organic social order. The final insult came for Cutler with his unsuccessful 1804 candidacy for brigadier general in the state militia. Washington County officers preferred him by "a clear majority of five votes in the brigade, and yet the major-general returned my opponent . . . as elected, and Governor Tiffin commissioned him!" Disgusted that "Democracy was in the ascendant, and . . . nothing in the political drama" interested him afterward. His defeat was simply too pernicious to bear. Rampant democracy and Jeffersonian demagoguery doomed the fortunes of Federalists like him, and for the next decade he found his time better spent locally as justice of the peace and leading new settlements around Marietta and Athens.[21]

Quickly, these Federalists found many ways to accomplish their goals outside of electoral politics. For Cutler and Putnam, promoting new educational institutions allowed them to continue affecting Western society. They envisioned new schools and colleges transforming the Ohio valley into a center of learning and virtue while bringing economic opportunity, and that attitude showed especially as Federalists tied to the Ohio Company focused on Ohio University. In December 1801, Ephraim Cutler introduced the bill to create a new university from the two townships reserved by the Ohio Company. The next month, a new law created American Western University from the grant, but college trustees—including Marietta Federalists like Rufus Putnam, Paul Fearing, and Dudley Woodbridge—waited until the Ohio General Assembly re-chartered it as Ohio University on February 18, 1804.[22] Progress was slow but steady afterward. Paucity of funds delayed the completion of the first building and creation of the first academic department until 1808, but Ohio University opened an academy offering secondary-level courses in June 1809 and granted its first bachelor's degrees in 1815.[23]

From its founding acts, Ohio University bore Federalist fingerprints. The acts to charter the university reflected Federalist ideals for education laid out in speculator plans of the 1780s, with both the 1802 and 1804 versions including a preamble stating, "institutions for the liberal education of youth, are essential to the progress of arts and sciences, important to morality, virtue and religion." While New England colleges of the era emphasized virtue and religion for their students, the university founders believed schools in general and Ohio University in particular should be "friendly to the peace, order, and prosperity of society, and honorable to the government." In the Federalist view, schools served greater social ends and imbued a spirit not of free inquiry but of obedience and deference to authority. The act also stated in its first section a priority list that included "promotion of good education, virtue, religion, and morality, and for conferring all the degrees and literary honors granted in similar institutions."[24] Listing the granting of degrees so far down the list is telling: Federalists wanted the university to produce exemplary citizens first.

The early years of Ohio University also reflected the values of its Federalist leaders. Rufus Putnam surveyed the town of Athens, established a leasing system in the university townships to raise revenue, informally led the university trustees, oversaw the construction of campus buildings, and helped design the initial curriculum. In addition, the first student code of conduct in 1814 stressed good behavior and punished misconduct harshly. Rules prohibited students from having or sharing "any lascivious, impious or irreligious book or ballad," and trustees stressed social harmony by disallowing any student to "quarrel with, insult or abuse a fellow student." Alcohol was another target of regulation, with students who wished to visit "a Tavern, Alehouse, Beerhouse, or any place of like kind" needing in writing, "special permission from someone of the faculty." Upon gaining permission, students still could not "keep company with a person whose character is notoriously bad" without facing punishment, up to expulsion for habitual offenders.[25] As the first code of conduct stressed in classic Federalist style, controlling conflicts, alcohol consumption, and even one's emotions were integral to becoming an educated gentleman and a worthy leader in the young republic.

Meanwhile, Ephraim Cutler aided local education and community development during his self-imposed exile from electoral politics. Establishing a homestead in Amesville, about thirty miles west of Marietta, Cutler hosted the first town school in his home. After citizens pooled their fur harvest to create the town's so-called Coonskin Library in 1804, Cutler also hosted it in his home and served as its librarian. By 1809, he had moved to Warren Township just north of Marietta and again volunteered his home for its first school, then built a log schoolhouse on his property that also served as a public meeting house and church. He supported schools and other political and social institutions, he wrote later, to aid the "progress of improvement in morals, intelligence, and property."[26] While making a prosperous farm for himself, Cutler continued the Federalist plan to make the West prosper culturally as well, especially by improving the morals and the education of Western citizens.

The efforts by Cutler, Putnam and the university trustees bore fruit in time, as the Amesville school helped to educate one of the first two graduates of Ohio University. Thomas Ewing attended the school in Cutler's Amesville home during three winters, and those classes only increased his appetite for learning. In 1802, teenaged Thomas "contributed ten Raccoon skins—being all my hoarded wealth" to the Coonskin Library. When the first fifty-one books returned, he wrote, "It seemed to me like an almost unbounded intellectual treasure—the library of the Vatican and all other libraries of which I had read were trifles—playthings—compared with it."

As it grew, he enjoyed "abundant and excellent reading for the seven or eight years that I afterwards remained at home."[27] Ewing was a success story for Federalist leadership, receiving an education from their efforts that later propelled him to success in the U.S. Senate and multiple presidential cabinets, including serving as the first Secretary of the Interior.

In the early years of statehood, Federalists enjoyed few victories at the ballot box, but they capitalized on new opportunities to encourage westward expansion and the construction of a well-ordered republican society. While Federalists farther east still pursued office actively and fought Jefferson even on such popular issues as the Louisiana Purchase, Ohio Federalists chose more promising forms of public service, especially in education, that let them advance their political and social visions. Thus, they were already separating themselves from their brethren to the east. The first few years of statehood may have brought many defeats that tested the resolve of many Federalists, but they found ways to stay relevant in Ohio politics and society.

The State of Fiscal-Mercantilism
The Pro-Business Politics of Ohio

The transition from Federalist to Republican rule in Ohio reflected trends in Indiana and Illinois, as Republicans often accepted and in some cases advanced Federalist creations. Particularly in the economy, Jeffersonians followed up on policies created by Federalists that actively aided commerce, like internal improvements and an inspection service for exports. Voters also approved of this approach, and after 1807, Federalists staged a minor comeback in the wake of Jefferson's embargo while continuing to seek an active role for government in economic development. This approach to developing markets bore fruit between statehood and the War of 1812, as Ohio's political leaders saw salutary reasons to maintain and even extend a close relationship between government and growing commerce.

Even before statehood, Ohioans held far-reaching economic ambitions New settlers tended to work for subsistence, primarily raising corn on partially cleared fields and hogs left to forage in wooded areas. Selling excess pork and making whiskey from corn presented the first participation in wider markets by white settlers in Ohio. As they rose above subsistence levels, many farmers moved to products meant almost entirely for export. They planted apple and peach orchards, cleared pastures for cattle, and grew wheat since it sold better and preserved much longer than corn.[28]

Products spread quickly, as French traveler François André Michaux reported in 1802 that Marietta had already shipped produce to Jamaica, and the next year Ohio exported more goods than Delaware, Vermont, and New Jersey. Some of that cargo even left Ohio on oceangoing vessels built in Marietta; the *Muskingum* and *Eliza Green*, both built in 1801, sent cargo to New Orleans and carried cotton to Liverpool in 1802.[29]

During those early years, Federalists were in the thick of commercial activities. Benjamin Ives Gilman spearheaded the nascent shipbuilding industry at Marietta that produced at least a dozen oceangoing merchant vessels between 1800 and 1806, and other shipbuilders in town built gunboats for the United States Navy.[30] The Putnams, especially Rufus and brother Israel, helped to introduce apple orchards to Ohio, bringing in 1796 a wagon with some forty different apple varieties to establish the first tree nursery west of the Appalachians. For the next twenty-five years, their nursery sold to Ohio farmers seeking to start their own orchards and export apples and cider. Ephraim Cutler also took the lead in exporting cattle east from Ohio, beginning annual drives to Baltimore in 1800 and continuing them for thirty years. While he said "Small profit generally resulted to me," his leadership in this new market led him to record with pride that through his business, "many poor families were placed in very flourishing circumstances," estimating that he "aided some two hundred families to acquire homes."[31] Once again, the absence of electoral majorities did not deter Ohio Federalists from taking important social and economic roles in the early years of statehood.

Rising ambitions and increased abilities of Ohioans to connect with outside markets led them to realize their economic future depended upon greater state involvement. Suggesting that the Market Revolution identified by Charles Sellers came to Ohio earlier than he identified nationally, Ohioans adopted state-friendly positions to include government in building markets in three key forms.[32] First, Ohio depended on a growing population for healthy local markets and increased production, and new arrivals required land sold by the U.S. government. Second, Ohioans recognized that access to distant markets would drive economic growth, so they pressed early and often for internal improvements. Third, a bright economic future depended upon a good reputation for Ohio produce, and they attempted to assure one through the statewide inspection service first established under Federalist territorial rule. In all three aspects, Ohio voters and politicians relied on a vision in which government would help to develop American commerce; ultimately, this fiscal-mercantile state based in Federalist assumptions and actions greatly influenced politics in Ohio for decades.

The population grew rapidly during the early years of statehood, and a good deal of it came with federal land office sales and the security of federally backed titles. Ohio's population almost quintupled from 1802 to 1808, from slightly above 40,000 to nearly 200,000 people, and its representation in the U.S. House grew from one to six after the 1810 Census. Cincinnati exhibited that rapid growth, increasing from around 500 inhabitants in 1795 to over 2,500 in 1810 and up to 4,000 in 1814. Ohioans spread across the land, too, as many lived within a few miles of waterways in the southern end of the state in 1802 but had filtered into much of the state by the War of 1812. The new arrivals provided real economic opportunities for longer-tenured Ohioans as well. Statewide agricultural production rose while new settlers offered a ready market for seed, livestock, food, and other important supplies. Until they cleared enough land and gained reliable, self-sustaining yields, those new settlers meant a revenue source for their neighbors.[33]

The federal government aided that growth, too. New land offices opened at Zanesville, Wooster, and Canton between 1803 and 1807 to sell public lands in central Ohio, joining offices established by the Land Law of 1800 at Steubenville, Marietta, Cincinnati, and Chillicothe. Between 1802 and 1807, settlers bought 1.9 million acres from them, taking on one million dollars of debt to the federal land office between October 1803 and October 1805. Federal land sales also helped Ohio to overtake Kentucky in population and economic importance by 1808, with the greater security of land deeds in Ohio being a major draw for many new Westerners.[34] In sum, federal backing helped Ohioans grow in numbers, spread across space, and increase their overall importance in the early nineteenth century.

Greater prospects lay in accessing markets across the nation and abroad, so Ohioans consistently supported internal improvements. They built roads privately, with speculators and locals looking to enhance property values and workers seeking supplemental incomes. However, public roads captured the public imagination. Ohioans often voted for Republicans but also chose to place government power at the cutting edge of the Market Revolution and its reliance on transportation. They used the three percent fund from public land sales promised in the Enabling Act of 1802 to build 1,030 miles of new roads in Ohio by June 1805, while counties improved existing roads in the state. As John Lauritz Larson noted, too, Federalists joined the push for internal improvements. The Cumberland Road bill passed through Congress in 1805 because of Federalist and Western support, and the *Washington Federalist* declared it an "important Law . . . far beyond any calculation yet formed on the subject" that held out "great Commercial Benefits," especially for Ohio.[35] Meanwhile, Republican Senator from Ohio Thomas Worthington offered a flurry of resolutions in late February 1807, culminating in a request that Secretary of the Treasury Albert Gallatin consider a national system of roads and canals "objects of public improvement, [which] may require and deserve the aid of Government." That same week, the Senate approved a commission for a new canal around the dangerous Ohio River rapids, a surefire stimulus to Western exports.[36] Thus, Ohioans found allies among the Federalists and federal officials while pursuing economic prosperity.

To assure lasting prosperity through high-quality exports, Ohioans also followed Federalist precedent with a government inspection system. Arthur St. Clair originally proposed the inspection system to the territorial legislature in late 1801, believing it "of the very first importance, that the articles sent to foreign markets should be of the best quality." Thus, he proposed to intertwine governmental oversight with Ohio's exports by affixing "some public stamp" on packages to prove regulations were followed. In addition, he called for the new regulations to be "guarded by very strong sanctions" to discourage low-quality, clandestine exports that would undermine the purpose of the system.[37] St. Clair's proposal represented the beginning of a fiscal-mercantile state in which government resources were directed to encourage as well as control economic activity. In essence, the state would stimulate and protect Western economic development, and the inspection offices were an important early element of it.

The territorial House agreed and appointed a committee including Republican Jeremiah Morrow, Ohio's lone Congressman before 1810, to draft a bill shortly after the speech. It passed, and on January 11, 1802, St. Clair signed the act requiring counties to appoint inspectors to oversee "as many deputies or packers, to pack and inspect under him, as the nature of the case may require."[38] They were to collect prescribed fees for each inspection, stamp approved items, and even pack (if necessary) all flour, meal, corn, biscuit, butter, lard, pork, and beef leaving the territory. The act even standardized size, construction, and sealing for containers of all types. For example, for the export of pork and beef:

> Barrels shall be made of good, sound, seasoned white-oak materials, clear of sap, tightly bound, with fourteen sufficient hoops, or ten flat hoops, at least two inches broad, secured in all cases with four nails, at least, in each chine hoop, and four wooden pins or pegs in each outward bilge hoop, and shall be packed with good, sound meat, with not less than two hundred nor more than two hundred and twenty-five pounds weight of meat in each barrel.[39]

Anyone avoiding inspections risked a $500 fine, and counterfeit stamps were treated as forgery. Like the Trade and Intercourse Acts passed by the U.S. Congress in the previous decade, the act also deputized the public by rewarding an informer with half of the fines collected from an offender.

After statehood, the Republican majority in the Ohio General Assembly passed a series of laws that elaborated on the inspection system and regulated commercial activity more closely. In early 1805, they nearly replicated the 1802 inspection law and capped milling fees, both aimed at better supervising agricultural business, while acts in February 1812 regulated the founding of manufacturing companies and added potash, lime, and fish to the inspection system. Even so, records related to the inspections are scant. Either the law was widely disregarded or the service's decentralized form, with county-appointed officers keeping private records, meant records may be lost in the fog of history.[40] Nonetheless, the renewals and refinements of the service suggest inspections were taken seriously. Taking cues from the Federalists, leaders in Ohio stood guard against unprincipled greed with regulations and offices clearly intended to guide economic growth and development.

In such a pro-business state, the embargo of 1807 created numerous economic difficulties for Ohioans. Rufus Putnam noted that the embargo brought Ohio "scarcity of money & the stopage of business," and the national economy fared little better. In 1808, American exports (at least officially) dropped from $108 million to $22 million, and agricultural exports fell to one-sixth of the previous year. This sudden and very steep drop in exports glutted local markets, leading commodity prices to nosedive. The depression also essentially killed Marietta's shipbuilding industry, with no new oceangoing vessel leaving the town after 1808.[41] The flow of settlers into Ohio waned as well, as potential settlers lacked both the funds to migrate west and the market access they needed to afford public land purchases on credit. Thus, real estate became difficult to sell. Rufus Putnam complained of inability to sell off land entrusted to him, while son William remarked, "land at this time is of no value."[42]

Other complaints made the broader problems clearer, but the Republican-led General Assembly offered a tone-deaf reply. In March 1808, the most prominent Western Federalist newspaper, the *Pittsburgh Gazette*, offered a stinging critique of the embargo. One writer asked on behalf of Westerners, "What does all this mean?" He had a simple answer: "The Mechanic is obliged to dismiss his journeymen—his customers desert him . . . on account of the embargo," while "The Farmer finds no market for his produce. . . . His oats, hay and corn were to be sold, but no body will buy." By December 1809, Ohio farmers expressed their pain through a petition reprinted in the *Dayton Repertory* that underlined the interlocked nature of economic problems. Signers complained to Congress that they could not pay their public land mortgages without specie influxes, reliable markets for their goods, and new immigrants who often brought money with them. Even so, the Republican-led legislature was committed to the embargo, resolving in February 1809 that British perfidy led Ohioans to "highly approve" of the federal embargo and other "pacific measures . . . for the preservation of our property, our seamen and our national honor."[43]

In response, Ohio Federalists found their pro-business policies and their vicious attacks on Jefferson's embargo more popular, and they reemerged on the political scene in a variety of ways. The embargo had spurred an observable Federalist revival nationally by 1808 as well, documented by Charles Sellers in his sweeping study of the national economy and Philip Lampi in his exhaustive voting data. In Ohio, this trend was clear especially quickly. Enough Federalists and allies won office in 1807 that they could elect Philemon Beecher as Speaker of the House, and Beecher also had built enough goodwill among Republican legislators and loyal Federalists to run for the U.S. Senate in 1806 and the U.S. House in 1808, even if unsuccessfully.[44]

By 1809, Federalists in Ohio were organizing and showing strength through local societies and publications as well. Taking a cue from their Atlantic brethren, Federalists in Marietta, Zanesville, Springfield, and rural southeast Ohio established four of some two hundred Washington

Benevolent Societies throughout the nation that promoted Federalist principles, opposed the embargo, and celebrated the life of George Washington. As publications indicate, the chapter in Marietta even remained active after the War of 1812. New newspapers also testified to the surging Federalist presence. In October 1808, Federalists founded the *Supporter* at the state capital Chillicothe, and in early 1810 Dayton saw the first issue of the *Ohio Centinel* edited by Isaac Burnet, brother of Jacob Burnet. Both papers attacked the embargo and Jeffersonian foreign policy overall, with the *Centinel* especially pressing for neutrality modeled on the foreign policy of George Washington. Even as the War of 1812 began, new Federalist newspapers, the *Zanesville Express* and St. Clairsville's *Ohio Federalist*, emerged to criticize Republican rule statewide and nationally while advocating Federalist positions.[45]

Meanwhile, the *Pittsburgh Gazette* used the embargo to outline in 1807 and 1808 a policy program of commercial development and a strong military that sounded familiar to long-tenured Ohioans. One piece claimed that "the United States was naturally a commercial country, as its commerce was the grand source of its prosperity," so Federalists had always supported a stronger American navy. On the other hand, a February 1808 piece argued that for the Jefferson administration, "Affection for our merchants is all a farce." The *Gazette* was also sure to note how the embargo undercut business elsewhere and reported high prices and strong demand for American produce in the Caribbean and Europe. Normally, they noted, "there is a tide in the affairs of men of industry and business, which, taken at the full, leads on to fortune," but the embargo forced Americans to accept nothing instead.[46]

The remedy, prescribed by the *Pittsburgh Gazette*, was support for Federalist policies once again. Articles urged Republicans to end the embargo, which "bound their fellow citizens, hand and foot" with restrictions "so unexpected, so pregnant with mischief," in order to allow prosperity and immigration to resume in the Northwest as the national economy recovered. Further, they favored internal improvements, an issue that had excited Federalists since the early 1790s. The paper argued one Republican legislator's plan for turnpikes throughout Pennsylvania deserved "the applause of every patriot," even if the proposed funding was "greatly inadequate to the magnitude of the object." Finally, as Federalists had advocated since the late 1780s, the nation required a strong military to confront threats, even in peacetime. As one correspondent argued forcefully, "Let us act from the conviction that . . . POWER is more respected than REASON. Let us possess the one to enforce the other."[47] The *Pittsburgh Gazette* consistently sought energetic government, from seeking a stronger military to greater funding for road projects.

A testament to the advantage Republicans held in Ohio politics, Federalists could not muster majority votes on their own even with all the momentum on their side, but Federalists again proved resourceful by allying with Republican factions who shared their policy objectives. In 1808, only one-quarter of voters backed Federalist Presidential electors, and Philemon Beecher won Fairfield County (around Lancaster) and Washington County in the U.S. House election but received only 28.5 percent of the vote against Republican Jeremiah Morrow.[48] However, the concomitant collapse of the state's Jeffersonian consensus offered Federalists a real opportunity. While one faction looked to strengthen Republican organization to better control election results, the Federalists took interest in the faction that held the court system in high regard and believed it a higher authority for citizens and a guardian of public order.

Their shared interest in preserving public order helped to form a new political faction that proved quite effective by 1808. For the most part, the faction involved Federalists backing pro-court Republicans. Federalist meetings in Marietta and Cincinnati led by Rufus Putnam and Arthur St. Clair, Jr., respectively, endorsed conservative Republican Samuel Huntington during his successful gubernatorial run in 1808. When the General Assembly met in December, it elected Return Meigs, Jr. to the U.S. Senate by a wide margin. The difference between Federalists and conservative Republicans was not so clear outside the state. The *New York Evening Post* listed Huntington alongside Philemon Beecher on Ohio's "Federal ticket" and reported in December that Huntington, "a federalist, is elected Governor."[49]

The alliance of Federalists and conservative Republicans worked well for two reasons. First, Huntington and other conservative Republicans emphasized morality and public order, priorities that naturally appealed to Federalists. In his inaugural address, Huntington reached out to them as well, declaring "diversity in political sentiment is neither pernicious nor useless" while decrying "the malignant spirit of party" as too often "disturbing private friendship and social harmony, and dissolving the ties of moral obligation." Such public references to morality appealed to Federalist ideals of an organic social order, and his annual message to the General Assembly the next year made it much clearer. Sounding more like St. Clair than Jefferson, Huntington warned against "unprincipled characters; men of restless, ambitious and mischievous dispositions . . . who are perpetually fomenting discord among the people."[50]

Second, members of the new political alliance shared an affinity for pro-business policies. Huntington spoke of government aiding prosperity "by the wisdom and justice of our laws" in a December 1808 address to the Ohio General Assembly, while successor Return Meigs, Jr. was more strident about placing state power behind commercial development. In his December 1810 inaugural address, he spoke optimistically about negotiations with Indians that might soon produce the right to build new roads linking Ohioans to the Great Lakes and elsewhere. In 1811, he urged the legislature to pass a bill regulating new manufacturing companies so that "capital might associate . . . under the sanction of law," and he called for action to support the planned Erie Canal. The General Assembly complied on January 15, 1812, becoming the only state outside New York to offer public support for the Erie Canal.[51] The alliance between Federalists and conservative, pro-business Jeffersonian Republicans proved powerful, winning statewide elections on programs meant not only to use state power to bring back prosperity in Ohio but to encourage obedience and public order in a fashion that would make Federalists proud.

The support Meigs received from Federalists in 1810 also reflected the nature of the alliance between Federalists and pro-business Republicans, and it was crucial to his victory. In Dayton, the new *Ohio Centinel* was fluid about party labels, backing the Republicans Meigs and Jeremiah Morrow for Governor and U.S. Representative, respectively. Appealing to his fellow Federalists, Isaac Burnet called his preferred slate of candidates "THE CONSTITUTIONAL TICKET." A correspondent to the Federalist *Chillicothe Supporter* in September went by the name Timothy Trowell and was frank about the alliance, too. He wrote of Meigs, "He is a moderate Republican. . . . he is no Federalist," but was still "the least evil of the two" Republican candidates. Striking a more stirring tone, Trowell hoped that the new alliance under the leadership of Meigs might mean "the words *federalists, lawyers, republicans*, &c. would loose their *magic charms*, and truth would prevail." Therefore, he urged, "Federalists come forward, take hold of our political ark. . . . Unite with all honest men in the election of judge Meigs." Ultimately, Meigs trounced rival Thomas Worthington around Federalist strongholds in Cincinnati, Dayton, and Marietta, indicating the popularity of this line of thinking. In fact, Dayton chose him by a 200–2 margin, even though local favorite Jeremiah Morrow endorsed

Worthington. Overall, the counties containing the three cities were key to Meigs's victory, giving him 1,867 of his 1,942-vote majority.[52]

From statehood until the War of 1812, political events overall reflected the legacy of Federalist rule in Ohio and suggested the direction political allegiances would continue afterward. In that first decade of statehood, Ohioans of both parties clearly benefitted and even came to demand that government be active in developing the region's economy. Federalists had supported internal improvements since the 1790s, and many Republicans joined them by the embargo era. Furthermore, this new bipartisan alliance envisioned a state able to power economic growth, the uniting ideal behind an alliance of Federalists and conservative Republicans until the War of 1812. That alliance also embraced Federalist ideals of morality and public order, showing Federalists could encounter a great deal of success even if the Federalist name had become political anathema. The short-lived Federalist-Republican alliance also portended the Whig Party in the trans-Appalachian West that developed by the late 1820s. Overall, Federalists in Ohio had reason to be optimistic even if they were potentially a permanent minority.

The Ordeal of 1812
Ohio Federalists and the War with Britain

While historians often talk of the political ramifications of the War of 1812 in national terms, Ohio defied standard interpretations of the war. New England Federalists made the Madison administration's titanic struggle against the world's most powerful empire and fierce Indian resistance throughout the trans-Appalachian West all the more difficult—and even toyed with treason later in the war—while Ohioans reacted very differently. Immediate security concerns were a prime mover in political reactions to the war across Ohio, and those reactions strayed from party lines. Meanwhile, many Ohio Federalists saw opportunity in the war. They redoubled their support for pro-business policies and maintained steadfast antagonism toward the embargo, while forward thinkers fashioned a stout but above all loyal opposition to Madison and his war that fueled their political survivals well into the future.

Standard interpretations of the War of 1812 include as a matter of course the death of Federalism. After years of supporting a stronger military, Federalists suddenly switched course to oppose the war, and became the greatest obstacle to Mr. Madison's War. Every Federalist in Congress

voted against the declaration of war, and their continued, organized opposition was unfortunate at best and treasonous at worst. They obstructed
funding requisitions, resisted or ignored calls for troops, and constantly
complained about the taxes used to pay for the war and the tactics used by
military leaders. For its duration and across most of the nation, Federalists maintained a monolithic opposition to the war until they graduated to
open treason with the Hartford Convention near the war's end. That final,
desperate grasp at power by a waning party assured its destruction. Soon,
Federalists were gone from the political landscape, a fitting punishment
for their betrayal of the republic when Americans most needed unity.[53]

Ohio defied those patterns in the War of 1812 for three primary reasons related to security and economics. First, the war created threats to
the lives and livelihoods of Ohioans. Republicans were largely enthusiastic about it, but arch-Republican Senator Thomas Worthington opposed
the declaration of war because—as he told Madison personally—it would
jeopardize his constituents' security.[54] Ohio's proximity to the Northwest
War of 1811 and raids by Tecumseh's confederacy persistently caused
worries that British troops would only exacerbate. Those threats were all
too real for settlers in northwest Ohio, which Indians ceded only in 1805.
So worried were the residents of Canton that a stray gunshot outside of
town sparked a full alarm on August 3–4, 1812. In fact, these fears led
many northwest Ohioans to abandon their homesteads during the first
year of the war.[55]

British provocation of Americans and interference with American interests stirred patriotism among Ohioans, the second reason residents
responded differently to the war. Ohio Federalists deplored the embargo, but Britain did itself no favors. News of the *Chesapeake* incident in
1807 prompted Federalist Jacob Burnet of Cincinnati to help author the
city's anti-British resolutions. By 1812, many Ohioans of both parties had
seen enough from Britain. Republicans and Federalists alike backed an
anti-British resolution the General Assembly passed on New Year's Day
that stated, "The conduct of Great Britain towards this country, is a gross
departure from the known and established law of nations." In turn, they
promised to "rally round the standard of freedom" and "not shrink from
the dangers of war."[56] Once the war began, the Federalist press also stood
behind the war. The new Federalist newspaper in Franklinton (near Columbus) called on Americans to rally behind the flag and war effort despite
party labels, and the *Chillicothe Supporter* announced its support on July
4. Relating news of the declaration of war, the newspaper once accused by

a Republican competitor of promoting "England and tory principles" for "echoing and re-echoing, rebellion and treason" threw its weight behind the new war effort. "However we may differ in political sentiments," an editorial declared of the news, "it now becomes the duty of every citizen to cling to his country and rise or fall with it."[57]

Finally, the war presented many Ohioans economic opportunities. Despite continued restrictions on British trade, Westerners could still export to Spanish colonies in Florida and the Caribbean, and flour exports to those colonies grew from 105,000 barrels in 1809 to 939,000 barrels in 1812. The war helped Ohio flour to sell well abroad and at home, too; in Ohio, wheat prices doubled and whiskey prices tripled during the war due to both rising exports and the need to feed American soldiers in the area. The war also offered transportation projects, with the military building a series of roads around the state that eased the flow of commerce and let more Ohioans gain access to reviving markets.[58] References to economic opportunities were rare in contemporary political discussions, but they doubtlessly had subtle effects on the ways Ohio residents reasoned through their positions on the War of 1812.

Many Federalists remained openly opposed to Madison and his war, and while they found new outlets for their positions, they also were careful to express their patriotism. In St. Clairsville on the eastern end of the state, Charles Hammond founded the *Ohio Federalist* in 1813 to be the preeminent Western voice against both the war and the Madison administration while promoting Federalist views and candidates. In Cincinnati, Federalists also found a new forum for their protests when the Republican *Western Spy* turned politically neutral and printed Federalist and antiwar items.[59] Despite their opposition, Federalists quickly and proudly took up arms for the war effort when needed. For example, despite his Federalist father's distaste for the war, Thomas Ewing joined a handful of Ohio University students in a mounted volunteer company. Meanwhile, when provisions needed to be delivered across the state from Urbana, "patriotic spirit" motivated "the federalist, the republican, the farmer, the mechanic, the lawyer and the merchant indiscriminately determined to shoulder muskets" and carry out the mission. This commitment to duty, newspapers noted, was "that true spirit of patriotism, which, when required, steps forth with alacrity, to defend her country's rights."[60] Even if many of them disagreed with the war, Ohio Federalists made it clear their patriotism would never falter.

Even with such assurances, Ohio's Federalist candidates that fall had mixed success at best. They were active in campaigns throughout the state, and in the Western Reserve, John S. Edwards won election to Congress; unfortunately, he passed away before he could take office. Nationally, DeWitt Clinton promised "vigorous" government that drew the support of the *Chillicothe Supporter* and other Federalists who saw in the Republican Clinton a greater chance for victory in the 1812 Presidential election than a conventional Federalist, but he drew less than 30 percent of the popular vote and no electoral votes from Ohio. That defeat is even more significant because the race was surprisingly close nationwide. The gubernatorial race went poorly, too. Clintonian candidate Thomas Scott drew only 38 percent of the vote against Return J. Meigs, Jr., who had backed the war wholeheartedly.[61] These defeats can in part be traced to the war, which grabbed most of the public interest in the summer and fall, as military campaigns rather than political ones captured the attention of many. James B. Gardiner of the Franklinton *Freeman's Chronicle* attested that politics that year were not "near as animated . . . had not the events of the war given the electioneering gentry something else to do." Nationwide, incumbents won by greater majorities during the war, so in a solidly Republican state like Ohio, Federalist prospects dimmed again.[62]

Federalists also had trouble assuring a suspicious public of their loyalty while spreading their political message. Perhaps the most innovative approach came from Charles Hammond's amalgamation of patriotism, partisanship, and republican virtue in his *Ohio Federalist*. Hammond was already a controversial figure as a fiery Federalist lawyer and newspaper essayist when he entered the publishing fray; only the *Freeman's Chronicle* welcomed his newspaper into the public sphere.[63] Blessed with intelligence and a sharp wit but lacking restraint, Hammond entertained and educated supporters while often offending detractors with his Federalist polemics. The war was central to his writing, and his opposition to the war centered on four Federalist hallmarks: support for mercantile development, opposition to French interests and sympathizers (whom he often slurred as Jacobins), wariness of immigrants, and demands for republican virtue. His unorthodox approach to writing about the war led Hammond into some interesting positions that sometimes had overtones of conspiracy theory, but it also let him remain a viable political activist and candidate after the war.

Quite often, Hammond expressed his antiwar position in terms of economic policy. In April 1814, he assessed the embargoes against Britain as "loathsome and most foolish," and news that the embargo's "anti-commercial plans" might soon be lifted led him to declare, "we shall rejoice that this wretched system will soon be in its grave." In August, he declared bluntly, "The commerce of the country was destroyed, & its agriculture withered, by an Embargo, and by non importation laws," and war became necessary after the embargo failed to deter practices on the high seas.[64] Thus, he believed, ending the embargo would end the cause for war. In attacking the embargo that upset Federalists and many Ohioans, Hammond made a broader appeal to Ohioans that also allowed him to be patriotic. After all, he only wanted economic prosperity more than war, and held different priorities than Republicans.[65]

Hammond also proclaimed his loyalty by making the French Revolution and Napoleon effective proxies for his complaints, thereby promoting opposition to the war as the true path for American patriots. Relying on an old Federalist trope, Hammond derided his pro-war Republican foes as servants of French intrigue, and again the embargo proved handy. Hammond paired the embargo with Napoleon's Continental System as "more than twin sisters," both of which were falling together by 1814. He took a much clearer tack in June, writing that "America and England should be at peace" and would be, if only the Jeffersonians had not been "full of the light of French politics" that encouraged anti-British commercial measures.[66] Thus, when he spoke against the war, he was not attacking America but rather French domination over American politics. As the true friend of the republic, therefore, Hammond could cast himself and fellow Federalists in an honorable and patriotic light.

That suspicion also led Hammond to tap into a common Federalist worry that immigrants (especially foreign-born editors) exerted undue influence over American politics. Immigrant editors were instrumental to Republican victories in 1800 and afterward, and Hammond saw the same problems afoot during the war. In autumn 1813, he ran a letter alleging that public opinion for war was "kindled by the newspapers," and the next spring he accused an opponent of being "one of your thorough bred European jacobins." He worried Republicans prized the opinions of immigrant editors too highly, also. When an immigrant editor criticized President Madison in another paper, he carped that similar complaints from him "would have amounted at least to moral treason" but from the immigrant editor was "evidence of patriotism and virtue!!" The antipathy toward Republicans and their foreign-born editors led him into a bitter newspaper war during most of 1815 with Irish-born James Wilson from nearby Steubenville. Hammond barely hid his contempt in the *Ohio Federalist*, calling Wilson a "fool" and "two legged animal without feathers" while saying privately that Wilson lacked the proper character to deserve better treatment.[67]

Finally, Hammond believed his opponents lacked the disinterest and selflessness needed to serve the republic well. He worked to expose "designing and unprincipled" Republican demagogues while believing the "wild misrule of their angry passions" had led the American people astray. Overall, Hammond said in a fit of righteous indignation, the United States had become "no more stable than the will of mobs and demagogues," and he and other Federalists would always stand against that awful trend. The assumption behind Hammond's sense of republican virtue was the same one underlying Federalist ideals of public order: the republic best functioned under strong precepts and principled leadership. Virtuous men did not pursue the approval of a fickle public but rather led by force of right. That line of thinking, though politically self-destructive, reassured Federalists who were losing elections with increasing frequency after 1800. After all, Federalists needed not to rethink their politics, but rather needed to educate the public about republican truths and Republican demagogues. To Hammond, the *Ohio Federalist* served that purpose.[68]

To spread his message effectively, Hammond wrapped his criticisms in the flag. Perhaps the two clearest examples of this approach came in summer 1814, the first being a particularly outrageous piece of mail from a Jeffersonian opponent. On June 15, he printed a letter from Kentucky threatening that Hammond would "swing by the neck" if he traveled through the area since good, patriotic Americans "despise tories and traitors." It also contained a revolting enclosure: "You will discover the use I have made of your paper—wiped my backside with it, as every good and honest man should do." Hammond ridiculed the writer as a "specimen of the *dignified, liberal* and *republican* notions." Such unprincipled attacks had no place in Hammond's vision of the republic, and he claimed two months later not to be "intimidated by denunciations." After all, "my political sentiments originate in a deep and unshaken conviction, that the course I pursue, is the path of patriotism, honor and justice." It was his calling, even: "All Federalists are prepared, to meet the crisis as becomes Patriots and Republicans."[69] Hammond was offering a real innovation in American freedom, seeing true patriots as men who questioned their leaders in wartime. He was forming the philosophical core of a loyal opposition that let him remain patriotic and spread an alternative political message.

The other item came in July, when he proposed four "American Principles" that buttressed his opposition to the war. First, he argued the United States should, as Washington warned in his Farewell Address, avoid intimate connections with foreign powers. Madison and other Republicans were tied too closely with France, he claimed, and war had resulted. Second, Hammond said Americans should avoid foreign crises like the Napoleonic Wars that had sucked the United States into war against Britain. Third, they should make war only when forced to do so, and the War of 1812 was anything but a last resort. Finally, in agreement with many Republicans, Hammond called for free trade around the globe for American merchants, all the while deploring federal interference via embargoes and other trade restrictions.[70] Here, Hammond offered a new formulation of American freedom while standing against the war. True Americans questioned the War of 1812 and its motives, and thus his loyalty to the nation was beyond question.

Political successes Hammond realized during the war show that his message resonated with nearby voters. During his first autumn editing the *Ohio Federalist* in 1813, he narrowly won a seat in the Ohio Senate. He addressed voters directly in his newspaper, and it likely made a difference in his victory by just twenty-nine votes. While in the Senate, Hammond tried to put his principles into action by supporting new roads, banks, schools, and other projects meant to encourage economic development and serve the public good. Further, his work doubtlessly contributed to the popularity of other Federalist candidates. Throughout the state, Federalists won races in Ashtabula and Montgomery Counties as well, and while the Republican candidate won the Congressional race in Hammond's district, the party's margin of victory dipped by nearly 75 percent.[71]

Hammond nevertheless faced accusations of disloyalty that created problems for him in the Ohio Senate. His attacks on Madison and other war proponents garnered him enough scorn that he had to apologize publicly for some of his newspaper remarks. Perhaps the greatest challenge to Hammond's loyal opposition came from other Federalists through the Hartford Convention of late 1814. New England Federalists talked of secession to solve their problems with Madison, the war, and the overall direction of American politics. This final act of obvious disloyalty forced Hammond to distance himself from his party brethren. To do so, he split Federalists during the war into two broad types, the first being the "small but virulent class" of Hartford Convention attendees who obstructed the war by every possible means and the other being "the most numerous and respectable . . . on the side of their country." Hammond left no mystery as to which side he preferred. He successfully maintained his right to a loyal opposition to the war to the very end, even as his party committed political suicide nationally, and that distinction served him well in his political career after 1815.[72]

However, Hammond and other antiwar Federalists did not have to maintain their opposition for long after the Hartford Convention. On March 2, 1815, Hammond hailed the Treaty of Ghent as a "propitious event" in his newspaper and expressed "gratitude to the Almighty Sovereign of the Universe." Confirming his previous arguments, he also reported that news of the peace led markets in New York to see "sudden, and to many a shocking change." In the ensuing weeks, he described a "burst of joy" around the nation that proved "the real wishes of the people" who universally celebrated the war's end. Similarly, Ephraim Cutler celebrated the news by hosting a party at his home. One neighbor recalled, "The house was brilliantly illuminated, the word PEACE shining from the upper windows, and the judge came out upon the door-steps and made us a capital speech, to which we responded with hearty cheers and patriotic songs, and the discharge of our guns" before a celebratory feast.[73]

Overall, Federalists in the Buckeye State hoped the end of the war would bring a return to principled republicanism and, more importantly, to business as usual. A poem in the *Ohio Federalist* expressed that desire well: "Swelling Commerce opens all her ports. . . . To grateful industry converting—makes / The country flourish and the city smile."[74] Removing the threats of embargo and war meant Federalists could look forward to a radiant future for the Northwest, in which Westerners and their government would embrace mercantile growth once again. For proponents of the war like Jacob Burnet, their political futures remained bright and they were successful for decades afterward. Even opponents like Ephraim Cutler and Charles Hammond succeeded with voters and newspaper readers in Ohio, with their political careers picking up after 1815. In sum, the War of 1812 was an ordeal to which Ohio's Federalists were more than equal. The war may have killed Federalism in other places, but in Ohio it presented an opportunity for Federalists to shine.

The years from 1803 to 1815 severely tested the might and mettle of Federalists in Ohio. Never again did the party win elections outright and sweep into power as the Republicans had done in 1803, but they found other ways to affect the politics and society of their new state. In the first years of statehood, many of them turned to private pursuits or smaller-scale civic projects to continue spreading their ideals among settlers, while a few like Philemon Beecher looked to build a new coalition with Republicans that would earn Federalists victories in the legislature, even if not at the polls. The embargoes that ran from 1807 through the War of 1812 hastened the formation of that coalition, as Federalists found willing allies among conservative Republicans in building up a fiscal-mercantile state that would encourage economic growth when the federal government would not do so. In the process, Ohioans on both sides of the aisle embraced Federalist policies and programs from enthusiastic support for internal improvements to maintaining an inspection system for state exports. Federalist candidates competed well in many places, too, as their ideas remained central to state politics.

Even the War of 1812 did not destroy Federalists in Ohio, unlike their counterparts farther east. In fact, Ohio's Federalists largely survived and even thrived in wartime with responses to the war that were unique among Federalists partly because of peculiar circumstances. Even war opponents found innovative ways to express their frustrations with the war and with the Madison administration. With men like Charles Hammond leading the way, Federalists in Ohio complied with wartime requests and created a new response—as a committed, steadfast, but above all loyal opposition—that allowed them to deflect charges of being Tories or traitors. While Republicans imagined themselves refighting the American Revolution, Hammond and other Ohio Federalists waged a war for the future by expressing an alternative vision for the republic that offered real promise moving into and beyond 1815. They were never a majority party on their own, but the War of 1812 allowed Federalists in Ohio a real political future.

The return of peace also allowed them to look back to alliances developed during the embargo, and in the next twenty-five years they slowly solidified and then morphed into Western Whigs together. They did so because they found strength in their unions, both with conservative Republicans and with the rest of the nation, before 1815. Going forward, Federalists remained focused on energetic government, tying government to mercantile interests, and a clear sense of order while attracting new adherents among their Republican foes. Perhaps most importantly, Federalist politicians and principles eventually attracted a new generation of politicians in the Northwest, and this new combination would later pay real dividends to Federalists who leaned on the strength of their Union and the ideals of their party.

CHAPTER SIX

From Frontier Federalists to Western Whigs
The Rise of a New Coalition

On July 4, 1825, "a cavalcade of citizens" numbering at least 5,000 thronged to the small town of Newark, Ohio, to celebrate the ground-breaking of the Ohio Canal, connecting Lake Erie to the Ohio River. Travelers filled boarding houses for miles around and jammed onto all roads leading into Newark. At nine in the morning, they poured into the streets of Newark to cheer the many luminaries on hand for the special occasion, including Ohio's secretary of state and its entire Congressional delegation, plus many General Assembly members. However, the audience saved its greatest reverence for ceremony leaders Governor Jeremiah Morrow and former New York Governor DeWitt Clinton, hero of the Erie Canal and "father of internal improvements." That morning of the forty-ninth anniversary of American independence, one newspaper described the governors enjoying the hearty "congratulations of the assembled multitude."[1]

Clinton and Morrow arrived at the ceremony site along the Licking River at about 11:30 a.m., when "thousands rent the air with their loud huzzas of welcome" followed by celebratory cannonades. On a makeshift stage, Clinton offered his keynote address. He saw "a peculiar fitness" in opening the canal on a date that would soon celebrate not only independence but also "the prosperity of the American people, and still further exalt our national character." Soon, July 4 would celebrate a nation truly united: "the East and the West, the North and the South, by identity of interest, by frequency of communication." The new canal would be, Clinton declared, "a channel of commerce" and a "stimulus to manufactures" but more importantly, it would protect Westerners from the vices of idleness. Connection to markets and attendant opportunities "will be a guardian of morality," he assured them, "by rousing the human mind" and rewarding industriousness.[2]

To the crowd, Clinton's words were perfect for the occasion and drew such loud cheers that he had difficulty making himself heard at times. After he finished speaking, toasts praised him as a man "guided by the unerring light of Science" and the canal as the "great artery of America, which will carry abundance to all the extremities of the Union." Toward the end of the ceremony, Morrow and Clinton dug the first shovelfuls of earth together. The audience responded with deafening cheers and the joyous firing of hundreds of guns and cannons. At its crescendo, the whole spectacle of the groundbreaking ceremony overcame Clinton and briefly brought tears to his eyes.[3]

Clinton and others understood the celebration in Newark as the convocation of a new era in which commerce would unite America. He remarked two days later in Columbus that the Ohio Canal was "a cause in which every citizen & every state in our country, is deeply interested" and praised its "great centripetal power." He saw a series of canal projects across the nation forming "an adamantine chain that will bind the Union together in the most intimate connection of interest and communication." Elsewhere, newspapers grasped the significance of the day as well. From Worcester, Massachusetts, the *National Aegis* presented the Ohio Canal groundbreaking in grand terms: "When we talk of the political revolution which derived its origin from that day," it cheered, "let us be able to refer to . . . all the other great revolutions of our country."[4]

The great revolution to which the *Aegis* referred was the Market Revolution, and in the Northwest, the market's most energetic evangelists ultimately aligned in the Whig Party. The old Federalist guard constituted a crucial part of this new alliance, especially in Ohio, where they continued their political careers into the 1820s and 1830s. By the 1830s, too, they ran for office and supported candidates under the Whig banner, maintaining a similar agenda as proponents of public education, orderly westward expansion, and government-sponsored economic development. Those items had led Federalists to nominate DeWitt Clinton for President in 1812, who though a Republican, shared their interest in using internal improvements to link Americans together. Clinton's and Morrow's longtime supporters among energetic Republicans also formed the core of this new alliance. In supporting internal improvement projects and enlarged public education systems, Morrow and many other Western Republicans found the emerging partisan message appealing. Across the region, they aligned behind Western champions Henry Clay and William Henry Harrison to support programmatic approaches to schools and transportation to transform their adopted Western homes into great centers of commerce. These energetic Republicans formed the base for the National Republicans in the 1820s, and many coalesced as the largest component of the Western Whigs by the 1830s, advocating for government energy in society and in market development.[5]

Through this new combination, frontier Federalists bequeathed a twin legacy to the republic. On one side, a few survivors of the disintegrating Federalist Party and especially their policy prescriptions were integral components of the new Whig Party in the West, which looked to programmatic policies to propel the nation into a new era of industry and capitalism.[6] On the other, they had established an administrative state that Whigs sought to expand. Western Whig programs of tariffs, centralized banking, and internal improvements reflected how deeply Federalist institutional creations had altered relationships between citizens and their government in the Ohio River valley. No matter their party preference, Western citizens had come to expect government to address their concerns quickly, if not anticipate problems entirely. However, the Whig vision for the nation did not involve laissez-faire capitalism; their plans for protectionism and conscious state action reflected Alexander Hamilton more than Adam Smith. Therefore, after 1815, the pro-state tradition of Western politics became only more entrenched in American politics, economics, and society.

Federalists, Energetic Government, and the Continued Fight for the Frontier, 1815–1824

By all accounts, the Federalist Party was dead in Ohio and elsewhere by 1815.[7] However, former members did not slink away quietly after the War of 1812, and some familiar Federalist names found real political success after 1815. For example, Philemon Beecher served multiple terms in the U.S. House from 1817 to 1829. Jacob Burnet of Cincinnati was an Ohio Supreme Court justice from 1821 to 1828, and then became U.S. Senator until 1831. The state legislature that chose Burnet did so after hearing the third annual message of Governor Allen Trimble, another former Federalist who served in the State Senate starting in 1817 and twice as governor, first briefly in 1822 and again between 1826 and 1830. Formerly Federalist candidates did well in elections in eastern Ohio and the old Ohio Company purchase too, with Charles Hammond, Ephraim Cutler, and William Rufus Putnam all winning seats in the state legislature during the late 1810s and throughout the 1820s.

Whatever their particular party labels after 1815, these men succeeded in Ohio by evolving their message to voters but staying true to their principles. During the postwar economic boom and in the wake of the Panic of 1819, they remained advocates of internal improvements and public schools with stated policy goals that resembled old frontier Federalist ideals. They hoped more energetic government would encourage social and economic development in the Northwest. As a result, government policy and economic stimulation would steer citizens away from isolation and self-interest and toward a stronger sense of community and republicanism. Their efforts ultimately placed them within an emerging new Western ideology soon to be broadcast across the nation from the Ohio valley under the new Whig banner.

This political evolution of Ohio's Federalists occurred in a state that saw explosive population growth after the War of 1812. Its population doubled between 1810 and 1820 to nearly 600,000, and virtually all that growth came after 1815. Cincinnati grew even more quickly. Roughly 4,000 people were in the city during the War of 1812 but over 10,000 lived there by 1819. Federal treaty negotiators enabled that growth by clearing all Indian title to Ohio by 1818, and federal land office sales attest to the growing white settlement in central and northern parts of the state. In Canton, the land office sold more land in 1813–1814 than it sold in all previous years combined, and overall sales in the Northwest spiked by 150 percent from 1814 to 1819. Meanwhile, other government institutions kept pace with the population growth. Between 1818 and 1820, for example, the post office expanded from 98 to 301 local offices within Ohio.[8] Much like the 1790s, settlement in Ohio grew by leaps and bounds after Indian threats were neutralized, and the early American state stood once again at the fore.

That influx of people and their money underlay a postwar economic boom in the Northwest. New settlers usually brought money to spend on new homes, tools, implements, and various other needs that longer-tenured Ohioans happily provided for the right price. The end of foreign embargoes also allowed Ohio farmers to raise their incomes and, by extension, brighten economic prospects across the state. The new prosperity also buoyed enthusiasm for the Market Revolution in Ohio, and citizens seemed to embrace it with gusto. Perhaps nowhere was that fact more salient than in the rising industrial center of Cincinnati, which saw growth in wool, milling, and brewing industries. Pork production dwarfed the other industries after the war, too, with so many packing houses cropping up that the city was dubbed Porkopolis.[9]

Government aided that prosperity, too, especially through the Second Bank of the United States. Chartered in 1816, it offered credit that capital-starved Westerners could use to open new businesses, expand operations, and deepen connections to outside markets. The Bank also represented stability. As Jacob Burnet recalled of state banks, "no person felt entirely safe, in receiving their paper," so Ohio businessmen "united in opinion in favor of a National Bank, as the only agent that could restrain . . . unreasonable and injurious issues" of state bank notes. Residents of many Ohio towns showed their excitement for the new Bank of the United States by applying for local branches, with Cincinnati and Chillicothe each gaining one in 1817. Furthermore, Jacob Burnet was appointed Cincinnati's branch director, making him one of ten Federalists nationwide serving as Bank of the United States branch directors. Bank policies also fed business growth and revived speculative ventures after 1815, with the main office in Philadelphia telling Burnet to offer generous loans with discounts for prompt repayments.[10]

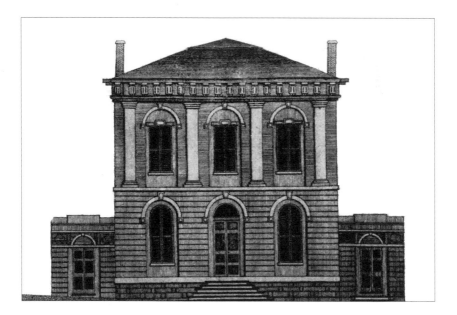

FIGURE 5. Bank of the United States, Cincinnati. Source: B. Drake and E. D. Mansfield, *Cincinnati in 1826* (Cincinnati: Morgan, Lodge, and Fisher, 1827).

However, that generous credit was soon overstretched and created a financial panic by late 1818. Distressed specie supplies led the Bank of the United States to contract the supply of their notes, but calling in loans in Ohio and elsewhere ruined clients and closed businesses in a steep economic downturn.[11] Ohioans noticed quickly, as one prominent Cincinnatian complained by November that citizens were "almost in a state of mutiny and insurrection in consequence of the Banks shutting up their vaults." Another Ohioan carped about "nothing in circulation in this Country but the paper of insolvent banks," and sluggish business pervaded the region. Commodity and real estate prices plummeted, and land sales effectively halted. According to Caleb Atwater, during the Panic of 1819 in Ohio, "The farmer was discouraged from raising much more, than what he really needed for his own immediate use; the trader feared to take bank paper, that might be of no value, before he could use it; and his old customers could no longer purchase any goods except mere necessaries." Worse for many yeoman farmers, part-time labor opportunities simply disappeared, and with them critical supplemental income that helped pay down land office loans.[12] Only a handful of years removed from Jefferson's embargo, a bad economy waylaid the people of Ohio once again.

While they staggered through the resultant economic depression into the 1820s, Ohioans responded in two very different ways that echoed past differences and presaged the political future of the Northwest. One reaction was populist and anti-statist in nature, with citizens and political leaders lashing out at the Bank of the United States. Their criticisms portrayed a federal government that had reached beyond its properly constituted powers. Simultaneously, they lambasted Bank proponents and apologists as elites who unduly controlled American politics, a line of argument that paralleled Jacksonian Democrats in the Bank War later. Meanwhile, the other side embraced energetic government. Composed largely of old Federalists, pro-business Republicans, and a new class of entrepreneurs, they blamed the Panic of 1819 on government doing *too little* for commerce and sought to embrace government action in the economy even more tightly. This coalition renewed arguments for internal improvements and a better public education system to create a happy, wealthy, and above all orderly public. All these central policy aims reiterated the politics of the state's Embargo-era Federalists and conservative Republicans while propelling those ideas into a new era.[13]

The push for stronger state action after the Panic began under Governor Ethan Allen Brown, who studied law under Alexander Hamilton before coming to Ohio. Though he later became a Jackson man, the plan Brown offered in his inaugural address of December 1819 reflected Hamilton's tutelage in a period when partisan positions were quite fluid. In Brown's view, "Manufactories, in the Western States" were the key to a prosperous future. Further reflecting the sentiments of Hamilton, Rufus Putnam, and other Federalists who presided over westward expansion, Brown claimed better transportation provided by government made for better economic prospects. "Forming Canals, and opening the natural channels of internal navigation" would allow Ohio's products to move about more cheaply and thereby become more profitable to producers. The next month, the state legislature showed that it shared his commitment, offering a resolution supporting "the practicability of connecting the Ohio river and Lake Erie by a canal" and asking the governor to provide more information on building it.[14] Clearly, the impulse to embrace government action gained traction quickly once the Panic of 1819 hit.

Ohioans pursued other programs to make their state more competitive economically, and behind those efforts stood the old alliance of Federalists and pro-business Republicans. On multiple levels, they sought better transportation through government aid. Ohio's first governor, Edward Tiffin, became Surveyor General of the United States in 1818, when he decided to "take it for granted that Columbus, the permanent Seat of Government of the State of Ohio" would be part of the National Road once it extended beyond the Ohio River. From there, he mapped out courses to St. Louis that crossed fertile farmland "certainly unequalled by any other portion of the United States." Further, he saw six new canals ready to connect the Great Lakes to Ohio and Mississippi valley waterways, requiring roughly 58 million cubic feet of earth to be moved. However, the funding was not as immediate as Tiffin expected. As Philemon Beecher noted in early 1819, "It is very doubtful" the National Road would be extended at that time, and he called it a "shameful & a losing game" since it would have to be extended eventually.[15]

Poor roads often impeded economic growth before 1819, so improving road travel continued to be a priority for Ohio politicians afterward. The Ohio legislature offered liberal charters to private companies that promised new turnpikes or improvements to existing roads, and Congressional support continued. Duncan McArthur used his single term in the House from 1823 to 1825 to convince Congress to extend the National Road west of the Ohio River. Further, he pressed for a road from Fort Meigs to Detroit for the benefit of northwest Ohioans. In his arguments for improving transportation, he showed an awareness of the burgeoning national marketplace. Arguing for the National Road, he cited first and foremost roads would "increase the revenue of the government" resulting from an "increase [in] the manufactures of the country," and overall believed in the "necessity of a home market" for agricultural states like Ohio.[16]

Ohio leaders found encouragement from the champion of the Erie Canal, DeWitt Clinton, who encouraged the construction of an Erie to Ohio canal on the back of his state's grand artificial river. In a series of letters to Governor and then Senator Ethan Allen Brown in 1821 and 1822, he pressed the case for a new canal and offered help behind the scenes. In April 1821, he declared "no doubt but that money can be obtained on the credit of Ohio in New York" based on "a vast unemployed capital . . . seeking investment." He also offered aid through hiring out a principal engineer on the Erie Canal to serve the state of Ohio, a man "of the senior grade" for a salary of $1,500 like he had taken in New York. As Clinton assured Brown, "The income will be great" on the canal, and if the Erie Canal was any guide, "you will be enabled . . . to pay off not only the interest but the principals of the debt incurred in its creation." Finally, as Daniel Walker Howe has noted, the Erie Canal was also a boon to settlement in the northern reaches of the state, as travel over water made the trek to homesteads and back to markets so much easier.[17]

In the private sector, the steamboat captured the imaginations of Ohioans and the rest of the Northwest with promising potential to conquer space, the greatest economic obstacle of the day for Westerners. The steamboat, Caleb Atwater noted, "roused into activity, the sleeping energies of the Western people" that provided Western travel "an inestimable blessing." The entire West seemingly joined the steamboat craze even in the throes of economic panic. The number of steamboats on Western rivers doubled from 35 to 72 between 1819 and 1820, and they nearly doubled again by 1823 to 130 steamers. By 1840, more than 500 steamboats carried goods and people along Western waterways.[18] Thus, even as markets seemed to collapse around them, forward-looking citizens of the Northwest embraced new technologies and programmatic economic policies that promised to enmesh Westerners further in those same markets.

While old allies like McArthur and protégés like Brown were important in the push for a more market-driven Ohio, Federalist politicians like Allen Trimble and Ephraim Cutler were centrally involved in three important policy initiatives in the state's response to the Panic of 1819. First, they worked doggedly to secure a new program of internal improvements in the state, especially the Ohio Canal stretching from Lake Erie to the Ohio River. Second, Federalists spurred bills to create a statewide public school system. Finally, they pressed for an overhaul of the state's tax system to pay for these new initiatives. In all three areas, Trimble in the State Senate and Governor's office and Cutler in the Ohio House of Representatives provided the leadership and determination to realize longstanding Federalist policy visions that had become National Republican ideals, too.

Trimble represented ambitious Ohio valley settlers of the early nineteenth century, even if his partisan politics did not align so well with most Ohioans. Part of the wave of new Ohioans who came after statehood, he settled in southwest Ohio shortly before his twenty-first birthday in 1804. He and his brother William volunteered for service when the War of 1812 began, but William eventually convinced Allen to return home and supervise family affairs. After the war, both brothers embarked on successful political careers. William continued to serve in the Army until his election to the U.S. Senate in 1819, where he remained until his premature death just two years later. However, Allen Trimble had a much longer and more impactful career, beginning nine years of service in the Ohio House and then Senate in 1816, and he was not the only Federalist in the state's General Assembly. Cutler, Charles Hammond, and David Jennings all represented counties in eastern Ohio during a brief Federalist renaissance in the late 1810s. Further, Trimble earned enough respect within the Ohio Senate to serve as its Speaker from his first term in 1817 until he left the chamber in 1825.[19]

As state senator, Allen Trimble was a tireless advocate for canals. He proposed, as did Clinton in letters to Ethan Allen Brown, using proceeds from Congressional land grants to pay for a new canal between Lake Erie and the Ohio River. In February 1820, he saw the proposal become law. Meanwhile, William tried to prepare Congress for the canal bill, noting he "succeeded in getting an able committee appointed in the Senate on Roads and Canals . . . and I have strong reasons to believe that they would favourably receive propositions on this subject from Ohio." The 1820 law did not result directly in the Ohio Canal, but it laid the legislative groundwork for its eventual construction. By 1824, Allen Trimble was central to planning it as a member of the state canal commission; he noted in his memoirs that he personally oversaw surveys and sales from the eventual Congressional land grant to fund the canal.[20]

In 1822, Allen Trimble was an especially effective canal advocate during his first stint as Governor. Succeeding Brown as governor after he won election to the U.S. Senate, Trimble argued in his inaugural address that an Erie to Ohio canal offered "agricultural, manufacturing and commercial advantages" and, perhaps more importantly, would "engage the attention of our industrious and enterprising citizens and bring into action the latent, hidden resources and energies of the State!"[21] The legislature apparently agreed with Trimble's Hamiltonesque reasoning, as Trimble signed a bill on January 31, 1822, creating a committee charged with outlining the course and likely expenses of the canal. Trimble's efforts won him praise from many Ohioans, but he returned to the Senate in the next session after losing a close election to fellow Ohio Canal committeeman Jeremiah Morrow.[22] After the tight race between the proponents of internal improvements who favored government energy in the economy, Trimble and Morrow continued working closely on the canal.

While Trimble argued for building canals, Ephraim Cutler continued his father Manasseh's quest for a strong public education system. Manasseh Cutler had worked to preserve public lands for schools and to found Ohio University on the Ohio Company's grant. Once Ephraim joined the Ohio House of Representatives in 1819, he offered bills to create a public school system, and other members rewarded his commitment to the issue with the chair of the House committee on schools. When Trimble gave his inaugural address in January 1822, he declared his intention to appoint Cutler to a committee to report on common schools. In his memoirs, Cutler called himself "an enthusiast in favor of the diffusion of education through all ranks of society" and gave the school committee "a willing mind, and . . . no small degree of personal labor and fatigue." That work soon bore fruit. The committee decided education was "the first care and highest duty of every parent, patriot and statesman," as it "polishes the manners, invigorates the mind and improves the heart."[23]

Public education was valuable to these advocates not because of the freedom it might bring but rather because, as Federalists once claimed, good schools made proper, obedient citizens. Items in the Cincinnati *Western Spy* in 1818 and 1819 reflected as much, with one writer claiming that too many Ohio children grew up "like noxious and useless weeds, without culture, without knowledge, and without principles." Another believed proper education would counteract self-interest, "enforc[ing] self-government" by teaching pupils the true nature of liberty and republicanism. Ultimately, a well-educated student should be able to "connect his own good with that of society." Cutler's close political ally Caleb Atwater, who moved from Massachusetts to Ohio after the War of 1812, often argued education would assure stability in the republic as well. He went so far as to tie the administration of school lands set aside in the Northwest Ordinance to other causes, including preventing squatting on public lands.[24]

To pay for the public schools and internal improvements, ex-Federalists argued their third great cause of the early 1820s: a new tax system to generate revenue. Ohio laid taxes solely on land holdings, based on fertility of the land but without regard to location. To redress the problems caused by this tax policy—such as thinly populated rural counties paying more in taxes than did Cincinnati's Hamilton County—supporters of the canal and school systems also took up tax reform in the name of fairness. Cutler and Atwater supported an *ad valorem* system that Cutler termed an "equal system of taxation" that would pay for internal improvements, too. Boosting tax revenue from population centers like Cincinnati would fund canals and roads, while increased property values created by new transportation would further grow revenues and pay for subsequent initiatives and projects. The new tax system could, in short, provide the basis for a fiscal-mercantile state apparatus in Ohio. Ephraim Cutler linked the three almost immediately after he joined the Ohio House in December 1819, also. As he told his wife, he wanted to achieve "a change in our system of taxation, . . . a law passed for establishing school districts and encouraging schools, and a state road" across southern Ohio.[25] New state institutions demanded new taxes, and Ohio's former Federalists led the way in pressing for both for the improvement of the state's character and commerce after the War of 1812.

Even into the early 1820s, Ohio politicians found success delivering pro-government messages. They succeeded because, like in the wake of Jefferson's embargo, hard times helped pro-business politicians find a program that resonated with voters. In their push for internal improvements, public education, and tax reforms, even old Federalists gained popularity and, in the case of Allen Trimble, competed in closely contested statewide elections. Moving forward, their three causes propelled the old Federalists in new directions with new allies during the 1820s and into the 1830s.

Energetic Republicanism and the New
States in the Era of Good Feelings

In Indiana and Illinois, energetic Republicans entered the uncertain new political era with confidence in a clear and prepared agenda. Their approach to government had advantages, not only in what it offered voters but also in the organizing ideas they shared. As Michael Holt has observed the decade following 1815, two developments negatively affected party organization in this period: party identities and voter identifications had not yet hardened, and statewide issues held primacy over national politics to voters.[26] As a result, energetic Republicans of Indiana and Illinois had little trouble continuing their agenda even as National Republicans struggled to gain traction elsewhere. They used the power of government to encourage public lands disposals to actual settlers, add transportation and public education systems, and foster domestic manufacturing, all while clinging to important Jeffersonian ideals. They were succeeding by the mid-1820s, too. Energetic Republicans advanced their political careers and won approval for policies they favored, and they saw real changes that distributed government power more broadly. In this Era of Good Feelings, then, energetic Republicans were forming the bases of a new political faction that would express an innovative national vision birthed in the West.

Indiana and Illinois continued to enjoy a postwar settlement boom into the first years of statehood, thanks to federal power keeping Indians at bay. Indiana leapt in population from 63,000 at the end of the War of 1812 to 147,178 by 1820, and more than doubled to 343,000 in the 1830 census. Illinois enjoyed less immediate growth, but even so, its population nearly tripled during the 1820s from 55,000 to over 157,000 people. New Illinois residents also purchased over 900,000 acres from government land offices ready and waiting to serve them. As Josiah Meigs of the General Land Office proudly wrote in 1819, "The United States have already established twenty Land-Offices . . . dispersed over a space of about thirteen degrees of Latitude, and ten of Longitude."[27]

Energetic Republicans elected to high offices in Indiana wanted to use public lands policy to enhance that growth. On December 31, 1816, James Noble had been U.S. Senator for only two weeks when he proposed dividing "a certain proportion of the quarter sections" for sale in the land offices. Meaning to make a farm more affordable, Noble saw his efforts rewarded with a new law in February 1817 to divide six sections of every township offered for sale into quarter and half-quarter sections (80 and 160 acres). Meanwhile, in the House of Representatives, William Hendricks hoped to aid Indiana's growth as part of the Committee on the Public Lands. On the floor, he advanced settlers' causes through multiple petitions, including one in January 1818 requesting a full township to create a Swiss immigrant colony, and another in December 1820 asking to relieve "purchasers of public lands under the old system."[28] From the new state capital at Corydon, Governor Jonathan Jennings also cheered news of price reductions for public lands. As he explained to the legislature, "Our lands constitute almost the entire mass of our solid capital," and reducing prices on land unsold after years on the market would provide "our labor and enterprize . . . active and useful employment."[29] Jennings left public life before the Second Party System took full shape and Hendricks ended up a Jackson man, but in the Era of Good Feelings, energy in government was a winning issue for everyone.

In the new state of Illinois, U.S. Senator Ninian Edwards also set out to align public lands policy to his ideals for westward expansion. He promoted his candidacy by promising to use public lands policy to aid Illinois as well, writing in September 1818, "my best talents shall be exerted to . . . promote the prosperity of our Infant State." He sought two particular goals: extinguishing all Indian claims south of the Illinois River and assuring "as much public land as possible, [was] immediately surveyed, and put into market with a view to make my fellow citizens to obtain lands" and with ample land available, they could take possession of their tracts "without too much competition."[30] Edwards was clearly eager to use federal power over public lands to promote the expansion of Illinois both in population and space, maintaining his energetic approach to Illinois settlement and government from his days as territorial governor.

Opening those lands for settlement, Edwards hoped, would allow every American to become an independent freeholder, and to that end he offered a series of amendments to public lands bills in February 1819. The Senator first proposed graduating land prices in a sort of reverse bulk pricing, by which purchasers of half-quarter sections would pay just fifty cents per acre, a quarter-section for seventy-five cents per acre, and up to a full section for one dollar per acre. When that failed, he offered two other unsuccessful amendments, offering preferences to actual settlers over speculators and then to reduce the price of all public lands to one dollar per acre. As he reported to his constituents afterward, "my best talents were arduously exerted" in order to make these amendments to attract "emigration to the State and [promote] the settlement and improvement thereof."[31]

Nationally, the National Republicans looked to internal improvements to promote economic development, and Illinois's first governor, Shadrach Bond, was fully committed to the cause in order to aid development and speed population growth. Bond spoke highly of the new state at the opening of the General Assembly, noting "the fertility of its soil, intersected and almost surrounded by lakes and rivers convenient for navigation." However, even with these advantages, he complained that Illinois lacked "the means requisite for the commencement of any internal improvement of consequence." Without it, he was concerned that population growth and real estate values would lag, but he saw hope in the "great forwardness" of the Erie Canal's construction. Adding to it, he proposed a canal linking the Illinois River and Lake Michigan, by which "a water communication from our very doors will be opened to the Atlantic." Such access offered opportunities and advantages "too obvious to require comment."[32] At the opening of the state government, Bond was already preaching the gospel of canals, immediately and intimately embedding the state government into Illinois's economic future.

Indiana's energetic Republican leaders embraced internal improvements even more tightly in the late 1810s and 1820s, beginning with its new state constitution and first governor. Its Enabling Act in 1816 created for Indiana a three percent fund from in-state public land sales for internal improvements, a fact Governor Jennings celebrated. As he saw it, the fund could "lay the foundation of a system of internal improvement" across the state, the first piece being a canal around the Falls of the Ohio at Jeffersonville directly across the river from Louisville. Then, he hoped to see Indiana follow up on the Erie Canal by extending "navigable communication between the great western and northwestern lakes and the Atlantic" through canals to improve navigation along the Ohio River and new roads to connect disparate parts of the state. Such a program, he assured, would have many positive effects. Internal improvements held promises of "lessening the expenses and time attendant" on transporting products, and they could "enhance the value of the soil by affording to the agriculturalist the means of deriving greater gain from his cultivation." In turn, better transportation would then offer "stronger inducements to industry and enterprize, and . . . invite to a more general intercourse between the citizens."[33] For Jennings, the three percent fund was a blessing, but the new state of Indiana could do so much more to provide its citizens with economic growth and opportunities.

William Hendricks reflected similar feelings in the House of Representatives. As his first official proposal, he asked for federal investment in the Jeffersonville company seeking to build the canal around the Falls of the Ohio. As he explained, the canal justified federal expenditures since it was so "intimately connected with the commerce and the general prosperity of the whole Western country." Afterward, the rest of the House agreed to his resolution to purchase shares in the Jeffersonville Ohio Canal Company, earning the praise of Governor Jennings for the "flattering prospect" of the canal that laid "still stronger claims upon the General Assembly to aid its ultimate execution."[34] Nearly immediately, Hendricks and Jennings had brought government energy to Jeffersonville for the good of Indiana commerce.

Hendricks paid attention to numerous other internal improvements projects as well. In March 1818, he gladly reported that the post office planned at least five new roads to and from Bloomington, Lawrence, Paoli, and Terre Haute (then Fort Harrison). "Pains have been taken," he told his constituents, "to connect the arrival and departure of the mails . . . to their steady progress through the country." In the next session, Hendricks continued to use the post office as a means to build more roads, calling on Congress to commission multiple new roads within the state and another from Elizabethtown, Kentucky to the Indiana state capital at Corydon, by way of two other southern Indiana towns. Beyond the post office, Hendricks also hoped to see the National Road extended for the benefit of Indiana residents, and he spoke hopefully of a bill in the 1821–1822 Congressional session to extend it "from Wheeling to the Mississippi, and making the seats of Government, in the states of Ohio, Indiana, and Illinois, points on the road." Federal benefits through the three percent fund of public land sales also had reached $60,000 by that spring.[35]

However, internal improvements had no greater friend among Indiana's early elected statewide officials than U.S. Senator James Noble. He made the National Road into one of his pet projects, and he supported John C. Calhoun's unsuccessful 1817 Bonus Bill to create a permanent fund from Second Bank of the United States dividends for internal improvements. Elsewhere, he aggressively chased internal improvement projects and funding with proposals for transparent accounting of the two-percent fund for transportation to and from Indiana, aid for a new canal from Lake Erie to the Wabash River, and additions to the National Road all the way to the Mississippi River. In his proposal for a new National Road bill in May 1826, he explained his reasoning well. Because "not one single tract of land bordering on the road, will remain long in the property of the United States," he argued, "we must have the road." In addition to augmenting land sales and values, he foresaw with the road better mail service and "our commercial men, and all other persons, would have the advantage of speedy conveyances . . . to the commercial cities, passing by many important places."[36] Using state power to improve government services and aid Hoosiers' business interests mattered greatly to Noble and the rest of Indiana's energetic Republican leaders.

The first governors of Indiana and Illinois also wanted to establish public school systems to invest in the futures of their new states, evidenced by each of their inaugural addresses. On November 7, 1816, Jonathan Jennings emphasized education in Indiana as a political and a moral good. "Under every free government, the happiness of the citizens must be identified with their morals," Jennings declared, and to that end, "useful knowledge will be indispensably necessary as a support to morals and as a restraint to vice." Promoting that useful knowledge required the legislature "to direct your attention to the plan of education" as soon as possible.[37] Similarly, Shadrach Bond gave education special attention in Illinois. Schools were not in the state constitution, but Congress set aside three percent of Illinois public lands receipts for education with one-sixth of it (one-half percent of all receipts) going to fund a university. In his inaugural, Bond told the General Assembly that it was their "imperious duty" to create a system of public schools with those funds so that "all classes of fellow citizens" would have "means of wisdom and of knowledge, which . . . will make the child of the poorest parent, a useful member of society, and an ornament to his country."[38]

However, progress varied. Indiana moved on public education quickly, with the first session of the legislature producing a law that required townships to appoint a superintendent to collect rents on the school section, provided for another superintendent over the state's township reserved for a seminary or college, and called for any township with a petition from twenty freeholders to form a public school. By the end of 1818, another new law allowed districts to build school buildings with some of the rents collected, and collecting rents suggested some townships had already founded school districts. The law encouraging school construction represented the first direct state funding for public schools. Later, an 1824 law required freeholding petitioners to form a township school district, allowed multiple schools within a township, and laid out requirements for teachers. Further, adult freeholding men had to contribute at least one day of labor per week to help build the school, or face fines to be applied to the local school. Thus, in Indiana, Hoosiers were obliged to pitch in and support their local schools.[39]

Efforts to promote public education in Illinois lagged behind Indiana while the state's population remained much lower throughout the 1810s and 1820s. While Bond hoped to see education become a legislative priority as early as 1818, the first major bill for education came in 1824 under Governor Edward Coles and newly elected State Senator Joseph Duncan. Coles opened the December 1824 session of the General Assembly calling for public education since "Intelligence and virtue are the main pillars in the temple of liberty." Propelling the message forward, Duncan proposed his bill to provide free public schooling to Illinois pupils, funded by local taxes and providing local control over school officers. Coles likely had a hand in its crafting, and the bill passed both houses and received the Governor's signature in late January 1825. The victory was but temporary in Illinois, though, as opponents of the new taxes severely weakened the collection powers of local schools.[40]

These energetic Republican policies echoed post-1815 Federalism in Ohio, but for Jeffersonian ends. The goal of Ninian Edwards's public lands policies was to offer land ownership to as many American settlers as possible. Like Jefferson, he believed tenants were "too subject to the influence of their landlords" and too many tenants were "dangerous and highly inimical to republicanism." In the U.S. Senate, he called for lower land prices and defended the credit system to help as many purchasers obtain land as possible. Joseph Duncan supported education to promote equality and liberty as well. To him, "the want of equal education" was responsible for "the great difference between man and man." Thus, he stated in the preamble to his Free School Law, "no nation has ever continued long in the enjoyment of civil and political freedom, which was not both virtuous and enlightened," while he saw in "the advancement of literature . . . the means of developing more fully the rights of man." Thus, government had a "peculiar duty . . . to encourage and extend the improvement and cultivation of the intellectual energies of the whole."[41]

In all these stances, energetic Republicans of the Northwest echoed not only Jeffersonian but also National Republican leadership in their policies and aims. As Charles Sellers has noted, National Republican leadership laid out a vision of an activist national state that embraced the Market

Revolution. John C. Calhoun even spoke loftily of Hamilton in this period, with ideas of reenacting much of his policy program. Nowhere did
that revolution and National Republican policies seem to have more ardent supporters than in the Northwest. John Lauritz Larson's research
has shown that Ohio, Indiana, and Illinois were the friendliest to projects
aimed at economic development. A series of questions before Congress
in 1818 about internal improvements received enthusiastic support from
the Ohio and Indiana delegations (with Illinois not yet a state). In 1824,
the General Survey Act authorizing the president to commission surveys
on important transportation routes also drew unanimous support from
House members in the three states.[42]

However, all these policies—better public education, effective public
lands disposals, and new internal improvements—headed toward a decidedly Hamiltonian cause: the promotion of domestic manufacturing. As a
good Jefferson man should, Ninian Edwards spoke highly of a republic of
freeholding farmers, but he also said in 1822, "Nothing but proper encouragement of domestic manufactures can free the western country from its
present embarrassments." In Indiana, Hendricks and Jennings supported
protective tariffs to aid American industry as well, with conspicuous notes
about their legislative progress in circulars. Jennings showed a broader
understanding of the tariffs, "protecting domestic industry and domestic
manufactures, in every part of the Union." As it stood in 1823, "Manufactures do not exist, but to a very limited extent, where there is a great
deficiency of active monied capital," and resolving the issue required "reflection and research, in order to apply the power . . . to the greatest and
best advantage of the nation."[43] To him, domestic manufactures required
a programmatic approach.

Westerners were also seeking private means to encourage industries in
their midst. In Kentucky, local boosters looked for ways to bring cotton
manufacturing to the state, with some going so far as to create a Society for
Domestic Manufactures in 1817. "Of great interest in the political economy of the country [is] the encouragement of domestic manufactures," its
circular declared, and they would achieve it "by consumption—by uni-
formly preferring domestic fabrics" and encouraging activist policies. The
lack of economic development also had effects in Albion, Illinois. Richard
Flower looked for good tailors and shoemakers while noting good prospects there for "a person understanding coarse cotton Manufacturing."[44]

By the mid-1820s, energetic Republicans of Indiana and Illinois saw
results for their policies that had become parallel to the causes Federalists

pursued in Ohio. In all three states, a broader political ideology was taking shape behind an overall pattern of energetic government, as internal improvements, better public education, protective tariffs, and domestic manufacturing ignited their political passions. Moving forward, the two factions needed a common ideal or, better, a common candidate to help them to coalesce into a new political movement. Luckily for them, a champion of this new Western ideology was already emerging, and the paths of Northwestern Federalists and energetic Republicans would continue to intertwine.

Making Western Whigs
Merging Ideology and Political Identity

The shared pro-business, pro-government concepts and approaches between old-line Federalists and energetic/National Republicans led to new political bonds that strengthened in the Northwest during the Presidential election of 1824. In Ohio, these new bonds continued into the ensuing legislative session of 1824–1825 as well. In this period, two elements of a nascent party organization are most salient. First, in the campaign and election of 1824 many residents in the region joined together to promote the American System, and thereby formed the backbone of support for its architect, Henry Clay. Second, not only did old Federalists join with pro-business Republicans, but the promise of state-powered economic development drew larger numbers, demonstrating that a clear vision for the economic future of the region could underlay future activities. Continuing into the 1830s, the solidifying alliances signaled that a new party broadcasting state-friendly political ideals from the Ohio River valley.

The initial steps toward Western Whiggery revolved around the leadership of Henry Clay. The Kentuckian had been a staunch advocate for Western interests in Washington since 1810, taking great pride in the growing manufacturing prowess of his home state while seeking wider commercial and political connections for the West overall. Known more as a War Hawk in his early years in Congress, Clay wanted government to sponsor economic development, too.[45] In his first recorded Congressional speech, he called domestic manufacturing essential to prosperity, but like other energetic Republicans, he did so in Jeffersonian terms. Rather than seek a commercial empire, Clay wanted to manufacture for domestic consumption and focus on exporting agricultural products, which would "enable us to supply our wants without withdrawing our attention from agriculture—that first and greatest source of national wealth and happiness."[46] Clay was as a fine example of a Western energetic Republican. Like Jefferson, he was wary of a commercial empire and lionized agriculture, but he reflected the influence of the early national state by supporting its continued penetration into the American economy.

Clay espoused this viewpoint more fervently over the next decade by joining the camp of National Republicans who saw merit in federal action to aid commercial growth. Like James Noble, Clay backed Calhoun's Bonus Bill and similar internal improvements measures, and his influence only grew with his election as Speaker of the House in 1823. In his new position, he crafted agendas to increase federal aid to commerce. His American System, a combination of centralized banking, protective tariffs, and federally-funded internal improvements, sought to insert the state directly into the economic development of the entire nation. Further, Clay "assumed that the Western States, from Ohio to the Gulf of Mexico, will be firmly and ardently united in my support." With the Missouri crisis recently opening schisms between North and South, Clay saw in the American System an effective tool to propel himself to the White House. "Of that," he wrote, "I entertain no doubt."[47]

Clay biographer Robert Remini called the American System "a bold reformulation of the relationship between government and society," but it had a clear antecedent in Hamiltonian policies that energetic Republicans had been reshaping for decades.[48] In the 1790s, Hamilton planned for a national economic empire through a central bank, internal improvements, and tariffs, and Clay's plan revolved around the same three elements. Based on Hamilton's plans for the first, Clay backed the Second Bank of the United States and even served as its legal counsel during his hiatus from Congress in the late 1810s. Like Hamilton and Washington in the 1780s and 1790s, Clay also argued for a broad system of internal improvements to improve commerce and link together disparate parts of the Union. Finally, Clay saw tariffs, a less intrusive form of taxation than Adams and Hamilton's direct or excise taxes, as an essential stimulus to American manufacturing that would also pay for his transportation programs. As a result, he shepherded the Tariff of 1824 through Congress, laying a 35 percent *ad valorem* tax on imports to form the first true protective tariff system in the United States.[49]

From the House floor on March 30 and 31, 1824, Clay defined the four-way Presidential contest of 1824 between himself, John Quincy Adams, William H. Crawford, and Andrew Jackson as a choice between two dueling philosophies. The first believed "American industry should be left to sustain itself" against cheap, widely available European goods. Clay set himself firmly on the other side, which supported manufacturing. More industry, he said, would "lessen our dependence on foreign nations, by securing a certain and ultimately a cheaper and better supply of our own wants from our own abundant resources." Such divisions correspond well to later Whig and Democratic differences. From there, he argued passionately for the American System, saying it was "the solemn duty of government to apply a remedy" and avoid seeing "industry languish and decay, yet more and more."[50] Looking ahead to that fall, Clay set himself at the vanguard of a new political movement that would use state power to bring prosperity to the nation.

The message resonated most effectively west of the Appalachians, where federal power was instrumental in settlement and economic development. By 1824, Ohio valley citizens began to see things as Federalists had: their future was intimately tied to the rest of the nation, and connections to the Atlantic coast meant a more prosperous future. The year prior, Republican editor James Wilson of Steubenville, Ohio began saying local manufacturing and agricultural products needed protected markets. Meanwhile, newspapers in Cincinnati discussed internal improvements as central to home manufactures. David Trimble of Kentucky also expressed these interests plainly before Congress in 1823, deeming canals linking the Ohio River and Atlantic Ocean of "very deep interest" to all Westerners because "trade of the Western Country would come Eastwardly for a market." He predicted a future "not far distant, when this country shall become entirely its own manufacturer." It was, quite simply, "the natural and irresistible progress of things."[51]

The Northwest also fervently supported protective tariffs and the politicians who backed such policies. For example, William Henry Harrison ran successfully for the Ohio State Senate in 1819 behind protective tariffs and other energetic approaches to the economic crisis. Once in office, he proposed resolutions backing new tariffs and seeking other revenues for "Roads, Canals and Domestic Manufactures." Kentucky and Missouri enthusiastically joined the movement for protective tariffs as well, seeking protections for local products like wool, lead, iron, and salt. Overall, support for elements of the American System in the West led Clay to count on support from Ohio, Indiana, Illinois, Kentucky, Missouri, and Louisiana. With so many contestants, Clay reasoned, no one would gain a majority of electoral votes, but once the election was in the House, Western support would help Clay maneuver to victory.[52]

Clay and his American System blurred old partisan lines in Ohio leading up to the election. As James Wilson noted in his *Steubenville Gazette*,
"the question is not now whether the candidate be a democrat or a federalist." Voters really wanted, he wrote, "a friend . . . to domestic industry
and internal improvements."[53] In Cincinnati, former Federalists and Jeffersonians alike lined up behind Clay. William Henry Harrison was a Clay
elector, and Charles Hammond (new to the city in 1823) became Clay's
campaign manager in Ohio. Hammond chose Clay because the American
System reflected his political philosophy, and he expressed his support for
Clay's plans in an 1824 pamphlet of the candidate's speeches entitled *An
American System for the Protection of Industry*.[54] Once carrying on a bitter newspaper war against each other during the War of 1812, Wilson and
Hammond joined the same side. Old party lines were crumbling for Clay's
backers, replaced by a vision of energetic state support for transportation
and mercantile development.

Despite his popularity, Clay faced stiff competition for Western votes
from John Quincy Adams, also a friend of the American System. He
appealed to voters in old Federalist strongholds like the former Ohio
Company purchase, where Adams carried three counties. In Indiana,
where the Federalist Party never truly established itself, voters backing
the American System turned their support to Adams as well, because he
supported protective tariffs and internal improvements while also oppos-
ing slavery like most Hoosiers. By the middle of 1824, most newspapers
in Indiana backed Adams as the man with the experience and character
necessary to serve in the nation's highest office. Indiana historian Donald
Carmony attributed that support to the benefits Hoosiers saw in past uses
of government power. Thus, the election of 1824 saw the unanimously
Republican newspaper editors of Indiana align behind a former New England Federalist.[55]

The final election tallies in all three states showed wide support for
Clay and even greater support for the American System. Clay found the
least enthusiasm in Illinois, which still boasted a fairly small population
and went on to be a Jacksonian bulwark. Andrew Jackson carried the
election with 1,901 votes, trailed by Adams at 1,542 and Clay in third
place at 1,047. Jackson also carried Indiana because of a split Adams/Clay
vote. Jackson received 7,343 votes in victory, while Clay received 5,215
votes and Adams only 3,095; meanwhile, Clay carried the most counties.
In Ohio, Clay ultimately prevailed thanks to the work of supporters like
Hammond, Harrison, and Wilson. He won a plurality of 19,255 votes over

Jackson's 18,849 and Adams's 12,280 votes. However, Ohio was one of only three states Clay carried in the election, leaving him in fourth place in the electoral vote and thus out of the final presidential votes in the House of Representatives.[56]

Despite Clay's losses, the election revealed that voters in the Northwest truly believed in the American System. In the House of Representatives, the Ohio delegation sided with their state's third-place finisher Adams, the friend of internal improvements and tariffs, over second-place finisher Jackson. They explained their choice in classic Federalist terms: leaders deserved to choose a candidate in the best interests of the people despite the ballot results. Former Jeffersonian and U.S. trade factor John Johnston declared that Adams was chosen by those "who are the best judges of qualification and who have the greatest Stake in the issue." Old Federalist Philemon Beecher had fewer qualms: "Adams is best qualified, and that is enough for me." Further, as known friends of the American System, Henry Clay and John Quincy Adams received a wide majority of votes over Andrew Jackson, a point not lost on many Clay and Adams supporters. Charles Hammond asked pointedly in his *Liberty Hall and Cincinnati Gazette* that while Jackson finished second, "If we, my friends, who voted for Mr. Clay prefer Mr. Adams . . . where is the proof that Gen. Jackson is preferred by the people. Eighteen thousand Jacksonians cannot constitute the people of Ohio."[57]

The American System and the election of 1824 reflected a distinct Western flavor to politics, and Federalists in Ohio saw much success when that year's statewide elections focused on their tripartite program of internal improvements, schools, and tax reforms. Federalist Allen Trimble lost a close gubernatorial election to Jeremiah Morrow by less than three percent, a repeat of the close 1822 contest that gave voters a choice between two solid proponents of a state canal system. Even better, Caleb Atwater wrote later, election results showed widespread support for old Federalist hobby horses. Legislative elections hinged on "the school system, the canal, and an equitable mode of taxation," he recalled, and in the end "the friends of all these measures, triumphed over all opposition."[58]

Opening the ensuing legislative session on December 7, 1824, Governor Morrow spoke optimistically about all three issues and presented the stark truth that energetic government had triumphed. Praising the "zeal and industry" of canal supporters and commissioners, Morrow supported a canal from Lake Erie to the Ohio River, nodded to tax reforms, and even talked about new taxes on "judicial process in civil cases—on capital employed in trade—on pleasure and travel carriages—on brass and other clocks, and on gold and silver watches" to pay for transportation projects. Meanwhile, he reminded the legislature of its responsibility "for the encouragement of learning, and in particular for the regulation and support of common schools." In the ensuing session, the General Assembly found itself engrossed by canals and revenues; by mid-December Ephraim Cutler reported proudly that his finance committee "agree[d] to the substance . . . for changing the whole revenue system, and adopting an equal one of taxing people according to their property" while another committee set the courses of the Ohio Canal from Cleveland to Portsmouth and the Miami Canal from Dayton to Cincinnati.[59] As the new year approached, Ohio was on the precipice of major victories for the old Federalist and energetic Republican alliance rechristened as National Republicans.

In addition to Cutler's efforts in the legislature, Charles Hammond's *Liberty Hall and Cincinnati Gazette* offered Federalist arguments for their passage. He castigated opponents as self-interested men who preferred "not a road, not a bridge, nor a canal, could ever be made at public expense. We should forever remain in a state of poverty, depression, and rudeness." On the other hand, maintaining an improvements plan would "bring capital into the state" as well as "excite and reward industry, and lay the foundation for other improvements." Hammond also argued for public education in terms that recalled the Ohio Company's original plan, because "We need moral as well as physical improvement," especially to guarantee "the happiness of society, and the perpetuity of our republican institutions."[60] Such an emphasis on disinterest and public morality was more than classical republicanism; it was classic Federalist thinking. After all, Hamiltonians consistently argued that government used its energies best when it assured that people were not only prosperous but morally upright and well-ordered.

Victories in all three areas came for the emerging coalition on February 3–5, 1825, by three new laws. The first law, a tax act passed February 3, made *ad valorem* taxation the feature of an intricate new taxation system on most real estate, many types of valuable personal property, and even on mercantile investments. The new system would guarantee more equitable taxation, as Atwater and Cutler argued for years, but it also promised to enhance revenues to fund projects in education and internal improvements.[61] Second, the next day Morrow signed a law to construct the Ohio Canal and Miami Canal. A board of canal commissioners including Ethan Allen Brown and Allen Trimble oversaw their funding, construction, and operation, with a decidedly Hamiltonian system of funded debts allowing the canal commission to borrow hundreds of thousands of dollars each year.[62] Hammond, Atwater, and other proponents of public schools got their wish in the final law. Guided through the Senate by Allen Trimble and the House by Ephraim Cutler, the law placed a one-twentieth of one percent *ad valorem* tax on property to support schools and established county school boards to create and oversee local schools. Thus, the 1825 school law was an important step toward fulfilling the promise of public schools for all that Cutler placed in the 1803 constitution.[63]

By 1825, Ohio saw important political victories for the cause of energetic government. As early as the 1780s, Federalists and allies like Manasseh Cutler and George Washington hoped government power might conquer space, pull Westerners from isolation, and broaden priorities beyond base self-interest, and men like Ephraim Cutler and Allen Trimble achieved those visions. By 1830, Ohio was well on its way to creating a public education system and new transportation links to the rest of the nation. These former Federalists were also still enjoying successful careers in Ohio, and their statist approach to westward expansion reaped real dividends. Their favored American System projected their state-friendly approach to forging economic prosperity from the Ohio valley to the rest of the nation. In a sense, the early American state had been born in the trans-Appalachian West, and by the 1820s it began to head eastward.

That success would continue, especially for Trimble, Hammond, and Burnet. Hammond continued to promote the old Federalist agenda and the emerging Whig cause in the weekly *Liberty Hall and Cincinnati Gazette* as well as his *Cincinnati Daily Gazette* until 1839, a year before his death.[64] Trimble won gubernatorial elections in 1826 and 1828, and he leaned heavily on the Federalist-National Republican-Whig cornerstones of public education, internal improvements, and protective tariffs. He also maintained Federalist arguments. He wanted a comprehensive public school system as an "enlightening influence on every mind" helping citizens avoid seeing "popular liberty . . . degenerated into licentiousness and anarchy." Once again, education was to be a force for inculcating order and reverence. In addition, Trimble saw many more internal improvements than the Ohio Canal on the horizon, as they ignited in Ohioans a "spirit . . . [that] cannot be stayed by the rivers Ohio and Potomac, but must and will penetrate beyond them with irresistible force." He concluded by alluding to the American System, noting that Ohioans who placed him into the Governor's office twice "look to extended improvements, and to the protection of Domestic Industry . . . as the basis of the independence and prosperity of our common country."[65] In short, Trimble not only delighted in a high point in his political career, but he also imagined a radiant future for his ideals.

Jacob Burnet also won election as U.S. Senator in 1828, replacing his friend William Henry Harrison. In a letter to old Federalist friend Wyllys Silliman of Marietta after his election, Burnet backed the American System, too. He explained plainly, "Our wealth . . . cannot be realized, unless we have a market for our produce, and increased facilities for transporting it in other words, unless the American System be sustained and extended by the General government." He also insisted on the need to "create a market at home" to aid "our manufactoring establishments." At the same time, he showed deepening partisan divides, saying with some bitterness toward Jackson that "I hope he will exert his influence in favour of the American System—that he will realize the expectations of his friends and disappoint the fears of his opponents—in short that he will feel and act, as the President of the Nation, and not of a party." That divide seemed clear to others by the late 1820s, too, with Trimble referring to "The Whig Party to which I belonged . . . during my term as Governor."[66]

New transportation projects also drew energetic and National Republicans. In Ohio, for example, Jeremiah Morrow worked alongside Allen Trimble for the Ohio Canal in the 1820s and stood with DeWitt Clinton at the Ohio Canal groundbreaking ceremony in 1825. By the next decade, Morrow opposed Andrew Jackson. Joseph Duncan also came to the Whig Party through his support for public education, internal improvements, and the Second Bank of the United States. Originally a Jackson supporter when he joined Congress in 1827, he was definitely a Whig when he won the 1834 gubernatorial election as an advocate for canal projects like the proposed linkage from the Illinois River to Lake Michigan. Even before then, Illinois Whigs liked Duncan, with Springfield newspaper editor Simeon Francis supporting Duncan in 1832 because "his course in Congress, as regards . . . the Bank of the U. States, the Tariff of Protection, and the system of Internal Improvements, has met with our cordial approbation."[67]

In addition to converted energetic Republicans, a new generation who came of age after the War of 1812 joined the ranks of Whig politicians like Noah Noble of Indiana. The younger brother of Sen. James Noble, Noah Noble was in his thirties when he ran for the governorship in 1831 with a pro-Clay platform of internal improvements, tariffs, and tax reforms. After winning office, and he quickly made building a statewide internal improvements system into a priority. With many Hoosiers having "large amounts of surplus produce," he told the General Assembly in 1833, farmers deserved state aid since "good roads and the improvement of our navigable streams, can only be effected, to any beneficial extent, by state authority."[68] Winning reelection in 1834, Noble and other Whigs were flourishing in Indiana, and they moved on *ad valorem* tax reforms like Ohio had previously done. "The burthen of taxation should be distributed equally . . . in proportion to the productive quality," Noble argued, to avoid letting speculators and others "escape contribution." The more equal system also would provide increased revenues, which he hoped to spend on "such internal improvements as will . . . increase the rewards of industry and enhance the general value of property."[69] With an *ad valorem* system as well, increasing property values meant increased tax revenue, and the cycle of using tax revenues to enhance transportation could continue.

The mid-1830s saw Noble lead a massive effort to implant the state government in economic development, of which the new taxation system was the centerpiece. Because of a growing population and increasing wealth in the state, Indiana's tax revenues rose steadily during Noble's tenure, most dramatically after the General Assembly voted the *ad valorem* system into law in 1835. The previous year, the legislature chartered the Second State Bank of Indiana, and such support for central banking was a nod to Hamiltonian policies and Clay's American System in the midst of Jackson's Bank War. The greatest and most consequential effort, though, came with the Mammoth Internal Improvements Act of 1836. A series of roads, canals, and railroads, the act committed the state to add to the Wabash and Erie Canal with $10.5 million in new transport projects.[70] The new law represented a major Whig victory and a signature event in the Noah Noble administration, and excitement for it even drew in the anti-Noble *Indiana Democrat*. Offering praise for Noble, the newspaper observed that Indianapolis residents "consider themselves one hundred per cent. richer than they were but one week since" and wished that "all party feeling might be swallowed up" in the spirit of improving the lives of Hoosiers.[71]

Similarly, Illinois saw energetic Republicans and the new generation combine to pass Whig legislation. Newly elected governor, Joseph Duncan, and a state representative, Abraham Lincoln, exemplified the impulse. Sitting for his first meeting as part of the General Assembly on December

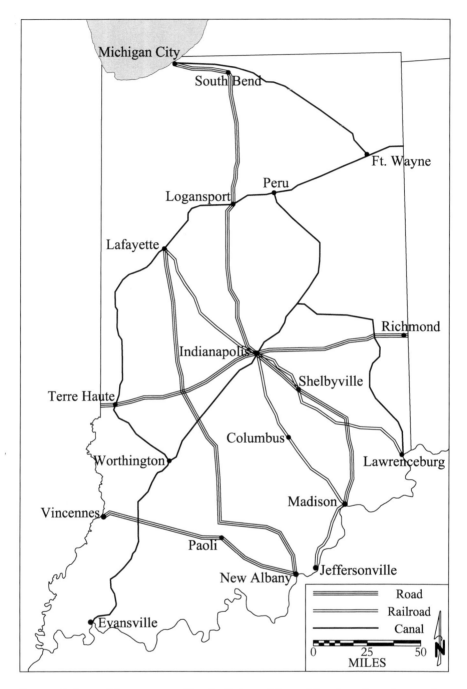

FIGURE 6. Internal Improvement Plan for Indiana. Many of the plans shown here in the "Mammoth" plan for Indiana, particularly many of the canal and railroad projects, went unfinished after the plan bankrupted the state. Map created by the author.

3, 1834, Lincoln listened to Duncan make a clarion call for the Whig vision
for America. Duncan asked the General Assembly to "use all the means
in its power . . . to establish some permanent system of common schools"
as well as to establish public colleges. His greatest attention, though, fell
upon internal improvements. He saw "a favorable time" in Illinois because
its population was still growing. "If roads, trackways, rail roads, and canals,
are now laid out, they can be made straight between most of the important
points, with very little expense and difficulty," he explained. Furthermore,
the prosperity brought by new roads, canals, and railroads would augment
revenues to fund more projects and public schools.[72]

Legislators differed as to how to proceed, but after the 1836 election,
they devised Illinois's own mammoth system of improvements. Always
an advocate of internal improvements, Lincoln and others in the Illinois
General Assembly voted for "a loan of several millions of dollars on the
faith of the State to construct Rail Roads," canals, and roads. Overall, in
early 1837 the legislature authorized over $10 million for new projects,
and both houses overrode Duncan's veto when he was concerned over
the size and scope of the plan.[73] Combined with the Illinois and Michigan
Canal approved in 1836, after years of planning and discussion, Illinois
had committed to a system even more ambitious than the projects under-
taken by Indiana. Politically, it was a watershed moment for Whigs and the
American System. The Illinois state government—in a Jacksonian Democratic stronghold, no less—had thrown its support behind the prime feature of the American System.

No combination of states embraced internal improvements and the
promises of the American System with the same passion as Ohio, Indiana,
and Illinois had done in the 1820s and 1830s, and their decisions had
multiple serious political consequences. Most immediately, each of the
states met extremely serious financial difficulties after the Panic of 1837
struck in the spring and summer. Ohio first opened its funded canal debt
in 1825 for the Ohio Canal. Its completion required more than $5 million,
and the bonds from the debt were not fully paid off until 1903.[74] Indiana
and Illinois fared much worse. Both states essentially became insolvent
servicing their debts from their mammoth improvement projects. They
had to abandon multiple projects as well, with Indiana only completing
one of multiple planned new canals after the state Board of Internal Improvement (headed by Noah Noble) ordered all other projects halted in
November 1839. Illinois saw numerous projects unfinished, bridges that

connected nonexistent roads, and other such problems. Illinois completed the Illinois and Michigan Canal, though, and the twelve-year construction project left a $6.5 million bill for the Prairie State that was not paid off until 1882.[75]

More importantly, despite dire financial straits, Westerners continued to see government action as a key to the region's and nation's future. In late 1837, when Governor Duncan urged the state legislature to repeal its previous improvement plans, the Illinois Senate actually passed a bill increasing the scope of improvements plans, and the House version gained Lincoln's vote. In Indiana, a series of private conventions attended by prominent Whigs as well as Democrats lobbied the General Assembly for increased funding for public education. Excitement for the National Road also persisted, indicating that enthusiasm for the economic opportunities held out by internal improvements remained even if the political will to carry them out waned due to financial troubles. The job opportunities and the increased traffic with easier travel still enticed Indiana residents to establish new businesses and purchase lands swiftly along the National Road.[76] The new canals and roads left residents in all three states more closely connected with the Atlantic coast, breaking their dependence on New Orleans for trade. Despite the strains placed on the states, internal improvements projects ultimately enabled citizens of the Northwest to dive headlong into the Market Revolution.

The so-called Era of Good Feelings was a crucial formative period for the Whig Party of the Northwest, and Federalism loomed large in two ways. First, Federalists continued into the new alliance and held many prominent positions even into the 1830s, and thus Ohio became the last bastion of a Federalist Party that had evaporated nationally. With leaders in the emerging Whig Party like Allen Trimble and Jacob Burnet, direct Federalist influence remained, too. Second, the American System reflected the Federalist approach to the trans-Appalachian frontier as well as the Western approach to government. After seeing government provide services in Indian wars and trade, land surveys and sales, transportation, and many other areas, Westerners had come to appreciate and even regularly expect energetic government. Those ideas were traveling eastward, but they were also planted in a new generation of Whigs entering the public sphere in the region. As the Whig Party solidified throughout the 1830s, that new generation rose to join their Federalist and energetic Republican colleagues, and through them the Federalist frontier would continue to leave an indelible imprint in American politics.

Up the Capitol Steps

Abraham Lincoln and the New Western Whigs

O~N~ N~OVEMBER~ 23, 1840, Abraham Lincoln had many reasons to be proud as he climbed the steps of the new capitol building to open the Illinois General Assembly's winter legislative session in Springfield. As a member of the "Long Nine," he was instrumental in moving the capital from Vandalia to his adopted hometown the previous year. On that Monday morning, Lincoln also was starting his fourth term as state representative and had already distinguished himself within the state Whig Party. By October 1841, the Whig newspaper and local party committee in Fulton (in northwestern Illinois) even proposed nominating Lincoln for governor in 1842, citing his "great talents, services and high standing." However, Lincoln protested that he did not want the office.[1] Most of all, though, Lincoln could be proud to have achieved so much by the tender age of thirty-one.

Far too often, this vision of Lincoln is overlooked. Biographers typically treat his early career as a prelude to his subsequent success in national politics. To them, Lincoln's career in the Illinois House was more of an apprenticeship to future greatness that receives comparatively scant attention. However, Lincoln was not ascending to glory that morning; rather he was carrying the legacies of the Federalist frontier up those Capitol steps. Far from an American Messiah ready to atone the nation for its sins of slavery, Lincoln as a state representative was eager to use government to change Western society. In 1840, his vision for America shared a great deal with the Federalists of older vintage: a virtuous, prosperous, and above all orderly people guided by wise and energetic leaders. Overall, Lincoln's political thought in his career as a state representative exemplified how Western Whigs of his generation often echoed the desires and policy goals of frontier Federalism.

FIGURE 7. Old State Capitol, Springfield, Illinois. Photograph taken by Nancy Maulden.

Abraham Lincoln's Illinois and the
Whig Party of the Northwest

Abraham Lincoln was a conventional and enthusiastic Whig when he climbed the steps that November day. William Lee Miller summarized him as "a loyal, active, and regular Whig," while Joel Silbey called him "an organization builder and political manager," "a total political operator," and more bluntly "a party hack."[2] Lincoln was indeed a regular Whig, and he shared three defining characteristics with other Whigs. First, they believed in the merits of energetic government, calling for new programs and active responses to resolve problems voiced by citizens. Second, they backed the American System, and Lincoln was among its most ardent supporters. Finally, many Whigs emphasized public order to accompany republican liberty. While other Whigs championed moral reforms, partic-ularly in New England and New York, Lincoln venerated the law and con-sistently stressed the importance of obeying authority. In all three ways, Lincoln and other Western Whigs united under a banner that showed the influence of Federalist administration in the Northwest.

Lincoln saw the benefits of federal power firsthand throughout his early life. After observing the problems his father Thomas encountered in Kentucky, Abraham Lincoln saw the benefits of the federal system of land surveys and sales. In his 1860 campaign autobiography, he blamed "the difficulty in land titles in Kentucky" for his family's removal to Indiana and recalled bitterly in 1864 that Kentucky "titles got into such an almighty mess with these pettifoggin' incumbrances turnin' up at evry fresh tradin' with the land." Messy Kentucky land titles led to lawsuits that Thomas lost, leading to his ejection from two different farms and whittling his land holdings from 816 acres to only 200. Worse, the elder Lincoln was without recourse. Once the family moved to Indiana, however, the federal system of surveying and sales gave Thomas the secure title that Kentucky could not.[3] For young Abraham, his father's struggles were an object lesson in the power of government to improve life on the frontier.

Abraham Lincoln joined the tradition among young Western men of fighting Indians by taking part in Black Hawk's War, but his support for the American System displays his belief in state power most prominently. Lincoln and his fellow Whigs understood the American System as using government to aid private enterprise. This view appealed to the young legislator's sensibilities about the positive effects of government in the West, but he could promote the American System in very limited ways. As a state representative he could not legislate or vote on tariffs, but he supported American manufacturing however he could from the very beginning of his career. On his first day in the state legislature on December 1, 1834, a former colleague recalled Lincoln "dressed in a very respectable looking suit of jeans . . . carrying out the protective idea of wearing home manufactures." While not the modern denim we imagine today, Lincoln wore this local homespun fabric adopted by many Whigs to support Henry Clay's plans.[4] Such symbolic gestures in the Illinois House clearly showed Lincoln's position on the American System and his support for American business and manufacturing.

Like many Western Whigs of the period, Lincoln also lined up squarely behind the second part of the American System, a strong central bank. Their stance originated with the First Bank of the United States, created by Hamilton in 1791 to, as he explained, "extend the active Capital of a Country" and ultimately "add new energies" to nascent American manufacturing. In the 1830s, Lincoln and other Whigs agreed that central banking was necessary to create economic prosperity throughout the nation. Members of the U.S. Congress supported the Second Bank of the United States created in 1816 and opposed Andrew Jackson's efforts to close it during the Bank War of the 1830s, while Lincoln made his best efforts to help from Vandalia. On January 8, 1835, during his first session in the state legislature, he stated that the Bank of the United States was "useful and expedient" because of its "salutary provisions . . . to promote the interests of the country."[5] Illinois benefitted especially from it because the state was capital-poor. The Bank of the United States provided a steady supply of available capital and credit that could attract new industries to Illinois in the 1830s and beyond. The Bank was an important stimulus to the Illinois economy, and for Lincoln government existed to promote private enterprise and general prosperity.

Once it became clear that Jackson and his fellow Democrats were determined to shutter the Second Bank of the United States, Lincoln voted to create the State Bank of Illinois in 1835. By the debates over renewing its charter on December 26, 1839, Lincoln took a more active role and spoke on the House floor. He defended the re-charter and attacked the Democrats for effectively closing the Bank of the United States. According to Lincoln, these choices caused the Panic of 1837 that threatened to ruin the deeply indebted Illinois state government. He praised central banks for keeping money in circulation and providing greater access to credit in the cash-poor West, while Democrats preferred to have "revenue . . . collected, and kept in iron boxes until the government wants it for disbursement; thus robbing the people of the use of it." Instead of using the State Bank of Illinois to make loans and invigorate commerce, Jacksonian Democrats wanted the money "performing no nobler office than that of rusting in iron boxes."[6]

Lincoln also saw Jacksonian opposition to central banks as a dishonor to public service, and he was vocal about his feelings. He consistently argued from old-fashioned republican virtue: to him, elected officials were duty-bound to provide constituents the greatest good possible, even when public opinion suggested another course of action. To Lincoln, central banks were nothing short of essential to a bright economic future, and he thought his opponents were shirking their responsibilities as public servants. As he said in the House in 1839, "A National Bank can establish and maintain a sound and uniform state of currency . . . and we further say, that no duty is more imperative on that Government, than the duty it owes the people, of furnishing them a sound and uniform currency." Here, Lincoln's rhetoric transcended normally sedate economic policy discussions and launched into invective against Democrats for breaching the public trust. He said as much in 1837, claiming that attacks on the Bank of the United States in Washington and in Illinois were part of a creeping "lawless and mobocratic spirit" threatening the very nature of the republic. His remarks resembled those made by the arch-conservative Federalist, Fisher Ames, who decried mobocracy in 1799 because it "strews the fruitful earth with promiscuous ruins" and likened it to "an earthquake . . . burying in an hour the accumulated wealth and wisdom of ages."[7] The connection is clear. Lincoln echoed Federalist political thought to defend central banking, a principal Federalist policy.

Most important to State Representative Lincoln was the American System's call for internal improvements to ease travel and the flow of commerce. His first public political speech in June 1830 focused on the need to improve transportation on the Sangamon River for the future of Decatur, where he had briefly settled with his father.[8] Two years later, he made his first campaign promise about improving the Sangamon River, telling Sangamon County voters that improving the river was "vastly important and highly desirable to the people of this county," and he would support "any measure in the legislature having this for its object." He followed through, too, co-authoring a bill to charter a Sangamon River canal company during his first session in the legislature; it passed in February 1835. His support for internal improvements also likely drew attention from voters whose enthusiasm for transportation projects was growing in the early 1830s. John Stuart, Lincoln's first law partner, described a "Railroad excitement" at that moment: "There was to be nothing but railroads. Railroad meetings were held everywhere, and the State was to become a gridiron at once." After his third run (and second win) for the Illinois House in 1836, Lincoln spent the next term in the legislature that embarked on a system of canals and roads so ambitious that it nearly bankrupted the state during the Panic of 1837.[9]

In addition to the material gains for Illinois, Lincoln also saw promise in the American System because it would allow reason and order to rule in frontier Illinois.[10] As he believed, central banks and other measures encouraged domestic manufacturing, allowing Illinois and the rest of the nation to not only prosper but become more logical and orderly. After all, the American System was a passionate embrace of the Market Revolution and the methods of rational production that went with it. Roads and railroads sped up overland travel for farmers and manufacturers alike, and canals imposed the logic of the emerging capitalist order onto the landscape. Lincoln heartily supported a canal to link the Illinois River and Lake Michigan, a project that later led to reversing the flow of the Chicago River (to make it flow south toward the Illinois River) in 1900. Meanwhile, other canals promised to correct the handiwork of God, creating rivers where the Almighty forgot to place them. With internal improvement projects, even nature became more orderly. Waterways were custom-made to carry two-way flatboat traffic, and rivers would be made to flow in the direction of progress.[11]

Such promise for the nation appealed to young Abraham Lincoln because he believed deeply in the power of reason. Lincoln fell squarely into what Daniel Walker Howe has categorized as an "improver" interested in personal growth and economic development. While other Whigs took greater interest in religious revival and moral reform amid the Second Great Awakening, Lincoln preferred Enlightenment-style rationalism. His law partner William Herndon even noted that Lincoln particularly liked Thomas Paine's *Age of Reason*, an impassioned attack on organized religion.[12] Instead of leaning on claims of understanding from ministers, Lincoln trusted reason and human ingenuity to resolve the mysteries of the universe. As such, he followed frontier Federalists as a reliable supporter of public education throughout his adult life.

In addition, Lincoln revered legal institutions and demanded unflinching obedience to the law by American citizens. He opposed preemption rights for squatters on public lands because granting such rights rewarded disrespect for the law and promoted a chaotic settlement process. Preemption would set a dangerous precedent, he and other Whigs worried, and it would ultimately discourage industrious settlers and men of means whom Illinois Whigs hoped to attract to their state. Furthermore, free land for squatters meant less revenue to fund transportation projects. Barely a month into his legislative career in January 1835, Lincoln proposed a resolution to instruct the state's congressional delegation to "procure the passage of any law" that would give the state of Illinois at least "20 per cent upon the amount annually paid to the Treasury of the United States, for public lands lying within the limits of the said State of Illinois" in order to build canals and railroads. Though it failed, the resolution clearly showed that Lincoln wanted obedience to the laws, and he showed ingenuity in his attempts to further the American System within Illinois.[13]

Above all else, Lincoln demanded reason and public order in rejection of both the violence of Jacksonian-era politics and lawlessness in frontier

FIGURE 8. *Sangamo Journal* Graphic. This advertisement for the 1840 election includes Lincoln among the electors for William Henry Harrison and John Tyler. Source: *Sangamo Journal* (Springfield, IL), Sept. 17, 1840.

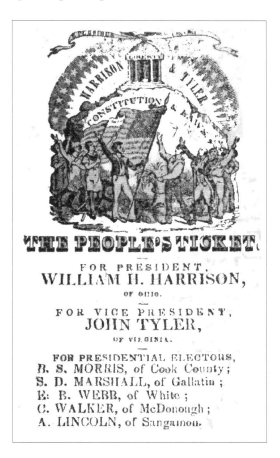

society. His 1838 speech to the Springfield Young Men's Lyceum, made shortly before his twenty-ninth birthday, was a plaintive call for reason and civility that was also perhaps his finest hour as a young politician. In a meditation on the murder of Alton abolitionist newspaper editor Elijah Lovejoy two months prior, Lincoln decried "an ill-omen amongst us" that included "increasing disregard for law . . . the growing disposition to substitute the wild and furious passions, in lieu of the sober judgment of Courts; and the worse than savage mobs, for the executive ministers of justice." These crowds were not virtuous republicans but men who "make a jubilee" of chaos and seek the "total annihilation" of government. They were the forebears, he said, of a "mobocratic spirit . . . now abroad in the land."[14]

Lincoln had a twofold purpose in denouncing the pro-slavery mob in Alton. First, he wanted to denounce his opponents among the Jacksonian Democrats. Though Lincoln supported universal white male suffrage, he was repulsed by the seeming disorder of Jacksonian politics.[15] Second, and perhaps most importantly to him, he wanted to promote his vision of public order. "Let every American, every lover of liberty . . . swear by the blood of the Revolution, never to violate in the least particular, the laws of the country; and never to tolerate their violation by others," he implored. He hoped to see:

> reverence for the laws . . . breathed by every American mother, to the lisping babe, that prattles on her lap—let it be taught in schools, in seminaries, and in colleges;—let it be written in Primmers, spelling books, and in Almanacs;—let it be preached from the pulpit, proclaimed in legislative halls, and enforced in courts of justice. And, in short, let it become the *political religion* of the nation. . . . Reason, cold, calculating, unimpassioned reason, must furnish all the materials for our future support and defence. Let those be moulded into *general intelligence, morality* and, in particular, *a reverence for the constitution and laws.*[16]

Clearly, a good American to Lincoln was an obedient and orderly American. On this point he would not yield: not in 1838 in the face of mob violence, and not in 1861 in the face of a broken Union. However, in the 1830s his view reflected the demands for order that went with the Federalist frontier.

Lincoln also was ascending the steps to the Springfield Capitol in the wake of the 1840 election that saw old frontier Federalists and young Western Whigs joining together to back Jeffersonian convert William Henry Harrison. After an unsuccessful run for President in 1836, Harrison remained a preferred candidate for many Whigs and was nominated by a national party convention in late 1839. The ensuing campaign has often been dismissed as one in which style triumphed over substance, when the political stunts and imagery of catchy slogans, hard cider, and log cabins prevailed over major issues.[17] However, it is significant in the Northwest because it shows the major branches of the Whig Party in the region working together to elect a man who was also, perhaps more significantly, a product of the Federalist frontier.

Harrison's path to the Presidency officially began on December 7, 1839, when sixty-nine-year-old Jacob Burnet rose to speak at the national Whig Party convention in Harrisburg, Pennsylvania. The aging Ohioan and still unrepentant Federalist had been chosen by friends and supporters of Harrison to make the formal nomination speech. Burnet gave a short biography of Harrison and spoke in soaring terms of his military prowess, selflessness, and administrative talents. Though they had once been political adversaries in Ohio under old party antagonisms, Burnet endorsed Harrison and pledged to support the old war hero and territorial governor. His reasons were simple: under Harrison's leadership the Whigs would continue to "stand for principles instead of men" because he had "talent and virtue enough" to save the nation from Jacksonian Democratic misrule.[18]

The speech was rousing, and its circumstances make it quite curious. According to most historians of the period, Burnet should not have been standing in that Harrisburg meeting. The Federalist Party was supposed to be anathema after the War of 1812, and its members were supposed to have scattered in the face of a new Republican consensus.[19] However, there stood Burnet. He was a living legacy of Federalist influence on the Old Northwest endorsing Harrison, himself a product of the institutional approach to white settlement in the region during the late 1700s and early 1800s. Harrison also promised to extend institutional influence throughout the nation as a supporter of the American System. The influence of Federalist-created institutions in the Northwest had finally arrived on its long journey from the Ohio valley.

Abraham Lincoln also took an active part in the campaign of 1840 from Springfield. According to a February edition of the local *Sangamo Journal*, he was one of five local Whigs who served as editors for Springfield's campaign organ, *The Old Soldier*. Running only from February until the fall election, the newspaper defended Harrison from attacks on his political and military record while promoting domestic manufacturing. Lincoln even became an elector for Harrison from Illinois, a show of party loyalty as well as ardent support for the candidate.[20] Even while the Northwest offered Harrison his widest margins of victory in 1840, Lincoln never had a chance to cast an electoral vote for him. Harrison carried Ohio and Indiana by over ten thousand votes each, but Illinois went to Martin Van Buren by fewer than two thousand votes.[21] Efforts to help Harrison at home may have fallen short, but Lincoln could still be happy to see his fellow Western Whig head to the White House.

Lincoln climbed those steps in November 1840 as a proud Whig and an already distinguished politician, but the involvement of the early American state in the Northwest had its clear influences, too. His family had moved to the former Northwest Territory to benefit from federal land distribution, and they had moved in the wake of the United States Army clearing away Indian threats from Indiana and Illinois. Lincoln had even participated in extirpating Indian threats through a short stint in the Illinois militia during Black Hawk's War. There in 1840 and onward, Lincoln hoped to bring those positive effects to the rest of the nation through the American System, another invention from the West that promised to enmesh government even more deeply into the everyday lives of Americans. This friendliness to government institutions from Westerners was the true legacy of the Federalist frontier, and Lincoln carried that legacy with him into the Capitol and far beyond.

Notes

Introduction: The Log Cabin on Washington Street

1. John Murrin, "The Great Inversion, or Court versus Country: A Comparison of the Revolution Settlements in England (1688–1721) and America (1776–1816)," in *Three British Revolutions, 1641, 1688, 1776*, ed. J. G. A. Pocock, 425; and Robert H. Wiebe, *The Opening of American Society: From the Adoption of the Constitution to the Eve of Disunion*, 132.

2. Rowena Buell, "The Ohio Company's Land Office," ca. 1900, Ohio Company Records (VFM 2736), OHS.

3. *Massachusetts Spy* (Worcester), June 19, 1788; Ohio Company, meeting, November 10, 1787, in Archer Butler Hulbert, ed., *Records of the Original Proceedings of the Ohio Company*, 1:20; Jervis Cutler, *Topographical Description of the State of Ohio, Indiana Territory, and Louisiana*, 17; Andrew R. L. Cayton, *The Frontier Republic: Ideology and Politics in the Ohio Country, 1780–1825*, 28; and John W. Reps, *The Making of Urban America: A History of City Planning in the United States*, 218.

4. See also Andrew R. L. Cayton, "'A Quiet Independence': The Western Vision of the Ohio Company," 26; and Andrew R. L. Cayton, "Radicals in the 'Western World': The Federalist Conquest of Trans-Appalachian North America," in *Federalists Reconsidered*, ed. Doron Ben-Atar and Barbara B. Oberg, 77–78.

5. Fortescue Cuming, "Sketches of a Tour to the Western Country," in *Early Western Travels, 1748–1846*, ed. Reuben Gold Thwaites, 4:123; Cutler, *Topographical Description*, 17–18; François André Michaux, "Travels to the West of the Alleghany Mountains," in *Early Western Travels*, ed. Thwaites, 3:177; and Reps, *Making of Urban America*, 225. Reps, as a scholar of urban design and architecture, wrote that even in the 1970s, the town kept its "early charm and stands as an excellent example of the benefits of sound community planning."

6. Manasseh Cutler, *An Explanation of the Map of Federal Lands*, 14. See also Andrew R. L. Cayton, "The Contours of Power in a Frontier Town: Marietta, Ohio, 1788–1803," 103; and Cayton, "'A Quiet Independence,'" 26.

7. Reps, *Making of Urban America*, 217. For more on the standardization and bureaucratization of public land sales in the land offices, see also Malcolm

J. Rohrbough, *The Land Office Business: The Settlement and Administration of American Public Lands, 1789–1837*.

8. Jacob Burnet, *Notes on the Early Settlement of the North-western Territory*, 43; Rufus Putnam to Fisher Ames, 1790, in *The Memoirs of Rufus Putnam and Certain Official Papers and Correspondence*, ed. Rowena Buell, 244; and Cayton, "'A Quiet Independence,'" 13.

9. Burnet, *Early Settlement of the North-western Territory*, 299.

10. Linda K. Kerber, *Federalists in Dissent: Imagery and Ideology in Jeffersonian America*, 135; and John C. Miller, *The Federalist Era, 1789–1801*, 273.

11. Thomas Jefferson to Levi Lincoln, October 25, 1802, quoted in Stanley Elkins and Eric McKitrick, *The Age of Federalism: The Early American Republic, 1788-1800*, 754; David Hackett Fischer, *The Revolution of American Conservatism: The Federalist Party in the Era of Jeffersonian Democracy*, 29; and Donald J. Ratcliffe, *Party Spirit in a Frontier Republic: Democratic Politics in Ohio, 1793–1821*, 21, 122.

12. William H. Bergmann, *The American National State and the Early West*, 7–9; John Lauritz Larson, *Internal Improvement: National Public Works and the Promise of Popular Government in the Early United States*, 5; and Charles Sellers, *The Market Revolution: Jacksonian America, 1815–1846*, 100–01. See also Rohrbough, *Land Office Business*; and Leonard D. White, *The Federalists: A Study in Administrative History*.

13. David Andrew Nichols, *Engines of Diplomacy: Indian Trading Factories and the Negotiation of American Empire*; David Andrew Nichols, *Red Gentlemen & White Savages: Indians, Federalists, and the Search for Order on the American Frontier*; Bethel Saler, *The Settlers' Empire: Colonialism and State Formation in America's Old Northwest*; and Silvana R. Siddali, *Frontier Democracy: Constitutional Conventions in the Old Northwest*.

14. Richard White, *"It's Your Misfortune and None of My Own": A History of the American West*, 57–58.

15. Doron Ben-Atar and Barbara B. Oberg, "The Paradoxical Legacy of the Federalists," in *Federalists Reconsidered*, ed. Ben-Atar and Oberg, 4; Elkins and McKitrick, *Age of Federalism*, 22; Fischer, *Revolution of American Conservatism*, 17; Ronald P. Formisano, "Federalists and Republicans: Parties, Yes—System, No," in *The Evolution of American Electoral Systems*, ed. Paul Kleppner et al., 37; and Miller, *Federalist Era*, 100.

16. Alexander Hamilton, "Conjectures about the New Constitution," September 17–30, 1787, in *The Papers of Alexander Hamilton*, ed. Harold C. Syrett, 4:275; Hamilton, "Report on Manufactures," December 5, 1791, in *Papers of Alexander Hamilton*, ed. Syrett, 10:249; and Broadus Mitchell, *Alexander Hamilton: A Concise Biography*, 219–20.

17. Kerber, *Federalists in Dissent*, 174–75; and Gordon S. Wood, *The Creation of the American Republic, 1776–1787*, 411. Adams's comments were overheard and recorded in Edgar S. Maclay, ed., *Journal of William Maclay: United States Senator from Pennsylvania, 1789–1791*, 349.

18. Miller, *Federalist Era*, 113, 115. See also Formisano, "Federalists and Republicans," 37; Ratcliffe, *Party Spirit*, 61; and Thomas Slaughter, *The Whiskey Rebellion: Frontier Prologue to the American Revolution*, 133.

19. Cutler, *Map of Federal Lands*, 21–22; Putnam to Fisher Ames, 1790, in Buell, *The Memoirs of Rufus Putnam*, 235; and Putnam to J. Habersham, February 26, 1800, in Buell, *The Memoirs of Rufus Putnam*, 430–31. For more on internal improvements as a political issue in the 1790s, see Larson, *Internal Improvement*, 19–21, 32–40; and for a discussion of Putnam's approaches, see Bergmann, *American National State*, 153.

20. Arthur St. Clair, "Remarks of Governor St. Clair before the Constitutional Convention," Nov. 1, 1802, in *The St. Clair Papers: The Life and Public Services of Arthur St. Clair: Soldier of the Revolutionary War, President of the Continental Congress, and Governor of the Northwestern Territory: With His Correspondence and Other Papers*, ed. William Henry Smith, 2:593; Cayton, "'A Quiet Independence,'" 17–19; and Kerber, *Federalists in Dissent*, 174–75.

21. *AC*, 7th Cong., 2nd sess., 95–96, 171; Lawrence D. Cress, "Republican Liberty and National Security: American Military Policy as an Ideological Problem, 1783 to 1789," 74; and Ratcliffe, *Party Spirit*, 75.

22. Putnam to Ames, in Buell, ed., *The Memoirs of Rufus Putnam*, 245. For a much more detailed treatment of the role of military force in the late eighteenth-century Ohio valley, see Patrick Griffin, *American Leviathan: Empire, Nation, and Revolutionary Frontier*.

23. Michael Mann, "The Autonomous Power of the States: Its Origins, Mechanisms and Results," in *States in History*, ed. John A. Hall, 114.

24. William Parker Cutler and Julia Perkins Cutler, eds., *Life, Journals, and Correspondence of Rev. Manasseh Cutler, LL.D.*, 1:146; and George Flower, diary entry, Oct. 12, 1816, Oversize BV1, Flower Family Papers, ALPL.

25. Cutler, *Map of Federal Lands*, 20; and Cutler, "Sermon Preached at Campus Martius, Marietta, North-west Territory," August 24, 1788, in *Rev. Manasseh Cutler*, ed. Cutler and Cutler, 2:449.

26. For a state-by-state breakdown of the resolution votes, see the table in Larson, *Internal Improvement*, 118. The actual votes appear in *AC*, 15th Cong., 1st sess., 1385–89.

27. Larson, *Internal Improvement*, 196, 205–10, 218; and John Lauritz Larson, *The Market Revolution in America: Liberty, Ambition, and the Eclipse of the Common Good*, 30. For more on internal improvements and funded debts, see E. L. Bogart, *Internal Improvements and the State Debt in Ohio*; and John H. Krenkel, *Illinois Internal Improvements, 1818–1848*.

Chapter One: A Contested Land

1. *Pittsburgh Gazette*, August 19, 1786.

2. *Pittsburgh Gazette*, August 19, 1786. As the soldier stated bluntly of the suspects, "It is the opinion of every body here that these two young fellows killed him."

3. See especially Henry Nash Smith, *Virgin Land: The American West as Symbol and Myth*, 6; and Patrick Griffin, *American Leviathan: Empire, Nation, and Revolutionary Frontier*, 260–61. As Smith declared in his classic study, "The American West was nevertheless, there, a physical fact of great if unknown magnitude. . . . It was potential wealth on an unprecedented scale."

4. Colin G. Calloway, *Crown and Calumet: British-Indian Relations, 1783–1815*, 3; Lawrence B. A. Hatter, "'Divided by a Common Language': The Neutral Indian Barrier and the British-Indian Alliance in the Old Northwest, 1783–1815," 44–45; Reginald Horsman, *Expansion and American Indian Policy, 1783–1812*, 21, 31; and Elizabeth A. Perkins, "Distinctions and Partitions amongst Us: Identity and Interaction in the Revolutionary Ohio Valley," in *Contact Points: American Frontiers from the Mohawk Valley to the Mississippi, 1750–1830*, ed. Andrew R. L. Cayton and Fredrika J. Teute, 206.

5. Colin G. Calloway, *The Victory with No Name: The Native American Defeat of the First American Army*, 17; François Furstenberg, "The Significance of the Trans-Appalachian Frontier in Atlantic History," 656–57; William R. Shepherd, "Wilkinson and the Beginnings of the Spanish Conspiracy," 490–506; and Mary K. Bonsteel Tachau, *Federal Courts in the Early Republic: Kentucky, 1789–1816*, 48.

6. William H. Bergmann, *The American National State and the Early West*, 12–13; Colin G. Calloway, *The Shawnees and the War for America*, 8–13; David Dixon, "'We Speak as One People': Native Unity and the Pontiac Indian Uprising," in *The Boundaries between Us: Natives and Newcomers along the Frontiers of the Old Northwest Territory, 1750–1800*, ed. Daniel P. Barr, 47; and R. Douglas Hurt, *The Ohio Frontier: Crucible of the Old Northwest, 1720–1830*, 10.

7. Andrew R. L. Cayton, *Frontier Indiana*, 18–20, 98–99; Griffin, *American Leviathan*, 52–53, 152–53; and Richard White, *The Middle Ground: Indians, Empires, and Republics in the Great Lakes Region, 1650–1815*, 340.

8. John D. Barnhart and Dorothy L. Riker, *Indiana to 1816: The Colonial Period*, 191, 213–14; Colin G. Calloway, *The American Revolution in Indian Country: Crisis and Diversity in Native American Communities*, 53–54; Calloway, *The Shawnees*, 64; Jessica Choppin Roney, "1776, Viewed from the West," 659; and Jack M. Sosin, *The Revolutionary Frontier, 1763–1783*, 104, 140, 142.

9. Barnhart and Riker, *Indiana to 1816*, 182; Calloway, *American Revolution*, 30–31; and Sosin, *Revolutionary Frontier*, 105.

10. Barnhart and Riker, *Indiana to 1816*, 239–41; Calloway, *American Revolution*, 36–38, 59; Calloway, *The Shawnees*, 74–75; Francis Paul Prucha, *The Great Father: The United States Government and the American Indians*, 42–43; and Timothy D. Willig, *Restoring the Chain of Friendship: British Policy and the Indians of the Great Lakes, 1783–1815*, 14–16.

11. George Washington to James Duane, September 7, 1783, in *The Writings of George Washington: From the Original Manuscript Sources, 1745–1799*, ed. John C. Fitzpatrick, 27:133–34. Emphasis as in the original.

12. *Journals of the Continental Congress, 1774–1789*, ed. Worthington C. Ford et al., 25:682–83.

13. "Treaty of Fort McIntosh," January 21, 1785, in *ASP:IA*, 1:11.

14. Emer de Vattel, *The Law of Nations; or, the Principles of the Law of Nature Applied to the Conduct and Affairs of Nations and Sovereigns*, trans. Joseph Chitty, 98, 427; Calloway, *Crown and Calumet*, 8–9; and Horsman, *Expansion and American Indian Policy*, 28, 31. Cited often in the late 1700s as the preeminent theorist of international law, Vattel argued that sovereignty meant "the nation directs and regulates at its pleasure every thing that passes in the country." By having Indian agreement that their relationship was an internal matter, Vattel's reasoning bolstered American sovereignty: "Foreign nations are not to interfere in the internal government of an independent state. It belongs not to them to judge between . . . the prince and his subjects."

15. Dorothy V. Jones, *License for Empire: Colonialism by Treaty in Early America*, 150–51; David Andrew Nichols, *Red Gentlemen & White Savages: Indians, Federalists, and the Search for Order on the American Frontier*, 19–20, 36; and Wiley Sword, *President Washington's Indian War: The Struggle for the Old Northwest, 1790-1795*, 25–26.

16. "Speech of the United Indian Nations, at their Confederate Council, held near the mouth of the Detroit river," November 28, and December 18, 1786, in *ASP:IA*, 1:9; Calloway, *The Shawnees*, 78; Prucha, *The Great Father*, 62–63; and Willig, *Restoring the Chain of Friendship*, 22–23.

17. Calloway, *Victory with No Name*, 6; and Gregory Evans Dowd, *A Spirited Resistance: The North American Indian Struggle for Unity, 1745–1815*, 91, 94. Dowd points particularly to Alexander McGillivray, who wrote to a Spanish trader that Indians in the trans-Appalachian West would need to maintain "the formidable Indian Confederacy of the late war against the Americans" in order to be "a great check on the States in . . . all the western Countrys."

18. J. M. P. Le Gras to Harmar, June 26, 1787, in *Outpost on the Wabash, 1787–1791*, ed. Gayle Thornbrough, 24–25; John May to Samuel Beall, May 4, 1786, transcription binder, Beall-Booth Family Papers (MSS A B365), FHS; May to Beall, May 1786, Folder 5, Beall-Booth Family Papers, FHS; John Hamtramck to Harmar, November 3, 1787, in *Outpost on the Wabash*, ed. Thornbrough, 44; and White, *Middle Ground*, 418.

19. Jones, *License for Empire*, 121–22, 125. For arguments that conquest ended in 1786 (or near then), see Andrew R. L. Cayton, *The Frontier Republic: Ideology and Politics in the Ohio Country, 1780–1825*; Horsman, *Expansion and American Indian Policy*; R. Douglas Hurt, *The Indian Frontier, 1763–1846*; and Prucha, *The Great Father*.

20. *Journals of the Continental Congress*, 33:696–97.

21. *Journals of the Continental Congress*, 32:105, 329.

22. *Journals of the Continental Congress*, 32:331.

23. *Boston Gazette*, August 5, 1793; Richard H. Kohn, *Eagle and Sword: The Federalists and the Creation of the Military Establishment in America*, 97; and Nichols, *Red Gentlemen & White Savages*, 37. The *Boston Gazette* estimated the army at 500 men, but Kohn used various primary sources to place the army at around 600.

24. *Pennsylvania Mercury* (Philadelphia), Jan. 13, 1786. See also Nichols, *Red Gentlemen & White Savages*, 77–79.

25. Josiah Harmar to Henry Knox, May 14, 1787, in *St. Clair Papers*, ed. William Henry Smith, 2:21; Harmar to Knox, August 7, 1787, in *St. Clair Papers*, ed. Smith, 2:29; Sword, *President Washington's Indian War*, 89; and Bergmann, *American National State*, 38–39.

26. Inhabitants of Jefferson County, "Appeal for Aid against Indians," July 1786, Folder 6, Bullitt Family Papers (MSS A B937c), FHS; and Alexander S. Bullitt to the Governor of Virginia, May 16, 1787, Folder 6, Bullitt Family Papers, FHS.

27. Washington to the President of Congress, June 17, 1783, in *Writings of George Washington*, ed. Fitzpatrick, 27:17.

28. *Pennsylvania Mercury* (Philadelphia), Jan. 13, 1786; and Owen S. Ireland, *Religion, Ethnicity, and Politics: Ratifying the Constitution in Pennsylvania*, 279. A statistical analysis of items appearing in the *Mercury* revealed that 94% of the pieces favored ratification, making it the publication most strongly allied with the Constitution in Philadelphia.

29. John Jay, "No. 3: Jay," in *The Federalist Papers*, ed. Clinton Rossiter, 44–45.

30. Hamilton, "No. 7: Hamilton" and "No. 24: Hamilton," in *The Federalist Papers*, ed. Rossiter, 61, 161.

31. Hamilton, "No. 24: Hamilton," in *The Federalist* Papers, ed. Rossiter, 161.

32. Max M. Edling, *A Revolution in Favor of Government: Origins of the U.S. Constitution and the Making of the American State*, 58, 122.

33. Rufus Putnam, "Thoughts on a Peace Establishment for the United States of America," 1783, in *The Memoirs of Rufus Putnam and Certain Official Papers and Correspondence*, ed. Rowena Buell, 202–04.

34. "Coppy of Petition for the Ohio Country," May 7, 1783, in *Memoirs of Rufus Putnam*, ed. Buell, 216. Emphasis as in original. The prescribed border was Lake Erie to the north, Pennsylvania to the east, the Ohio River to the east and south, a north-south line beginning on the Ohio 24 miles west of the mouth of the Scioto River and ending at the Miami River, and the Maumee River (mistakenly named as the Miami) to the north flowing into Lake Erie.

35. "Coppy of Petition for the Ohio Country," May 7, 1783, in *Memoirs of Rufus Putnam*, ed. Buell, 216; Putnam to Washington, June 16, 1783, in *Memoirs of Rufus Putnam*, ed. Buell, 216, 218; and Washington to the President of Congress, June 17, 1783, in *Writings of George Washington*, ed. Fitzpatrick, 27:17.

36. Linda Elise Kalette, "Arthur St. Clair," in *The Papers of Thirteen Early Ohio Political Leaders*, 8; and Gordon S. Wood, *The Radicalism of the American Revolution*, 83.

37. Cayton, *Frontier Republic*, 3; Randolph C. Downes, "Ohio's Squatter Governor: William Hogland of Hoglandstown," 274–75; and William Irvine to Benjamin Harrison, April 20, 1782, in *The Washington-Irvine Correspondence: The Official Letters which Passed between Washington and Brig–Gen. William Irvine and between Irvine and Others Concerning Military Affairs in the West from 1781 to 1783*, ed. C. W. Butterfield, 267.

38. John Emerson, "Advertisement," March 12, 1785, in *St. Clair Papers*, ed. Smith, 2:5n. For more on the statehood movement of 1785, see Downes, "Ohio's Squatter Governor," 273, 277.

39. Cayton, *Frontier Republic*, 7; and Nichols, *Red Gentlemen & White Savages*, 43, 56. For the full text of the Ordinance of 1785, see Clarence E. Carter, ed., *Territorial Papers of the United States*, 2:12–18.

40. United States Congress [Confederation], "The Regulation of Indian Affairs," Aug. 7, 1786, in Carter, ed., *Territorial Papers of the United States*, 2:21; and Prucha, *The Great Father*, 46–47.

41. Smith, ed., *St. Clair Papers*, 1:116–17; and St. Clair to Thomas Jefferson, February 13, 1802, in *St. Clair Papers*, ed. Smith, 2:574.

42. Jacob Burnet, *Notes on the Early Settlement of the North-western Territory*, 296–97; and "A Brief Sketch of the Life of Solomon Drowne, M.D.," Drowne Papers, Rhode Island State Historical Society, Providence, quoted in Andrew R. L. Cayton, "'A Quiet Independence,'" 11.

43. Craig Bruce Smith, *American Honor: The Creation of the Nation's Ideals during the Revolutionary Era*, 164; and Wood, *Radicalism of the American Revolution*, 22, 38.

44. Washington to Benjamin Harrison, October 10, 1784, in *The Papers of George Washington: Confederation Series*, ed. W. W. Abbot and Dorothy Twohig, 2:92. Washington communicated the same thoughts in very similar words to George Plater, October 25, 1784, in *Papers of George Washington*, ed. Abbot and Twohig, 2:108.

45. Samuel H. Parsons to William S. Johnson, November 26, 1785, quoted in Cayton, *Frontier Republic*, 8; Philip J. Deloria, *Playing Indian*, 21, 26, 44; and Roy Harvey Pearce, *Savagism and Civilization: A Study of the Indian and the American Mind*, 48. For another view on the perceived self-interest and "Indianness" of squatters, see Eric Hinderaker, *Elusive Empires: Constructing Colonialism in the Ohio Valley, 1673–1800*, 239.

46. W[illiam] North to unsigned, Aug. 7, 1786, Box 1, Folder 26, Northwest Territory Collection, IHS; and Manasseh Cutler, *An Explanation of the Map of Federal Lands*, 13.

47. Daniel Broadhead to George Washington, October 26, 1779, quoted in Downes, "Ohio's Squatter Governor," 274–75.

48. Josiah Harmar to Congress, May 1, 1785, in *St. Clair Papers*, ed. Smith, 2:3; John Armstrong to Josiah Harmar, April(?) 1785, in *St. Clair Papers*, ed. Smith, 2:4n; Bergmann, *American National State*, 27; and Downes, "Ohio's Squatter Governor," 278–82.

49. John Armstrong to Josiah Harmar, April(?) 1785, in *St. Clair Papers*, ed. Smith, 2:4n; and Knox to Congress, April 16, 1787, in *Journals of the Continental Congress*, 32:213; Alfred Byron Sears, "The Political Philosophy of Arthur St. Clair," 47; and Cayton, *Frontier Republic*, 11.

50. Harmar to Knox, May 14, 1787, in *St. Clair Papers*, ed. Smith, 21; and Knox to Congress, July 10, 1787, in *Journals of the Continental Congress*, 32:327–30.

51. Ohio Company, *Articles of an Association by the Name of the Ohio Company*, 3; and Cayton, *Frontier Republic*, 16.

52. Cutler to Nathan Dane, March 16, 1787, in *Life, Journals, and Correspondence of Rev. Manasseh Cutler, LL.D.*, ed. William Parker Cutler and Julia Perkins Cutler, 1:195; and Jeffrey L. Pasley, "Private Access and Public Power: Gentility and Lobbying in the Early Congress," in *The House and Senate in the 1790s: Petitioning, Lobbying, and Institutional Development*, ed. Kenneth R. Bowling and Donald R. Kennon, 73, 87.

53. Cutler, July 20–21, 25, 1787, "Diary of 1787," in *Rev. Manasseh Cutler*, ed. Cutler and Cutler, 1:295–96, 300; United States Congress [Confederation], "Committee Report on the Sale of Lands," July 23, 1787, in *Territorial Papers*, ed. Carter, 2:54–55; United States Congress [Confederation], "Report of Committee: Proposals of Cutler and Sargent," in *Territorial Papers*, ed. Carter, 2:63–64; United States Congress [Confederation], "Indenture between the Board of Treasury and the Agents of the Ohio Company," in *Territorial Papers*, ed. Carter, 2:80–81; Calloway, *Victory with No Name*, 48–51; and Malcolm J. Rohrbough, *The Land Office Business: The Settlement and Administration of American Public Lands, 1789–1837*, 11. Rohrbough claimed the depreciated certificates sold the land for as little as ten cents per acre, and of the whole affair, he claimed that it showed "the willingness of Congress to rid itself of the expense and difficulty of administering a large section of the public domain and to the need for immediate revenue of some kind. . . . The whole affair was a tribute to the lobbying skill of the Reverend Manasseh Cutler."

54. R. Douglas Hurt, "John Cleves Symmes and the Miami Purchase," in *Builders of Ohio: A Biographical History*, ed. Warren Van Tine and Michael Pierce, 14.

55. John Cleves Symmes, "Petition of John Cleves Symmes for a Grant of Land," August 29, 1787, in *Territorial Papers*, ed. Carter, 2:70; United States Congress [Confederation], "Report of the Board of Treasury: Proposal of Royal Flint and Joseph Parker," October 22, 1787, in *Territorial Papers*, ed. Carter, 2:77; and Charles J. Bayard, *The Development of the Public Land Policy, 1783–1820, with Special Reference to Indiana*, 136–37.

56. For historical works praising the Northwest Ordinance, see Beverley W. Bond, Jr., "An American Experiment in Colonial Government," 222; Andrew R. L. Cayton and Peter S. Onuf, *The Midwest and the Nation: Rethinking the History of an American Region*, 9–11; Peter S. Onuf, *Statehood and Union: A History of the Northwest Ordinance*, xiii; and Theodore C. Pease, "The Ordinance of 1787," 167.

57. Dane to Rufus King, July 16, 1787, in *Rev. Manasseh Cutler*, ed. Cutler and Cutler, 1:371–72; and Onuf, *Statehood and Union*, 58, 141–42. As he stated at the time, the prohibition against slavery was not in the original bill before Congress, but "finding the House favorably disposed on this subject, after we had completed the other parts, I moved the art., which was agreed to without opposition."

58. Cutler and Cutler, eds., *Rev. Manasseh Cutler*, 1:121, 130, 370.

59. Cutler, July 19, 1787, "Diary of 1787," in *Rev. Manasseh Cutler*, ed. Cutler and Cutler, 1:293.

Chapter Two: "To Show All Lawless Adventurers"

1. Knox to Washington, January 22, 1791, in *ASP:IA*, 1:112–13.

2. Knox to Washington, January 22, 1791, in *ASP:IA*, 1:112–13.

3. Andrew R. L. Cayton, "'Separate Interests' and the Nation-State: The Washington Administration and the Origins of Regionalism in the Trans-Appalachian West," 43.

4. Knox to Washington, January 22, 1791, in *ASP:IA*, 1:112–13; and Knox to St. Clair, March 21, 1791, in *ASP:IA*, 1:172.

5. Ebenezer Denny, *Military Journal of Major Ebenezer Denny, an Officer in the Revolutionary and Indian Wars*, 126–27.

6. Denny, *Military Journal*, 127–30; and Arthur St. Clair to John Jay, December 13, 1788, in *St. Clair Papers*, ed. William Henry Smith, 2:106.

7. "Treaty of Fort Harmar," January 9, 1789, in *ASP:IA*, 1:6; and Andrew R. L. Cayton, *Frontier Indiana*, 123.

8. John P. Duvall et al., to Washington, December 12, 1789, in *ASP:IA*, 1:85–86; St. Clair to Washington, May 2, 1789, in *Territorial Papers of the United States*, ed. Clarence E. Carter, 2:193; St. Clair to Washington, September 14, 1789, in *St. Clair Papers*, ed. Smith, 2:123; Reginald Horsman, *The Frontier in the Formative Years, 1783–1815*, 39–40; and Isabel Thompson Kelsay, *Joseph Brant, 1743-1807: Man of Two Worlds*, 433.

9. *AC*, 1st Cong., 1st sess., 83.

10. Knox to Washington, June 15, 1789, in *ASP:IA*, 1:13.

11. Knox to Washington, June 15, 1789, in *ASP:IA*, 1:13–14; and Wiley Sword, *President Washington's Indian War: The Struggle for the Old Northwest, 1790-1795*, 83.

12. *Connecticut Journal* (New Haven), November 4, 1789; St. Clair to Knox, May 1, 1790, Box 3, Folder 4, Arthur St. Clair Collection, OHS; and Hamtramck to St. Clair, December 2, 1790, in *St. Clair Papers*, ed. Smith, 2:197. For more on the British-Indian relationship in the period, see Colin G. Calloway, *Crown and Calumet: British-Indian Relations, 1783–1815*, 16; and Timothy D. Willig, *Restoring the Chain of Friendship: British Policy and the Indians of the Great Lakes*, 11, 30–31.

13. St. Clair to Washington, June 14, 1789, in *ASP:IA*, 1:15; and St. Clair to Washington, September 14, 1789, in *St. Clair Papers*, ed. Smith, 2:123–24.

14. St. Clair to Washington, September 14, 1789, in *St. Clair Papers*, ed. Smith, 2:124; Washington to St. Clair, October 6, 1789, in *St. Clair Papers*, ed. Smith, 2:126; and Washington to the Senate, September 16, 1789, in *ASP:IA*, 1:57.

15. *AC*, 1st Cong., 2nd sess., 969; and Richard H. Kohn, *Eagle and Sword: The Federalists and the Creation of the Military Establishment in America*, 86.

16. William Maclay, *Journal of William Maclay: United States Senator from Pennsylvania, 1789–1791*, ed. Edgar S. Maclay, 174–75, 239–240; *AC*, 1st Cong., 2nd sess., 972; and Max M. Edling, *A Revolution in Favor of Government: Origins of the U.S. Constitution and the Making of the American State*, 48–49.

17. "An Act for regulating the Military Establishment of the United States," April 30, 1790, in United States Congress, *United States Statutes at Large*, 1:119–21.

18. Hamilton to St. Clair, May 19. 1790, in *The Papers of Alexander Hamilton*, ed. Harold C. Syrett, 6:42; and Knox, "Summary Statement of the Situation of the Frontiers by the Secretary of War," May 27, 1790, in *St. Clair Papers*, ed. Smith, 2:146.

19. Knox to Harmar, June 7, 1790, in *ASP:IA*, 1:97; Knox to St. Clair, June 7, 1790, in *St. Clair Papers*, ed. Smith 2:148; and Kohn, *Eagle and Sword*, 104.

20. Knox to Harmar, June 7, 1790, in *ASP:IA*, 1:97. For more detailed narratives of the Harmar campaign, see especially Cayton, *Frontier Indiana*, 148–54; William H. Guthman, *March to Massacre: A History of the First Seven Years of the United States Army, 1784–1791*, 185–98; Howard H. Peckham, "Josiah Harmar and His Indian Expedition," 227–41; and Sword, *President Washington's Indian War*, 89–122.

21. Denny, *Military Journal*, 148–49.

22. Harmar to Knox, November 4, 1790, in *ASP:IA*, 1:104; St. Clair to Knox, November 6, 1790, in *St. Clair Papers*, ed. Smith, 2:190; Washington to Knox, November 19, 1790, in *Territorial Papers*, ed. Carter, 2:310; and David Andrew Nichols, *Red Gentlemen & White Savages*, 117–18.

23. *AC*, 1st Cong., 3rd sess., 1771.

24. *AC*, 1st Cong., 3rd sess., 1776.

25. *AC*, 1st Cong., 3rd sess., 1839; and Maclay, *Journal of William Maclay*, 349.

26. Stanley Elkins and Eric McKitrick, *The Age of Federalism*, 229, 557, 594; and Lance Banning, *The Jeffersonian Persuasion: Evolution of a Party Ideology*, 142–43.

27. Knox to Washington, January 5, 1791, in *ASP:IA*, 1:107; and *Providence Gazette*, February 5, 1791. For examples of these sorts of reprints, see *American Mercury* (Hartford, CT), February 14, 1791; and *Norwich Packet* (CT), March 25, 1791. A longer exploration into the Big Bottom Massacre appears in Patrick Griffin, "Reconsidering the Ideological Origins of Indian Removal: The Case of the Big Bottom 'Massacre,'" in *The Center of a Great Empire: The Ohio Country in the Early Republic*, ed. Andrew R. L. Cayton and Stuart D. Hobbs, 11–35.

28. Knox to the Miami Indians, March 11, 1791, in *ASP:IA*, 1:146–47.

29. Knox to the Miami Indians, March 11, 1791, in *ASP:IA*, 1:147; and Thomas Procter to Knox, July 9, 1791, in *ASP:IA*, 1:155.

30. Knox to Charles Scott, March 9, 1791, in *ASP:IA*, 1:129–30; Scott to Knox, June 28, 1791, in *ASP:IA*, 1:131; Cayton, *Frontier Indiana*, 156; and Sword, *President Washington's Indian War*, 139–41.

31. Arthur Campbell to unnamed [letter fragment], July 16, 1791, folder 4, Arthur Campbell Papers, FHS; John Grenier, *The First Way of War: American War Making on the Frontier, 1607–1814*, 5, 11, 171; and Kristopher Maulden, "A Show of Force: The Northwest Indian War and the Early American State," 32.

32. Knox to St. Clair, March 21, 1791, in *ASP:IA*, 1:171–72; and Knox to Washington, January 22, 1791, in *ASP:IA*, 1:113. Complaints about poor supplies can

be found in Denny, *Military Journal*, 157, 160; Winthrop Sargent, "Winthrop Sargent's Diary while with General Arthur St. Clair's Expedition Against the Indians," 245–46; and St. Clair to Knox, November 1, 1791, in *St. Clair Papers*, ed. Smith, 2:250. For more detailed accounts of the St. Clair expedition, see Colin G. Calloway, *The Victory with No Name: The Native American Defeat of the First American Army*, 83–92, 119–28; Guthman, *March to Massacre*, 220–43; and Sword, *President Washington's Indian War*, 160–95.

33. Denny, *Military Journal*, 162–63, 168–69; Gregory Evans Dowd, *A Spirited Resistance: The North American Indian Struggle for Unity, 1745–1815*, 106; Leroy V. Eid, "American Indian Military Leadership: St. Clair's 1791 Defeat," 71; Nichols, *Red Gentlemen & White Savages*, 138–40; Sargent, "Winthrop Sargent's Diary," 262, 265; and Sword, *President Washington's Indian War*, 188–95.

34. *AC*, 2nd Cong., 1st sess., 242; Knox to St. Clair, December 23, 1791, in *St. Clair Papers*, ed. Smith, 2:276; and Knox to Cornplanter, January 7, 1792, in *ASP:IA*, 1:226. For more on how the news of the defeat spread, see Calloway, *Victory with No Name*, 130–31.

35. For examples of the news spreading in New England, see *Boston Gazette*, December 19, 1791; *New-Hampshire Gazette* (Portsmouth), December 21, 1791; and *Connecticut Gazette* (New London), December 22, 1791.

36. *Federal Gazette* (Philadelphia), January 3, January 6, and January 18, 1792.

37. *National Gazette* (Philadelphia), January 2, 1792. Emphasis as in original. For more on the newspaper war, see Elkins and McKitrick, *Age of Federalism*, 282–92; and Jeffrey L. Pasley, *"The Tyranny of Printers": Newspaper Politics in the Early American Republic*, 48–78.

38. *National Gazette* (Philadelphia), January 26, 1792; and *Federal Gazette* (Philadelphia), January 21 and November 19, 1792.

39. *Gazette of the United States* (Philadelphia), January 14, February 4, and February 11, 1792; Seth Cotlar, "The Federalists' Transatlantic Cultural Offensive of 1798 and the Modern American Democratic Discourse," in *Beyond the Founders: New Approaches to the Political History of the Early American Republic*, ed. Jeffrey L. Pasley, Andrew W. Robertson, and David Waldstreicher, 276, 298.

40. Knox, "Statement Relative to the Frontiers Northwest of the Ohio," December 26, 1791, in *ASP:IA*, 1:198–99; and John Adlum, "John Adlum on the Allegheny: Memoirs for the Year 1794," quoted in Patrick Griffin, *American Leviathan: Empire, Nation, and Revolutionary Frontier*, 216.

41. *AC*, 2nd Cong., 1st sess., 337–48. Unfortunately, individual speeches were not separated from one another, so the journal is unclear as to who offered which points. Nonetheless, the day's speakers are listed at the end of the day's business.

42. *AC*, 2nd Cong., 1st sess., 349–50.

43. *AC*, 2nd Cong., 1st sess., 343; and Peter Silver, *Our Savage Neighbors: How Indian War Transformed Early America*, xx.

44. *AC*, 2nd Cong., 1st sess., 345–46.

45. Knox to Anthony Wayne, April 12, 1792, in *Anthony Wayne, A Name in Arms: Soldier, Diplomat, Defender of Expansion Westward of a Nation; The*

Wayne-Knox-Pickering-McHenry Correspondence, ed. Richard C. Knopf, 15; and Wayne to Knox, April 13, 1792, in *Anthony Wayne*, ed. Knopf, 17.

46. Daniel Bradley, *Journal of Capt. Daniel Bradley; an Epic of the Ohio Frontier*, ed. Frazer E. Wilson, 42–43; and Willig, *Restoring the Chain of Friendship*, 41–43.

47. Knox to Alexander Trueman, April 3, 1792, in *ASP:IA*, 1:229–30; Knox, "Speech from the Secretary of War," April 4, 1792, in *ASP:IA*, 1:230; Joseph Brant to Knox, July 28, 1792, in *ASP:IA*, 1:243; and William May to Knox, October 11, 1792, in *ASP:IA*, 1:243.

48. *AC*, 2nd Cong., 2nd sess., 762, 778–79, 802.

49. Wayne to Knox, August 10, 1792, in *Anthony Wayne*, ed. Knopf, 65–66; Knox to Wayne, November 9, 1792, in *Anthony Wayne*, ed. Knopf, 132; and Colin G. Calloway, *The Shawnees and the War for America*, 98. For a much more detailed account of the 1793 peace envoys, see Nichols, *Red Gentlemen & White Savages*, 146–51.

50. Nichols, *Red Gentlemen & White Savages*, 147.

51. Benjamin Lincoln, Beverley Randolph, and Timothy Pickering to John Simcoe, June 7, 1793, in *ASP:IA*, 1:347; Indian chiefs to Lincoln, Randolph, and Pickering, July 30, 1793, in *ASP:IA*, 1:352; Speech of the Seven Nations, Delawares, et al. to the American Commissioners, August 13, 1793, quoted in Nichols, *Red Gentlemen & White Savages*, 150; Lincoln, Randolph, and Pickering to Knox, August 21, 1793, in *ASP:IA*, 1:359; and Sword, *President Washington's Indian War*, 244–46.

52. Wayne to Knox, January 8, 1794, in *Anthony Wayne*, ed. Knopf, 298; Kohn, *Eagle and Sword*, 153; Calloway, *Crown and Calumet*, 225–26; Sword, *President Washington's Indian War*, 249–50, 272; and Willig, *Restoring the Chain of Friendship*, 55.

53. William Clark, "William Clark's Journal of General Wayne's Campaign," ed. R. C. Magrane, 419; and Kohn, *Eagle and Sword*, 156. Clark estimated the force at 2,000 regulars and 1,500 militia, a figure that Kohn accepts as accurate. Also, for more detailed accounts of Wayne's expedition, see Cayton, *Frontier Indiana*, 161–66; Paul David Nelson, *Anthony Wayne, Soldier of the Early Republic*, 259–68; Sword, *President Washington's Indian War*, 279–311; and James Wilkinson, "General James Wilkinson's Narrative of the Fallen Timbers Campaign," ed. M. M. Quaife, 81–90. For an account of the campaign from the British and Indian perspective, see Reginald Horsman, "The British Indian Department and the Resistance to General Anthony Wayne, 1793–1795," 279–86.

54. Wayne to Knox, July 27, 1794, in *Anthony Wayne*, ed. Knopf, 350; Clark, "William Clark's Journal," ed. Magrane, 424–27; and Wilkinson, "General James Wilkinson's Narrative," ed. Quaife, 83.

55. Tarke to the United States, September 26, 1794, in *ASP:IA*, 1:527; unsigned to Wayne, September 27, 1794, in *ASP:IA*, 1:528; Kohn, *Eagle and Sword*, 157; and Willig, *Restoring the Chain of Friendship*, 247.

56. "Jay's Treaty," November 19, 1794, in Samuel Flagg Bemis, *Jay's Treaty: A Study in Commerce and Diplomacy*, 444–45; Horsman, "British Indian Department," 286; and Willig, *Restoring the Chain of Friendship*, 57.

57. *AC*, 4th Cong., 1st sess., 1258–59. The entire text of Ames's speech is on 1239–63. Ames so moved many members of the House that the Federalists rose and demanded "The question," essentially asking for a vote after Ames roused their spirits.

58. Elkins and McKitrick, *Age of Federalism*, 439–40.

59. Sean M. Theriault, "Party Politics during the Louisiana Purchase," 297.

60. *Pittsburgh Gazette*, November 21, 1795; and Mary K. Bonsteel Tachau, *Federal Courts in the Early Republic: Kentucky, 1789–1816*, 48–51.

61. See especially Dorothy V. Jones, *License for Empire: Colonialism by Treaty in Early America*, 174.

62. "Minutes of a Treaty," July 15, 1795, in *ASP:IA*, 1:567; and Horsman, "British Indian Department," 289. For a much more detailed recent account of the treaty proceedings, see William H. Bergmann, *The American National State and the Early West*, 121–27.

63. Griffin, *American Leviathan*, 259; and Robert M. Owens, *Mr. Jefferson's Hammer: William Henry Harrison and the Origins of American Indian Policy*, 35.

64. "Report of the Board of Treasury," October 22, 1787, in *Territorial Papers*, ed. Carter, 2:77; Sword, *President Washington's Indian War*, 51, 204; and Charles Tilly, "Reflections on the History of European State Making," in *The Formation of National States in Western Europe*, ed. Charles Tilly, 42.

65. *AC*, 4th Cong., 1st sess., 11–13.

Chapter Three: The Speculator's Republic

1. St. Clair, "Governor St. Clair's Address at Marietta," July 15, 1788, in *St. Clair Papers*, ed. William Henry Smith, 2:53–55.

2. Putnam, "Reply of the Citizens of Marietta," July 15, 1788, in *St. Clair Papers*, ed. Smith, 2:56–57n.

3. Linda Elise Kalette, "Arthur St. Clair," in *The Papers of Thirteen Early Ohio Political Leaders: An Inventory to the 1976–77 Microfilm Editions*, 9; Ohio Company, meeting, October 26 and November 21, 1789, in *Records of the Original Proceedings of the Ohio Company*, ed. Archer Butler Hulbert, 1:126; Rufus Putnam, "Lands in the Ohio Company purchas [sic] drawn in the Name of Arthur St. Clair Esquire," September 10, 1790, Box 8, Folder 6, Arthur St. Clair Collection, OHS; St. Clair to John Cleves Symmes, December 7, 1790, Box 3, Folder 6, Arthur St. Clair Collection, OHS; Andrew R. L. Cayton, *The Frontier Republic: Ideology and Politics in the Ohio Country, 1780–1825*, 25, 47; and Patrick Griffin, "Reconsidering the Ideological Origins of Indian Removal," in *The Center of a Great Empire: The Ohio Country in the Early Republic*, ed. Andrew R. L. Cayton and Stuart D. Hobbs, 18. In company land records, Putnam listed six different tracts of land held by St. Clair, which included a total of 1,173 acres and House Lot 294 in Marietta.

4. William J. Novak, "The Myth of the 'Weak' American State," 769.

5. Manasseh Cutler, *An Explanation of the Map of Federal Lands*, 13.

6. Andrew R. L. Cayton, "'A Quiet Independence': The Western Vision of the Ohio Company," 24–25; and Alan Taylor, *William Cooper's Town: Power and Persuasion on the Frontier of the Early American Republic*, 5.

7. Cutler, *Map of Federal Lands*, 20–22; Cayton, "The Significance of Ohio in the Early American Republic," in *Center of a Great Empire*, ed. Cayton and Hobbs, 1; and John R. Van Atta, *Securing the West: Politics, Public Lands, and the Fate of the Old Republic, 1785–1840*, 50.

8. John Cleves Symmes, *To the Respectable Public*, 15–18; and R. Douglas Hurt, "John Cleves Symmes and the Miami Purchase," in *Builders of Ohio: A Biographical History*, ed. Warren Van Tine and Michael Pierce, 16–17.

9. Richard C. Wade, *The Urban Frontier: Pioneer Life in Early Pittsburgh, Cincinnati, Lexington, Louisville, and St. Louis*, 1.

10. Symmes, *To the Respectable Public*, 27.

11. Cutler, *Map of Federal Lands*, 13–14; Cutler, July 25, 1787, "Diary of 1787," in *Life, Journals, and Correspondence of Rev. Manasseh Cutler, LL.D.*, ed. William Parker Cutler and Julia Perkins Cutler, 1:300; and Andrew R. L. Cayton, "The Contours of Power in a Frontier Town: Marietta, Ohio, 1788–1803," 106.

12. Cutler and Cutler, eds., *Rev. Manasseh Cutler*, 1:133; and Symmes, *To the Respectable Public*, 26.

13. Cutler, *Map of Federal Lands*, 20–21; Cayton, *Frontier Republic*, 14; John W. Reps, *The Making of Urban America: A History of City Planning in the United States*, 216–17; and Van Atta, *Securing the West*, 51.

14. Ohio Company, meeting, July 1, 1790, in *Proceedings of the Ohio Company*, ed. Hulbert, 2:48; Ohio Company, meeting, December 8, 1790, in *Proceedings of the Ohio Company*, ed. Hulbert, 2:65; and Cutler, *Map of Federal Lands*, 20.

15. *Massachusetts Centinel*, 16 August 1786; and Cutler to Winthrop Sargent, March 16, 1787, in *Rev. Manasseh Cutler*, ed. Cutler and Cutler, 1:193.

16. Dudley Woodbridge to James Backus, December 9, 1788, Box 1, Folder 1, Backus-Woodbridge Family Papers, OHS; and S. W[oodbridge] to James Backus, December 29, 1788, Box 1, Folder 1, Backus-Woodbridge Family Papers, OHS.

17. Ohio Company, meeting, February 18, 1790, in *Proceedings of the Ohio Company*, ed. Hulbert, 2:2–3; Jacob Burnet, *Notes on the Early Settlement of the North-western Territory*, 416; and Symmes, *To the Respectable Public*, 19.

18. James M. Varnum, *An Oration, Delivered at Marietta, July 4, 1788, by the Hon. James M. Varnum, Esq. One of the Judges of the Western Territory*, 7.

19. Symmes, *To the Respectable Public*, 20; Varnum, *An Oration*, 5; St. Clair, "Governor St. Clair's Address at Marietta," July 15, 1788, in *St. Clair Papers*, ed. Smith, 2:54; and Daniel J. Boorstin, *The Americans: The National Experience*, 53.

20. Symmes, *To the Respectable Public*, 3, 21; Varnum, *An Oration*, 5; and Ohio Company (of Associates), *Articles of an Association by the Name of the Ohio Company*, 10, 16.

21. Ohio Company, meeting, March 6, 1788, in *Proceedings of the Ohio Company*, ed. Hulbert, 1:39; Ohio Company, meeting, April 4, 1791, in *Proceedings of the Ohio Company*, ed. Hulbert, 2:91–92; and Boorstin, *The Americans*, 53.

22. Cutler, *Map of Federal Lands*, 20–21; and *Rev. Manasseh Cutler*, ed. Cutler and Cutler, 2:33.

23. Andrew R. L. Cayton, "Radicals in the 'Western World': The Federalist Conquest of Trans-Appalachian North America," in *Federalists Reconsidered*, ed. Doron Ben-Atar and Barbara B. Oberg, 91.

24. *AC*, 1st Cong., 1st sess., 428–29, 654. See also Van Atta, *Securing the West*, 54–57.

25. *AC*, 1st Cong., 1st sess., 429, 651, 656.

26. Hamilton, "Plan for Disposing of the Public Lands," July 20, 1790, in *AS-P:PL*, 1:4.

27. John Lauritz Larson, *Internal Improvement: National Public Works and the Promise of Popular Government in the Early United States*, 14, 19; and Broadus Mitchell, *Alexander Hamilton: A Concise Biography*, 217, 222.

28. Hamilton, "Report on Manufactures," December 5, 1791, in *The Papers of Alexander Hamilton*, ed. Harold C. Syrett, 10:260, 269.

29. St. Clair to Knox, May 1, 1790, Box 3, Folder 4, Arthur St. Clair Collection, OHS; and St. Clair to Hamilton, August 9, 1793, in *St. Clair Papers*, ed. Smith, 2:318.

30. St. Clair to George Tod, April 21, 1802, in *St. Clair Papers*, ed. Smith, 2:582; and St. Clair to Washington, August 1789, in *Territorial Papers of the United States*, ed. Clarence E. Carter, 2:211.

31. St. Clair to Washington, August 1789, in *Territorial Papers*, ed. Carter, 2:212; and Brown, "Arthur St. Clair and the Establishment of U.S. Authority in the Old Northwest," in Van Tine and Pierce, *Builders of Ohio*, 29.

32. St. Clair to Hamilton, August 9, 1793, in *St. Clair Papers*, ed. Smith, 2:317.

33. *AC*, 1st Cong., 2nd sess., 1575; St. Clair to Knox, July 5, 1788, in *Territorial Papers*, ed. Carter, 2:48; Putnam, "Copy of an Address to the People of Vincennes," September 16, 1792, in *The Memoirs of Rufus Putnam and Certain Official Papers and Correspondence*, ed. Rowena Buell, 334–35; and Francis Paul Prucha, *The Great Father: The United States Government and the American Indians*, 98–99.

34. Symmes to Jonathan Dayton, August 15, 1791, in *The Intimate Letters of John Cleves Symmes and His Family*, ed. Beverley W. Bond, Jr., 149; and Thomas Wallcut, journal entry, February 2, 1790, in Thomas Wallcut, *Journal of Thomas Wallcut in 1790*, ed. George Dexter, 12.

35. Wallcut, "To His Excellency Arthur St. Clair, Esq., Governor and Commander-in-chief of the Territory of the United States North-west of the River Ohio," 1790 [undated but inferred], in *Journal of Thomas Wallcut*, 13n.

36. Buell, ed., *Memoirs of Rufus Putnam*, 107–10, 122; and Return J. Meigs, Jr. to Nathaniel Hubbard, Jr., August 30, 1792, Box 1, Folder 38, Northwest Territory Collection, IHS.

37. Ohio Company, meeting, July 29, 1790, in *Proceedings of the Ohio Company*, ed. Hulbert, 2:52; Ohio Company, meeting, September 7, 1790, in *Proceedings of the Ohio Company*, ed. Hulbert, 2:58; Ohio Company, meeting, January 5, 1791, in *Proceedings of the Ohio Company*, ed. Hulbert, 2:68, 70; and Ohio Company, meeting, March 21, 1791, in *Proceedings of the Ohio Company*, ed. Hulbert, 2:85–86.

38. Ohio Company, meeting, January 5, 1791, in *Proceedings of the Ohio Company*, ed. Hulbert, 2:70; Ohio Company, "To the Court of General Sessions of the Peace for the County of Washington," 1791, in *Proceedings of the Ohio Company*, ed. Hulbert, 2:71–73; and Putnam to Fisher Ames, 1790, in *Memoirs of Rufus Putnam*, ed. Buell, 244. Emphasis as in original.

39. Knox to Washington, March 19, 1791, Box 1, Folder 36, Northwest Territory Collection, IHS; and Putnam to Washington, February 28, 1791, in *Territorial Papers*, ed. Carter, 2:338.

40. Ohio Company, meeting, June 30, 1790, in *Proceedings of the Ohio Company*, ed. Hulbert, 2:33; "An Act authorizing the grant and conveyance of certain Lands to the Ohio Company of Associates," April 21, 1792, in United States Congress, *United States Statutes at Large*, 1:257; "Contract with John Cleves Symmes," February 9, 1797, in *ASP:PL*, 1:66–67; Winthrop Sargent, "As to Assembling at Public Worship without Arms," Sept. 18, 1792, in *St. Clair Papers*, ed. Smith, 2:309–10; and Symmes to Dayton, August 15, 1791, in *Letters of John Cleves Symmes*, ed. Bond, 153.

41. See especially John D. Barnhart and Dorothy L. Riker, *Indiana to 1816: The Colonial Period*, 273; Eric Hinderaker, *Elusive Empires: Constructing Colonialism in the Ohio Valley, 1673–1800*, 249; and Hurt, "John Cleves Symmes," in *Builders of Ohio*, ed. Van Tine and Pierce 18, 24.

42. Hinderaker, *Elusive Empires*, 248–49; and Reps, *Making of Urban America*, 225.

43. *Centinel of the North-Western Territory* (Cincinnati), November 9, 1793; and Cayton, *Frontier Republic*, 64–65.

44. *Centinel of the North-Western Territory* (Cincinnati), November 30, 1793, and October 4, 1794.

45. For more precise figures and other accounts of population growth in present-day Ohio after 1795, see Cayton, *Frontier Republic*, 36, 52; Jervis Cutler, *Topographical Description of the State of Ohio, Indiana Territory, and Louisiana*, 9–11; Donald J. Ratcliffe, *Party Spirit in a Frontier Republic: Democratic Politics in Ohio, 1793–1821*, 8; and Malcolm J. Rohrbough, *The Land Office Business: The Settlement and Administration of American Public Lands, 1789–1837*, 17.

46. St. Clair to Timothy Pickering, January 1796, in *Territorial Papers*, ed. Carter, 2:548.

47. Cayton, *Frontier Republic*, 52; David R. Contosta, *Lancaster, Ohio, 1800–1820: Frontier Town to Edge City*, 14; and Ratcliffe, *Party Spirit*, 17.

48. Putnam to Timothy Pickering, August 30, 1794, in *Memoirs of Rufus Putnam*, ed. Buell, 394; Pickering to St. Clair, March 25, 1795, Box 4, Folder 8, Arthur St. Clair Collection, OHS; and Pickering to the House Committee of the Military Establishment, February 3, 1796, in Charles W. Upham, *The Life of Timothy Pickering*, 3:144.

49. *AC*, 4th Cong., 1st sess., 353; and St. Clair, "Some Considerations as to the Dangers that Beset the Western Territory, and How It May Be Preserved as an Important Part of the Union," in *St. Clair Papers*, ed. Smith, 2:419–20. For a more detailed account of Congressional debates, see Van Atta, *Securing the West*, 62–67.

50. "An Act Providing for the Sale of the Lands of the United States, in the Territory Northwest of the River Ohio, and Above the Mouth of Kentucky River," May 18, 1796, in *United States Statutes at Large*, 1:466–67; "Pre-emption Rights

Northwest of the Ohio," May 12, 1796, in *ASP:PL*, 1:60; Wolcott, "Extension of Credit on Lands Sold," Jan. 30, 1797, in *ASP:PL*, 1:65; and Rohrbough, *Land Office Business*, 19, 21.

51. Pickering to the House Committee of the Military Establishment, February 3, 1796, in Upham, *Life of Timothy Pickering*, 3:144–45; Ephraim Cutler, "The First Settlement of Athens County, with Biographical Notices of Some of the Early Settlers," in *Biographical and Historical Memoirs of the Early Pioneer Settlers of Ohio, with Narratives of Incidents and Occurrences in 1775*, ed. S. P. Hildreth, 410, 412.

52. St. Clair to Pickering, January 1796, in *Territorial Papers*, ed. Carter, 2:543; and Sargent to Pickering, January 20, 1797, in *Territorial Papers*, ed. Carter, 2:587.

53. Burnet, *Early Settlement of the North-western Territory*, 292, 298. Emphasis in the original.

54. Cayton, *Frontier Republic*, 52; and Ratcliffe, *Party Spirit*, 32.

55. Burnet, *Early Settlement of the North-western Territory*, 306; St. Clair to Joseph Parks, December 13, 1798, in *St. Clair Papers*, ed. Smith, 2:436; and St. Clair, "Speech of Governor St. Clair to the Legislature," December 19, 1799, in *St. Clair Papers*, ed. Smith, 2:475–76. As Burnet notes, St. Clair's opponents claimed he should be removed because he vetoed so many bills.

56. David Zeisberger, et al., to St. Clair, October 28, 1798, in *St. Clair Papers*, ed. Smith, 2:433–34; and Burnet, *Early Settlement of the North-western Territory*, 312.

57. Burnet, *Early Settlement of the North-western Territory*, 33; St. Clair to James Ross, December 1799, in *St. Clair Papers*, ed. Smith, 2:482.

58. Burnet, *Early Settlement of the North-western Territory*, 306; "Petition to Congress from Inhabitants of the Scioto," February 1, 1798, in *Territorial Papers*, ed. Carter, 2:638; and Ratcliffe, *Party Spirit*, 34. Albert Gallatin presented a similar petition for Northwestern lands: see "Applications for Land at Reduced Prices," May 19, 1798, in *ASP:PL*, 1:73.

59. Burnet, *Early Settlement of the North-western Territory*, 395–96; and Hinderaker, *Elusive Empires*, 249.

60. Cayton, *Frontier Republic*, 75–76; Mary Alice Mairose, "Thomas Worthington and the Quest for Statehood and Gentility," in *Builders of Ohio*, ed. Van Tine and Pierce, 62; and Ratcliffe, *Party Spirit*, 42, 44, 57.

61. *Scioto Gazette*, January 29, 1801.

62. "Remarks of Mr. Fearing and Mr. Griswold in the House of Representatives on the Report of the Select Committee Respecting the Admission of the Northwestern Territory as a State into the Union," Mar. 31, 1802, in *St. Clair Papers*, ed. Smith, 2:576–77, 580.

63. Cutler, diary entry, April 7, 1802, in *Rev. Manasseh Cutler*, ed. Cutler and Cutler, 2:105; and Burnet, *Early Settlement of the North-western Territory*, 350–51.

64. "Speech of Governor St. Clair at Cincinnati," 1802, in *St. Clair Papers*, ed. Smith, 2:589.

65. "Remarks of Governor St. Clair before the Constitutional Convention," November 1, 1802, in *St. Clair Papers*, ed. Smith, 2:592–96; Burnet, *Early Settlement of the North-western Territory*, 352–53; Julia Perkins Cutler, *Life and Times of Ephraim Cutler: Prepared from His Journals and Correspondence*, 68; and Ohio Constitutional Convention, *Journal of the Convention of the Territory of the United States North-west of the Ohio, Begun and Held at Chillicothe, on Monday the First Day of November, A.D. One Thousand Eight Hundred and Two, and the Independence of the United States the Twenty-Seventh*, 9; Cayton, *Frontier Republic*, 77; and Mairose, "Thomas Worthington," in *Builders of Ohio*, ed. Van Tine and Pierce, 62.

66. Cutler, *Ephraim Cutler*, 71, 73; and Ohio Constitution of 1802, Art.III, sec. 3, 10.

67. Cutler, *Ephraim Cutler*, 70, 74–77; and Ohio Constitution of 1802, Art. VIII, sec. 3. Cutler claimed personal credit for both parts of Article VIII, writing, "I prepared and introduced all that part which relates to slavery, religion, and schools or education." Also, for another Federalist opinion on the 1802 constitution, see Burnet, *Early Settlement of the North-western Territory*, 358–59, 363–64.

68. "Address of Governor St. Clair to the People of the North-western Territory," December 8, 1802, in *St. Clair Papers*, ed. Smith, 2:597–98; and St. Clair to James Madison, December 21, 1802, in *St. Clair Papers*, ed. Smith, 2: 599–600.

69. Cutler, diary entries, March 1–3, 1803, in *Rev. Manasseh Cutler*, ed. Cutler and Cutler, 2:118.

70. Cayton, *Frontier Republic*, 53–55; Ratcliffe, *Party Spirit*, 103; and Lee Soltow, "Inequality Amidst Abundance: Land Ownership in Early Nineteenth Century Ohio," 137, 147.

71. Cayton, "Radicals in the 'Western World,'" in *Federalists Reconsidered*, ed. Ben-Atar and Oberg, 92–93.

Chapter Four: Energy and Republicanism

1. "Petition of the Inhabitants of Post Vincennes," July 26, 1787, in *Territorial Papers of the United States*, ed. Clarence E. Carter, 2:58–59; and Magistrates of Kaskaskia to Harmar, August 25, 1787, in *Territorial Papers*, ed. Carter, 2:67.

2. The literature on this topic is vast, but for recent examples from broader histories, see Daniel Walker Howe, *What Hath God Wrought: The Transformation of America, 1815–1848*, 37–38; John Lauritz Larson, *Internal Improvement*, 39; Sean Wilentz, *The Rise of American Democracy: Jefferson to Lincoln*, 106–07; and Gordon S. Wood, *Empire of Liberty: A History of the Early Republic, 1789–1815*, 276, 291, 357.

3. William Henry Harrison, "Harrison's Address to the General Assembly," July 29, 1805, in *Messages and Letters of William Henry Harrison*, ed. Logan Esarey, 1:156.

4. *AC*, 6th Cong., 1st sess., 316; Freeman Cleaves, *Old Tippecanoe: William Henry Harrison and His Time*, 24; Robert Gray Gunderson, "William Henry

Harrison: Apprentice in Arms," 21; and Robert M. Owens, *Mr. Jefferson's Hammer: William Henry Harrison and the Origins of American Indian Policy*, 35.

5. A similar claim focused on the trade factories appears in David Andrew Nichols, *Engines of Diplomacy: Indian Trading Factories and the Negotiation of American Empire*, 44.

6. For more on the meteorological records of the General Land Office, see also the Maryland Weather Service, "The System of the U.S. Land Office, 1817," in *Maryland Weather Service*, 1:355; and Redfield Proctor, *Annual Report of the Secretary of War for the Year 1891*, 4:334.

7. William H. Bergmann, *The American National State and the Early West*, 65–67; and Andrew R. L. Cayton, "'Separate Interests' and the Nation-State: The Washington Administration and the Origins of Regionalism in the Trans-Appalachian West," 54.

8. Bergmann, *American National State*, 188–89; and Nichols, *Engines of Diplomacy*, 69.

9. "An Act Making Provision for the Purposes of Trade with the Indians," March 3, 1795, in *United States Statutes at Large*, 1:443; Reginald Horsman, *Expansion and American Indian Policy, 1783–1812*, 63; Nichols, *Engines of Diplomacy*, 32; and Francis Paul Prucha, *The Great Father: The United States Government and the American Indians*, 115–16.

10. *AC*, 4th Cong., 1st sess., 230, 232.

11. *AC*, 4th Cong., 1st sess., 230, 241, 284; and Bergmann, *American National State*, 172–73.

12. *AC*, 4th Cong., 1st sess., 329, 339, 405–06; Malcolm J. Rohrbough, *The Land Office Business: The Settlement and Administration of American Public Lands*, 18–19; and Raymond Walters, Jr., *Albert Gallatin: Jeffersonian Financier and Diplomat*, 95.

13. Jacob Burnet, *Notes on the Early Settlement of the North-western Territory*, 302; St. Clair to Adams, in *The St. Clair Papers*, ed. William Henry Smith, 2:488; Carter, ed., *Territorial Papers*, 7:13n; Cleaves, *Old Tippecanoe*, 28–30; Owens, *Mr. Jefferson's Hammer*, 45, 48–50; and Rohrbough, *Land Office Business*, 23.

14. Henry Dearborn to Jefferson, December 8, 1801, in *ASP:IA*, 1:654; Nichols, *Engines of Diplomacy*, 44; Prucha, *The Great Father*, 118–19; and Walters, *Albert Gallatin*, 143–45.

15. John D. Barnhart and Dorothy L. Riker, *Indiana to 1816: The Colonial Period*, 323–25; Harrison, "Proclamation: Forbidding Settling, Hunting, and Surveying on Indian Lands," May 9, 1801, in *William Henry Harrison*, ed. Esarey, 1:24; and Owens, *Mr. Jefferson's Hammer*, 46.

16. "Petition to Congress by Trustees of Jefferson Academy," December 31, 1801, in *Territorial Papers*, ed. Carter, 7:44.

17. "An Act Making Provision for the Disposal of the Public Lands in the Indiana Territory, and for Other Purposes," March 26, 1804, in *United States Statutes at Large*, 2:279; Carter, ed., *Territorial Papers*, 7:44n; George E. Greene, *History of Old Vincennes and Knox County, Indiana*, 1:893–94; and "Petition to Congress

by Trustees of Vincennes University," November 20, 1807, in *Territorial Papers*, ed. Carter, 7:492–93.

18. Barnhart and Riker, *Indiana to 1816*, 369; Cleaves, *Old Tippecanoe*, 51; and Owens, *Mr. Jefferson's Hammer*, 41.

19. Dearborn to Jefferson, December 8, 1801, in *ASP:IA*, 1:655; Horsman, *Expansion and American Indian Policy*, 108; and Nichols, *Engines of Diplomacy*, 4–6, 35–36. Dearborn reported to Jefferson of the trade factories that "The intercourse . . . has a powerful tendency towards strengthening and confirming the friendship of the Indians to the people and Government of the United States." Nichols makes this point about the diplomatic advantages of the trade factory system much more thoroughly in his book.

20. Dearborn to Harrison, February 23, 1802, in *William Henry Harrison*, ed. Esarey, 39–40; and Prucha, *The Great Father*, 119. For the text of laws reauthorizing trade factories, see "An Act to Revive and Continue in Force, an Act Intituled 'An Act for Establishing Trading Houses with the Indian Tribes,'" April 30, 1802, in *United States Statutes at Large*, 2:173; and "An Act for Continuing in Force a Law, Intituled 'An Act for Establishing Trading Houses with the Indian Tribes,'" March 26, 1804, in *United States Statutes at Large*, 2:207.

21. Gallatin to Joseph H. Nicholson, January 2, 1804, in *ASP:PL*, 1:167; and "An Act Making Provision for the Disposal of the Public Lands in the Indiana Territory, and for Other Purposes," March 26, 1804, in *United States Statutes at Large*, 2:277–83.

22. Andrew R. L. Cayton, *Frontier Indiana*, 203–04; Charlotte Reeve Conover, *Concerning the Forefathers: Being a Memoir, with Personal Narrative and Letters of Two Pioneers, Col. Robert Patterson and Col. John Johnston*, 25–27; Nichols, *Engines of Diplomacy*, 46–47; and Leonard U. Hill, *John Johnston and the Indians in the Land of the Three Miamis*, 22.

23. Gayle Thornbrough, introduction to *The Correspondence of John Badollet and Albert Gallatin, 1804–1836*, 9–13, 19; and Findley and John Smilie to Jefferson, March 28, 1804, in *Territorial Papers*, ed. Carter, 7:188.

24. Charlotte Reeve Conover, *Concerning the Forefathers: Being a Memoir, with Personal Narrative and Letters of Two Pioneers, Col. Robert Patterson and Col. John Johnston*, 39; John D. Haeger, "The American Fur Company and the Chicago of 1812–1835," 123; and John Johnston to unnamed, September 30, 1804, John Johnston Records, IHS, Indianapolis, Indiana.

25. Jefferson, Message to Congress, January 18, 1803, in *ASP:IA*, 1:684; Johnston, "Colonel John Johnston's Indian Agency Account Book, 1802–1811," in *Fort Wayne, Gateway of the West, 1802–1813: Garrison Orderly Books, Indian Agency Account Book*, ed. Bert J. Griswold, 409, 421, 427; Bergmann, *American National State*, 189; and Nichols, *Engines of Diplomacy*, 81.

26. Jefferson to Dearborn, August 12, 1802, in *Territorial Papers*, ed. Carter, 7:68–70; Jefferson to Harrison, February 27, 1803, in *Territorial Papers*, ed. Carter, 7:91; and Prucha, *The Great Father*, 123, 125.

27. Walters, *Albert Gallatin*, 145–46; Gallatin to Joseph H. Nicholson, January 2, 1804, in *ASP:PL*, 1:167; and "An Act Making Provision for the Disposal of

the Public Lands in the Indiana Territory, and for Other Purposes," March 26, 1804, in *United States Statutes at Large*, 2:282. Section 14 of the Land Law of 1804 required examinations of the register's and receiver's records at least once per year.

28. "An Act Making Provision for the Disposal of the Public Lands in the Indiana Territory, and for Other Purposes," March 26, 1804, in *United States Statutes at Large*, 2:281; Ninian W. Edwards, *History of Illinois, from 1778 to 1833; and Life and Times of Ninian Edwards*, 104; and Walters, *Albert Gallatin*, 175.

29. Badollet to Gallatin, August 31, 1805, in *John Badollet and Albert Gallatin*, ed. Gayle Thornbrough, 47–48; Gallatin to Badollet, October 23, 1805, in *Territorial Papers*, ed. Carter, 7:312; and Edwards, *History of Illinois*, 104.

30. "An Act for Establishing Trading Houses with the Indian Tribes," April 21, 1806, in *United States Statutes at Large*, 2:402; Leonard U. Hill, *John Johnston and the Indians in the Land of the Three Miamis*, 40; and Prucha, *The Great Father*, 120–21. For Johnston's full account book, see Griswold, ed., *Fort Wayne, Gateway of the West*, 405–663.

31. Jefferson to Congress, January 18, 1803, in *ASP:IA*, 1:684; "Treaty of St. Louis," November 3, 1804, in *ASP:IA*, 1:694; and Prucha, *The Great Father*, 134.

32. Johnston to John Mason, February 4, 1808, in *Territorial Papers*, ed. Carter, 7:521; and Gomo, speech to Ninian Edwards, April 16, 1812, in Edwards, *History of Illinois*, 63.

33. Jefferson, "Proclamation of Public Land Sales," November 19, 1807, in *Territorial Papers*, ed. Carter, 7:491; and Payson Jackson Treat, *The National Land System, 1785–1820*, 410.

34. The credit system is summarized well by Andrew Gregg in "Credit on Public Lands," April 5, 1806, in *ASP:PL*, 1:265. For more on the specific duties (and compensation) for land officers, see Rohrbough, *Land Office Business*, 31–32. Rohrbough noted that registers represented "a direct link between the purchaser and the government," while receivers controlled funds and the credit system involved with sales. The complex interest and discount system meant "calculation of the accounts alone was a burdensome and exacting chore."

35. John D. Hay to Gallatin, August 1, 1810, in *Territorial Papers*, ed. Carter, 8:36; Richard Ferguson to Gallatin, August 3, 1810, in *Territorial Papers*, ed. Carter, 8:38; and Rohrbough, *Land Office Business*, 32.

36. Gallatin to Badollet and Ewing, October 11, 1806, in *Territorial Papers*, ed. Carter, 7:396; and Jefferson, "Proclamation of Public Land Sales," October 10, 1806, in *Territorial Papers*, ed. Carter, 7:397; and Gallatin to Badollet, March 9, 1807, in *Territorial Papers*, ed. Carter, 7:436.

37. Gallatin to Badollet, March 9, 1807, in *Territorial Papers*, ed. Carter, 7:436; Rohrbough, *Land Office Business*, 75; and Treat, *National Land System*, 406.

38. "An Act for the Establishment of a General Land-Office in the Department of the Treasury," April 25, 1812, in *United States Statutes at Large*, 2:716–18; and Rohrbough, *Land Office Business*, 35, 48–49.

39. Griswold, introduction to *Fort Wayne, Gateway of the West*, 23–25; Hill, *John Johnston*, 41; and Nichols, *Engines of Diplomacy*, 47–48. Johnston paid

$1.25 for skins from bucks and $1.00 from does, 50¢ for raccoon skins, and as much as $5.00 for bear skins.

40. Delivery document, March 10, 1808, Box 1, Folder 1, John Johnston Papers, OHS; and delivery document, April 9, 1808, Box 1, Folder 1, John Johnston Papers, OHS.

41. John Mason to William Eustis (enclosure), January 13, 1812, in *ASP:IA*, 1:784; Conover, *Concerning the Forefathers*, 41; and Nichols, *Engines of Diplomacy*, 107. According to Mason's report, the entire factory system turned a total profit of $14,171.30 between December 31, 1807 and September 30, 1811. In comparison, Chicago and Fort Wayne made $14,228.23 in profits during the same period.

42. Population figures vary among numerous sources, but the figures given here reflect those in Owens, *Mr. Jefferson's Hammer*, 166. For other sources on the territorial population, see Barnhart and Riker, *Indiana to 1816*, 320; Arthur Clinton Boggess, *The Settlement of Illinois, 1778–1830*, 91; and "Census Schedule," July 4, 1801, in *Territorial Papers*, ed. Carter, 7:25.

43. Harrison to Dearborn, July 15, 1801, in *William Henry Harrison*, ed. Esarey, 1:26–27; Cayton, *Frontier Indiana*, 199; and R. David Edmunds, *The Shawnee Prophet*, 4–5.

44. Barnhart and Riker, *Indiana to 1816*, 80; Edmunds, *Shawnee Prophet*, 4; Logan Esarey, *A History of Indiana: From Its Exploration to 1850*, 23; and Griswold, introduction to *Fort Wayne, Gateway of the West*, 24.

45. Cayton, *Frontier Indiana*, 201; Dearborn to Harrison, September 3, 1802, in *Territorial Papers*, ed. Carter, 7:74; and Harrison, "Proclamation: Selling Liquor to Indians," October 24, 1802, in *William Henry Harrison*, ed. Esarey, 1:60.

46. Harrison, "Message to Legislature," Nov. 3, 1806, in *William Henry Harrison*, ed. Esarey, 1:199; and Edmunds, *Shawnee Prophet*, 4–5, 20.

47. St. Clair to John Marshall, August 5, 1800, in *St. Clair Papers*, ed. Smith, 2:497; Dearborn to Harrison, February 23, 1802, in *Territorial Papers*, ed. Carter, 7:49.

48. Harrison, "Proclamation: Forbidding Settling, Hunting, and Surveying on Indian Lands," May 9, 1801, in *William Henry Harrison*, ed. Esarey, 1:24; Harrison, "Proclamation: Forbidding Traders from Selling Liquor to Indians in and around Vincennes," July 20, 1801, in *William Henry Harrison*, ed. Esarey, 1:31; and Harrison, "Proclamation: Against Trading with the Indians," August 31, 1801, in *William Henry Harrison*, ed. Esarey, 1:32.

49. Cayton, *Frontier Indiana*, 204; Jefferson to Harrison, February 27, 1803, in *Territorial Papers*, ed. Carter, 7:90; and Johnston to unnamed, September 30, 1804, John Johnston Collection, IHS.

50. Dearborn to William Lyman, July 14, 1801, in *Territorial Papers*, ed. Carter, 7:26; Jefferson to Harrison, February 27, 1803, in *Territorial Papers*, ed. Carter, 7:90–91; and Jefferson to chiefs of the Wyandot, Ottawa, Chippewa, Potawatomi, and Shawnee, January 10, 1809, quoted in Horsman, *Expansion and American Indian Policy*, 108.

51. Harrison, "Address to Indian Council," August 12, 1802, in *William Henry Harrison*, ed. Esarey, 1:53–55; Nichols, *Red Gentlemen & White Savages*, 196; and Owens, *Mr. Jefferson's Hammer*, 59.

52. "Treaty of Fort Wayne," June 7, 1803: in *ASP:IA*, 1:688; "Treaty of Vincennes," August 18, 1803, in *ASP:IA*, 1:687; "Treaty with the Piankeshaw," August 18, 1804, in *ASP:IA*, 1:690; Horsman, *Expansion and American Indian Policy*, 145–46; Owens, *Mr. Jefferson's Hammer*, 80; Mary K. Bonsteel Tachau, *Federal Courts in the Early Republic: Kentucky, 1789-1816*, 133; and Treat, *National Land System*, 404.

53. "A Treaty between the United States of America and the Tribes of Indians Called the Delawares, Pattawatamies, Miamies, Eel River, and Weas," August 21, 1805, in *ASP:IA*, 1:696–97; Harrison to Dearborn, August 26, 1805, in *William Henry Harrison*, ed. Esarey, 1:162–64; Horsman, *Expansion and American Indian Policy*, 144, 151; and Owens, *Mr. Jefferson's Hammer*, 104–07.

54. Harrison to Dearborn, January 1, 1806, in *William Henry Harrison*, ed. Esarey, 1:184. For the treaty, see "Articles of a Treaty Made at Vincennes," December 30, 1805, in *ASP:IA*, 1:704–05.

55. Oulaqua, "The Answer of Pawatamo, Chasso, and Oulaqua," December 16, 1805, in *William Henry Harrison*, ed. Esarey, 1:179.

56. Troy Bickham, *The Weight of Vengeance: The United States, the British Empire, and the War of 1812*, 37–38; Alfred A. Cave, "The Shawnee Prophet, Tecumseh, and Tippecanoe: A Case Study of Historical Myth-Making," 6 4 1 , 644; Cayton, *Frontier Indiana*, 205; and Owens, *Mr. Jefferson's Hammer*, 123, 186. Cave describes the religious message well, but see also Edmunds, *Shawnee Prophet*, 28–40.

57. Bergmann, *American National State*, 223–26; and Edmunds, *Shawnee Prophet*, 37.

58. Barnhart and Riker, *Indiana to 1816*, 371; and Cave, "The Shawnee Prophet," 644.

59. Harrison to Delawares, early 1806, in *William Henry Harrison*, ed. Esarey, 1:184; Harrison to Shawnee chiefs, August 1807, in *William Henry Harrison*, ed. Esarey, 1:248; and William Wells to Dearborn, December 5, 1807, in *Territorial Papers*, ed. Carter, 7:498.

60. Harrison to Shawnee chiefs, August 1807, in *William Henry Harrison*, ed. Esarey, 1:251; Cayton, *Frontier Indiana*, 209; Owens, *Mr. Jefferson's Hammer*, xiv, 62; Alan Taylor, *The Civil War of 1812: American Citizens, British Subjects, Irish Rebels, & Indian Allies*, 126; and Timothy D. Willig, *Restoring the Chain of Friendship: British Policy and the Indians of the Great Lakes, 1783–1815*, 215.

61. Cave, "The Shawnee Prophet," 647; Edmunds, *Shawnee Prophet*, 70–72, 92–93; and John Sugden, *Tecumseh: A Life*, 171–75.

62. Harrison to the Prophet, June 24, 1808, in *William Henry Harrison*, ed. Esarey, 1:293–94.

63. Harrison, "Message to the Legislature," August 17, 1807, in *William Henry Harrison*, ed. Esarey, 1:232–33; Harrison to Dearborn, September 1, 1808, in

William Henry Harrison, ed. Esarey, 1:302; Harrison, "Annual Message, Second Session, Second Assembly," September 27, 1808, in *William Henry Harrison*, ed. Esarey, 1:305; Cayton, *Frontier Indiana*, 213–14; and Prucha, *The Great Father*, 77.

64. Harrison to Eustis, May 16, 1809, in *William Henry Harrison*, ed. Esarey, 1:346; Eustis to Harrison, June 5, 1809, in *William Henry Harrison*, ed. Esarey, 1:347; and "Journal of the Proceedings of the Indian Treaty at Fort Wayne and Vincennes September 1 to October 27, 1809," in *William Henry Harrison*, ed. Esarey, 1:362, 364.

65. Cave, "The Shawnee Prophet," 648; Cayton, *Frontier Indiana*, 215; Edmunds, *Shawnee Prophet*, 80; Harrison to Eustis, November 15, 1809, in *William Henry Harrison*, ed. Esarey, 1:392; and Treat, *National Land System*, 404. For the full treaty, see "A Treaty between the United States of America and the Tribes of Indians called the Delawares, Puttawatamies, Miamies, and Eel River Miamies," September 30, 1809, in *ASP:IA*, 1:761. The estimates on the land cession vary widely. Cayton claimed the cession incorporated 2.5 million acres, Harrison sent a sketch of the cession and declared it "upwards of 2,900,000 acres," Cave and Edmunds placed the cession at more than three million acres, and Treat listed the cession at exactly 3,257,600 acres. Since the numbers vary so widely, the figure given here is not meant to be a final accounting of the cession but rather a conservative estimate based on existing claims.

66. Michel Brouillette, affidavit, June 30, 1810, Box 2, Folder 25, Albert Gallatin Porter Collection, IHS; Eustis to Harrison, November 1809, in *William Henry Harrison*, ed. Esarey, 1:387; Harrison, "Annual Message to the Third General Assembly," October 17, 1809, in *William Henry Harrison*, ed. Esarey, 1:381; Harrison to Eustis, November 3, 1809, in *William Henry Harrison*, ed. Esarey, 1:389; Bickham, *Weight of Vengeance*, 38; Cave, "The Shawnee Prophet," 648; Cayton, *Frontier Indiana*, 216; Edmunds, *Shawnee Prophet*, 81–82; and R. David Edmunds, *Tecumseh and the Quest for Indian Leadership*, 123.

67. Harrison to Eustis, October 5, 1810, in *William Henry Harrison*, ed. Esarey, 1:474–75; Harrison to Eustis, June 19, 1811, in *William Henry Harrison*, ed. Esarey, 1:520–21; and Eustis to Harrison, July 17, 1811, in *William Henry Harrison*, ed. Esarey, 1:536.

68. Cayton, *Frontier Indiana*, 220; Prucha, *The Great Father*, 77; and Sugden, *Tecumseh*, 237–49.

69. For particularly well-written accounts of the march from Vincennes and the Battle of Tippecanoe, see Owens, *Mr. Jefferson's Hammer*, 214–22; and Sugden, *Tecumseh*, 226–36.

70. Harrison to Eustis, November 1811, quoted in Prucha, *The Great Father*, 78; and Owens, *Mr. Jefferson's Hammer*, 222.

71. Edwards to Gomo, March 1812, in Edwards, *History of Illinois*, 55–56; and Edwards, address at Cahokia, April 16, 1812, in Edwards, *History of Illinois*, 56–57.

72. Edwards to Charles Scott, August 4, 1812, Folder 1, Ninian Edwards Papers (SC 447), ALPL; M[artin] D. Hardin to Edwards, May 25, 1813, in Edwards,

History of Illinois, 100; Bickham, *Weight of Vengeance*, 113–14, 137; Prucha, *The Great Father*, 78; Sugden, *Tecumseh*, 294–306; Taylor, *Civil War of 1812*, 150–51; and Willig, *Restoring the Chain of Friendship*, 244.

73. Harrison to Eustis, August 12, 1812, in *Territorial Papers*, ed. Carter, 8:190–91.

74. Edwards, address to the Territorial Legislature, November/December [undated] 1812, in Edwards, *History of Illinois*, 81, 83; Edwards to Isaac Shelby, February 16, 1813, Folder 1, Ninian Edwards Papers (SC 447), ALPL; Shadrach Bond to Edwards, February 7, 1813; February 25, 1813; and February 12, 1814, all in *The Edwards Papers: Being a Portion of the Collection of the Letters, Papers, and Manuscripts of Ninian Edwards*, ed. E. B. Washburne, 94, 97, 109.

75. Beverley W. Bond, Jr., "William Henry Harrison in the War of 1812," 501–02, 510; Owens, *Mr. Jefferson's Hammer*, 223–27, 283n; William Sterne Randall, *Unshackling America: How the War of 1812 Truly Ended the American Revolution*, 252; J. C. A. Stagg, *Mr. Madison's War: Politics, Diplomacy, and Warfare in the Early American Republic, 1783–1830*, 213; and Taylor, *Civil War of 1812*, 242–43.

76. Bickham, *Weight of Vengeance*, 231; Bond, "William Henry Harrison," 503; Randall, *Unshackling America*, 276–77; Stagg, *Mr. Madison's War*, 328–30; Sugden, *Tecumseh*, 372–75; and Taylor, *Civil War of 1812*, 244–46.

77. "A Treaty of Peace and Friendship between the United States of America and the Tribes of Indians called the Wyandots, Delawares, Shawanese, Senecas, and Miamies," in *ASP:IA*, 1:826; Harrison to Johnston, October 25, 1813, quoted in Hill, *John Johnston*, 75; Johnston, "Recollections of Sixty Years," in Hill, *John Johnston*, 168–69.

78. Nichols, *Red Gentlemen & White Savages*, 199.

79. Haeger, "The American Fur Company," 125, 129; Prucha, *The Great Father*, 83–84; and Taylor, *Civil War of 1812*, 429, 435.

80. Haeger, "The American Fur Company," 124, 124n; Matthew Irwin to Thomas L. McKenney, March 10, 1817, in "The Fur Trade and Factory System at Green Bay 1816–21," ed. Reuben Gold Thwaites, *Report and Collections of the State Historical Society of Wisconsin* VII (1873–1876): 270; Irwin to McKenney, June 18, 1818, and August 10, 1818, in "The Fur Trade and Factory System," ed. Thwaites, 276. For more on Prairie du Chien's short-lived successes, see Nichols, *Engines of Diplomacy*, 141–44.

81. Irwin to McKenney, ca. 1819; Irwin to McKenney, [1819]; and Irwin to McKenney, February 15, 1820, in "The Fur Trade and Factory System," ed. Thwaites,278, 279; Jedidiah Morse, 1820, in "The Fur Trade and Factory System," ed. Thwaites, 283; Haeger, "The American Fur Company," 123; and Prucha, *The Great Father*, 126, 134.

82. Irwin to McKenney, September 29, 1817, in "The Fur Trade and Factory System," ed. Thwaites, 275; and Morse, 1820, in "The Fur Trade and Factory System," ed. Thwaites, 285; and Nichols, *Engines of Diplomacy*, 1.

83. "Petition to Congress by Citizens of the Territory," June 15, 1812, in *Territorial Papers*, ed. Carter, 8:184; Rohrbough, *Land Office Business*, 58; and Treat,

National Land System, 407. To be exact, Jeffersonville's sales of over 35,000 acres in 1810–1811 and in 1811–1812 slipped to 31,655 in 1812–1813.

84. Michael Jones and Shadrach Bond to Edward Tiffin, October 28, 1814, quoted in Rohrbough, *Land Office Business*, 60; Benjamin Parke to James Brown, November 23, 1813, Box 1, Folder 11, Albert Gallatin Porter Collection, IHS; Rohrbough, *Land Office Business*, 61, 63; and Treat, *National Land System*, 407–08.

85. Rohrbough, *Land Office Business*, 92–93, 131; and Treat, *National Land System*, 408–10. Treat's figures from the Jeffersonville and Vincennes offices in Indiana and the Edwardsville, Kaskaskia, and Shawneetown offices in Illinois show a total of 2,282,134 acres sold from 1814 to 1819, and Indiana accounted for 1,296,328 acres in all.

86. "An Act to Enable the People of the Illinois Territory to Form a Constitution and State Government," April 18, 1818, in *United States Statutes at Large*, 3:428–31; Barnhart and Riker, *Indiana to 1816*, 361, 427; Cayton, *Frontier Indiana*, 252, 258, 267; and James E. Davis, *Frontier Illinois*, 155–63. For a detailed narrative of the convention and analysis of the Indiana Constitution of 1816, see Barnhart and Riker, *Indiana to 1816*, 439–60.

87. Indiana Constitution of 1816, art. IX, sec. 1–2, 5.

88. Indiana Constitution of 1816, art. X; and Illinois Constitution of 1818, art. VIII, sec. 21.

89. William E. Bartelt, "The Land Dealings of Spencer County, Indiana, Pioneer Thomas Lincoln," 211; Lowell H. Harrison, *Lincoln of Kentucky*, 23; Tachau, *Federal Courts in the Early Republic, 1789–1816*, 167, 175; and Louis A. Warren, *Lincoln's Youth: Indiana Years, 1816–1830*, 12–13. Warren laid out Thomas Lincoln's struggles, noting he ultimately held onto only 200 of the 816.5 acres he purchased in Kentucky.

90. Bartelt, "The Land Dealings," 213, 218–21; David Herbert Donald, *Lincoln*, 24; and Harrison, *Lincoln of Kentucky*, 28.

91. Morris Birkbeck, Letter XV, February 24, 1818, in *Letters from Illinois*, 67.

92. Flower, diary entry, Oct. 12, 1816, Oversize BV1, Flower Family Papers, ALPL.

93. Joshua Meigs to Henry Eddy, August 28, 1819, Box 1, Folder 1, Henry Eddy Papers, ALPL; and Treat, *National Land System*, 410–11.

94. John Dumont, speech at Vevay, July 4, 1817, Box 1, Folder 14, Harlow Lindley Collection, IHS.

Chapter Five: "Our Strength Is Our Union"

1. Ohio House Journal, 1810–1811, 42–43.

2. Ohio House Journal, 1810–1811, 45; Jeffrey Paul Brown, "Frontier Politics: The Evolution of a Political Society in Ohio, 1788–1814," 305; and Andrew R. L. Cayton, *The Frontier Republic: Ideology and Politics in the Ohio Country, 1780–1825*, 88.

3. "Ohio 1807 Governor," NNV, https://elections.lib.tufts.edu/catalog/02870v887 (last accessed January 29, 2011). According to Philip Lampi's tabulations, Meigs

won 115 votes in Marietta while competitors received none, and 225 Cincinnatians voted for him while only 76 voted for competitor Nathaniel Massie. Meanwhile, Athens County voted for Meigs by a 134–2 margin, and Trumbull County residents, many of them from Connecticut, preferred Meigs over Massie by a tally of 879–62. For more detailed accounts of the controversy surrounding Meigs's eligibility for office during the 1807 election, see also Brown, "Frontier Politics," 347–48; and Cayton, *Frontier Republic*, 99–100.

4. Ohio House Journal, 1810–1811, 44–45; and Ohio House Journal, 1811–1812, 10–11.

5. Brown, "Frontier Politics," 305; Cayton, *Frontier Republic*, 79; Ronald P. Formisano, "Federalists and Republicans: Parties, Yes—System, No," 39 [table]; and Donald J. Ratcliffe, *Party Spirit in a Frontier Republic: Democratic Politics in Ohio, 1793–1821*, 138. Brown's chapter title even declared early Ohio a one-party state.

6. Formisano, "Federalists and Republicans," 35. For similar definitions, see especially Philip J. Lampi, "The Federalist Party Resurgence, 1808–1816: Evidence from the New Nation Votes Database," 256–57; Jeffrey L. Pasley, "The Cheese and the Words: Popular Political Culture and Participatory Democracy in the Early American Republic," in *Beyond the Founders: New Approaches to the Political History of the Early American Republic*, ed. Jeffrey L. Pasley, Andrew W. Robertson, and David Waldstreicher, 39; and David Waldstreicher, *In the Midst of Perpetual Fetes: The Making of American Nationalism, 1776–1820*, 11–12.

7. Ratcliffe, *Party Spirit*, 122.

8. "Ohio 1803 Governor," NNV, https://elections.lib.tufts.edu/catalog/z316q161n (last accessed February 21, 2011). Overall, Tiffin picked up 5,377 votes, and he was the unanimous choice of Belmont, Clermont, and Jefferson Counties. In addition to St. Clair and Gilman, Bezaleel Wells received 89 votes in Fairfield County while Ohio Company members and Marietta residents Rufus Putnam and Paul Fearing picked up three and one, respectively.

9. Brown, "Frontier Politics," 316; and William T. Utter, "Ohio Politics and Politicians, 1802–1815," 30, 42. Brown and Utter listed Ohio Senators Bezaleel Wells and Zenas Kimberly as well as Representatives Rudolph Blair, Zacheus A. Beatty, Thomas Elliot, and Isaac Meeks among the Federalists of the first session of the General Assembly.

10. *New-York Evening Post*, February 8, 1803; Sean M. Theriault, "Party Politics during the Louisiana Purchase," 297, 302–03; and Betty Houchin Winfield, "Public Perception and Public Events: The Louisiana Purchase and the American Partisan Press," in *The Louisiana Purchase: Emergence of an American Nation*, ed. Peter J. Kastor, 43.

11. *AC*, 7th Cong., 2nd sess., 95–96, 113.

12. *New-York Evening Post*, March 17 and March 22, 1803.

13. Jerry W. Knudson, *Jefferson and the Press: Crucible of Liberty*, 88, 98–99; and Winfield, "Public Perception," in *The Louisiana Purchase*, ed., Kastor, 44–45. Federalist newspapers also claimed $15 million was an outrageous price to restore American trading rights at New Orleans.

14. *Columbian Centinel* (Boston), July 2 and July 13, 1803; Knudson, *Jefferson and the Press*, 96; and John R. Van Atta, *Securing the West: Politics, Public Lands, and the Fate of the Old Republic, 1785–1840*, 72.

15. *Columbian Centinel* (Boston), July 16, 1803.

16. *New-York Evening Post*, July 5, 1803; and Winfield, "Public Perception," in *The Louisiana Purchase*, ed., Kastor, 48.

17. *Scioto Gazette* (Chillicothe, OH), October 1, 1803; and Samuel Huntington to Thomas Worthington, October 3, 1803, quoted in Utter, "Ohio Politics and Politicians," 44.

18. Ohio House Journal, 1803–1804, 36–37, 39; and Jeffrey P. Brown, "The Political Culture of Early Ohio," in *The Pursuit of Public Power: Political Culture in Ohio, 1787–1861*, ed. Jeffrey P. Brown and Andrew R. L. Cayton, 13.

19. *Trenton Federalist*, May 4, 1807; S. P. Hildreth, *Biographical and Historical Memoirs of the Early Pioneer Settlers of Ohio, with Narratives of Incidents and Occurrences in 1775*, 310; and Brown, "Frontier Politics," 312–14.

20. Ratcliffe, *Party Spirit*, 77–78, 95.

21. Julia Perkins Cutler, *Life and Times of Ephraim Cutler: Prepared from His Journals and Correspondence*, 84–85.

22. "An Act Establishing an University in the Town of Athens," in Ohio University, *Resolutions and Acts Passed by the Ohio and Territorial Legislatures, Relative to the Ohio University, at Athens*, 5–6; "An Act Establishing an University in the Town of Athens," December 18, 1804, in Ohio University, *Resolutions and Acts Passed*, 12–13; Cutler, *Ephraim Cutler*, 177; Thomas N. Hoover, *The History of Ohio University*, 17–18; and William E. Peters, *Legal History of the Ohio University, Athens, Ohio*, 88–89. Hoover and Peters reported the date as February 18, and Ohio University calls February 18 its founding date. The December date in *Resolutions and Acts* seems to be a misprint.

23. Cutler, *Ephraim Cutler*, 177; Hoover, *History of Ohio University*, 24; R. Douglas Hurt, *The Ohio Frontier: Crucible of the Old Northwest, 1720–1830*, 386; and Peters, *Legal History*, 89, 113.

24. "An Act Establishing an University in the Town of Athens," in Ohio University, *Resolutions and Acts Passed*, 5–6, 12; and Craig Bruce Smith, *American Honor: The Creation of the Nation's Ideals during the Revolutionary Era*, 49, 57.

25. Brown, "Frontier Politics," 312; and Hoover, *History of Ohio University*, 21–23, 27–28.

26. Cutler, *Ephraim Cutler*, 88; Sarah J. Cutler, "The Coonskin Library," 59, 68; and John B. Nicholson, Jr., "'The Coonskin Library': A Legend of Books in the Wilderness," 6.

27. Clement L. Martzolff, ed., "The Autobiography of Thomas Ewing," 141, 150–51, 161.

28. Kim M. Gruenwald, *River of Enterprise: The Commercial Origins of Regional Identity in the Ohio Valley, 1790–1850*, 49; Hurt, *Ohio Frontier*, 217, 259.

29. *Columbian Centinel* (Boston), February 16, 1803; Samuel P. Hildreth, "Ships Built at Marietta, 1800–1806," vol. 2, item 33, Samuel P. Hildreth Collection,

Marietta College Library, Marietta, Ohio; Hurt, *Ohio Frontier*, 213; François André Michaux, "Travels to the West," in *Early Western Travels, 1748–1846*, ed. Reuben Gold Thwaites, 3:177.

30. *Trenton Federalist* (New Jersey), May 4, 1807; Hildreth, "Ships Built at Marietta, 1800–1806," vol. 2, item 33, Samuel P. Hildreth Collection, Marietta College Library, Marietta, Ohio; and Michaux, "Travels to the West," in *Early Western Travels*, ed. Thwaites, 3:177.

31. Cutler, *Ephraim Cutler*, 89–90; and Hurt, *Ohio Frontier*, 243–45.

32. Charles Sellers, *The Market Revolution: Jacksonian America, 1815–1846*, 19. Sellers centered government promotion of economic growth as a key element of emerging market economies.

33. Brown, "Frontier Politics," 306; and Gruenwald, *River of Enterprise*, 81–83, 88–90.

34. Andrew Gregg, "Credit on Public Lands," April 5, 1806, in *ASP:PL*, 1:265; Gruenwald, *River of Enterprise*, 83; Malcolm J. Rohrbough, *The Land Office Business: The Settlement and Administration of American Public Lands, 1789-1837*, 30; and Payson Jackson Treat, *The National Land System, 1785–1820*, 406.

35. *AC*, 7th Cong., 2nd sess., 85; *Washington Federalist* (DC), April 2, 1806; William H. Bergmann, *The American National State and the Early West*, 151; Ernest Ludlow Bogart, *Financial History of Ohio*, 20–21; Hurt, *Ohio Frontier*, 222, 255, 257; John Lauritz Larson, *Internal Improvement: National Public Works and the Promise of Popular Government in the Early United States*, 55–56; and Sellers, *Market Revolution*, 32.

36. *AC*, 9th Cong., 2nd sess., 88–92, 95; and Ernest Ludlow Bogart, *Internal Improvements and the State Debt in Ohio*, 12.

37. *Journal of the House of Representatives of the Territory of the United States, Northwest of the Ohio*, 2nd General Assembly, 1st sess., 14–15.

38. "An Act Providing for the Inspection of Certain Articles of Exportation Therein Enumerated," January 9, 1802, in *The Statutes of Ohio and of the Northwestern Territory*, ed. Salmon P. Chase, 1:333; and *Journal of the House of Representatives of the Territory of the United States, North-west of the Ohio*, 2nd General Assembly, 1st sess., 16, 131.

39. "An Act Providing for the Inspection of Certain Articles of Exportation Therein Enumerated," January 9, 1802, in *The Statutes of Ohio*, ed. Chase, 1:334.

40. "An Act for the Inspection of Certain Articles of Exportation Therein Enumerated," February 20, 1805, in *The Statutes of Ohio*, ed. Chase 1:474–76; "An Act for the Incorporation of Manufacturing Companies," January 11, 1812, in *The Statutes of Ohio*, ed. Chase, 2:764–66; "An Act to Amend the Act for the Inspection of Certain Articles of Exportation Therein Enumerated," January 15, 1812, in *The Statutes of Ohio*, ed. Chase, 2:766; and Bogart, *Financial History of Ohio*, 22.

41. Putnam to John May, May 7, 1808, in Elbert Jay Benton, ed., "Side Lights on the Ohio Company of Associates from the John May Papers," 202; R. Carlyle Buley, *The Old Northwest: Pioneer Period, 1815–1840*, 1:107; Donald R. Hickey, *The War of 1812: A Forgotten Conflict*, 21; William Sterne Randall, *Unshackling*

America: How the War of 1812 Truly Ended the American Revolution, 134; Ratcliffe, *Party Spirit*, 141; and George Rogers Taylor, "Agrarian Discontent in the Mississippi Valley Preceding the War of 1812," in *The Old Northwest: Studies in Regional History, 1787–1910*, ed. Harry N. Scheiber, 36, 41–42, 51.

42. Gruenwald, *River of Enterprise*, 84; William Rufus Putnam to May, September 22, 1808, in Benton, "Side Lights on the Ohio Company," 203; and Taylor, "Agrarian Discontent in the Mississippi Valley," in *The Old Northwest*, ed. Scheiber, 30, 42.

43. *Acts of Ohio*, Seventh General Assembly, 1st sess., 223–24; *Dayton Repertory* (Ohio), December 14, 1809; and *Pittsburgh Gazette*, March 8, 1808.

44. Lampi, "Federalist Party Resurgence," 256, 259; Ratcliffe, *Party Spirit*, 140–43; and Sellers, *Market Revolution*, 37.

45. Brown, "Frontier Politics," 403; Jeffrey P. Brown, "The Ohio Federalists, 1803–1815," 266–67, 271–73; Lampi, "Federalist Party Resurgence," 273; and Douglas C. McMurtrie, *Early Printing in Dayton, Ohio*, 14–17.

46. *Pittsburgh Gazette*, August 11, 1807, and February 2 and March 8, 1808.

47. *Pittsburgh Gazette*, August 11, 1807, and March 1 and 8, 1808. For more on Federalist defense policy, see Donald R. Hickey, "Federalist Defense Policy in the Age of Jefferson, 1801–1812," 64–67.

48. "Ohio 1808 Electoral College," NNV, https://elections.lib.tufts.edu/catalog /ms35t9448 (last accessed April 26, 2011); https://elections.lib.tufts.edu/catalog /p5547s070; "Ohio 1808 U.S. House of Representatives," NNV, (last accessed July 3, 2019); Brown, "The Ohio Federalists," 264; and Cayton, *The Frontier Republic*, 96.

49. *New-York Evening Post*, September 12 and December 10, 1808; Brown, "The Ohio Federalists," 267–68. For more on the Jeffersonian Republican schism, see especially Cayton, *Frontier Republic*, 95–109.

50. Ohio House Journal, 1808–1809, 43; and Ohio House Journal, 1809–1810, 28.

51. Ohio House Journal, 1808–1809, 43; Ohio House Journal, 1809–1810, 45; Ohio House Journal, 1811–1812, 13; and Ohio Historical Society, *History of the Ohio Canals: Their Construction, Cost, Use and Partial Abandonment*, 9.

52. *Chillicothe Supporter*, September 22, 1810; *Ohio Centinel* (Dayton), October 4, 1810; "Ohio 1810 Governor," NNV, https://elections.lib.tufts.edu/catalog /qb98mg259 (last accessed January 29, 2011); and Brown, "The Ohio Federalists," 273.

53. Raymond W. Champagne, Jr. and Thomas J. Reuter, "Jonathan Roberts and the 'War Hawk' Congress of 1811–1812," 447; George Dangerfield, *The Era of Good Feelings*, 86–88, 98; Donald R. Hickey, "Federalist Party Unity and the War of 1812," 24–26, 38; Hickey, "Federalist Defense Policy," 64; Hickey, *War of 1812*, 53, 255; Merrill, D. Peterson, *The Great Triumvirate: Webster, Clay, and Calhoun*, 4–5, 44; and J. C. A. Stagg, *Mr. Madison's War: Politics, Diplomacy, and Warfare in the Early American Republic, 1783–1830*, 90–91, 111–14.

54. Stagg, *Mr. Madison's War*, 114. For a more detailed discussion of Worthington's stance on the War of 1812, see Alfred Byron Sears, *Thomas Worthington, Father of Ohio Statehood*, 159–74.

55. R. Douglas Hurt, "The Firelands: Land Speculation and the War of 1812," in *The Sixty Years' War for the Great Lakes, 1754–1814*, ed. David Curtis Skaggs and Larry L. Nelson, 305, 311–13; Ratcliffe, *Party Spirit*, 171; and Alan Taylor, *The Civil War of 1812: American Citizens, British Subjects, Irish Rebels, & Indian Allies*, 204.

56. *Niles' Weekly Register* (Baltimore), January 18, 1812; Brown, "Frontier Politics," 397; and Ratcliffe, *Party Spirit*, 172. The Register was misdated 1811 on its front page.

57. *Chillicothe Supporter* (Ohio), July 4, 1812; *Cincinnati Whig*, May 4, 1809; Brown, "The Ohio Federalists," 277; and Ratcliffe, *Party Spirit*, 171–73.

58. Bergmann, *American National State*, 243; Hickey, *War of 1812*, 117; Hurt, *Ohio Frontier*, 344; and Ratcliffe, *Party Spirit*, 203.

59. Brown, "The Ohio Federalists," 275; Ratcliffe, *Party Spirit*, 179; and Barbara Jo Triplett, "A Biography of Charles Hammond," 32.

60. *Greensburgh and Indiana Register* (Indiana, PA), August 6, 1812; and Martzolff, ed., "Autobiography of Thomas Ewing," 157–58.

61. "Ohio 1812 Electoral College," NNV, https://elections.lib.tufts.edu/catalog/r207tq33w (last accessed May 2, 2011); "Ohio 1812 Governor," A New Nation Votes: American Election Returns, 1787–1825, https://elections.lib.tufts.edu/catalog/fx719n30c (last accessed May 2, 2011); Brown, "The Ohio Federalists," 277; Hickey, *War of 1812*, 101; Lampi, "Federalist Party Resurgence," 267, 272; and Stagg, *Mr. Madison's War*, 83.

62. *Freeman's Chronicle* (Franklinton, OH), September 5, 1812.

63. Brown, "Frontier Politics," 406; and Francis Phelps Weisenburger, "A Life of Charles Hammond: The First Great Journalist of the Old Northwest," 344–46.

64. *Ohio Federalist* (St. Clairsville, OH), April 13 and August 24, 1814.

65. James Murray Murdoch, "Charles Hammond: Egalitarian-Whig: An Analysis of the Political Philosophy of a Federalist-Whig Editor and Its Implications Concerning the Traditional Concept of Jacksonian Democracy," 75.

66. *Ohio Federalist* (St. Clairsville, OH), April 13 and June 15, 1814.

67. *Ohio Federalist* (St. Clairsville, OH), September 15, 1813 and May 18, 1814; and Murdoch, "Charles Hammond," 30–33. For more on immigrant Republican editors, see Michael Durey, "Thomas Paine's Apostles: Radical Emigrés and the Triumph of Jeffersonian Republicanism," 662–88.

68. *Ohio Federalist* (St. Clairsville, OH), September 29, 1813 and May 18 and August 24, 1814; Brown, "Frontier Politics," 407; Murdoch, "Charles Hammond," 16, 46; and Ratcliffe, *Party Spirit*, 191–94.

69. *Ohio Federalist* (St. Clairsville, OH), June 15 and August 24, 1814. Emphasis in the original.

70. *Ohio Federalist* (St. Clairsville, OH), July 27, 1814; and Murdoch, "Charles Hammond," 24–26.

71. "Ohio 1813 State Senate, Belmont County," NNV, https://elections.lib.tufts.edu/catalog/f7623d498 (last accessed May 7, 2011); Brown, "Frontier Politics," 407; Lampi, "Federalist Party Resurgence," 273; and Triplett, "Biography of Charles Hammond," 37–39. Triplett claimed a 67-vote margin for Hammond, but the tabulations collected by Philip Lampi revealed a closer election of 738 votes for Hammond against 709 for opponent Joseph Sharp. According to Brown, the margin of Republican victory in the U.S. House elections in the district shrank from 200 to 53 between 1812 and 1814.

72. *Cincinnati National Republican*, February 13, 1827, quoted in Murdoch, "Charles Hammond," 55; and Ratcliffe, *Party Spirit*, 200.

73. *Ohio Federalist* (St. Clairsville, OH), March 2, 9, and 30, 1815; and Cutler, *Ephraim Cutler*, 107.

74. *Ohio Federalist* (St. Clairsville, OH), March 23, 1815.

Chapter Six: From Frontier Federalists to Western Whigs

1. *National Gazette* (Philadelphia), July 12, 1825; *Columbian Centinel* (Boston), July 23, 1825; *Daily National Intelligencer* (Washington, D.C.), July 18, 1825; and Caleb Atwater, *A History of the State of Ohio, Natural and Civil*, 266. Atwater wrote the July 4 crowd "amounted to many thousands," while accounts in the *Centinel* claimed at least 5,000, and the *National Intelligencer* stated 8,000 were present.

2. Atwater, *History of the State of Ohio*, 266; and DeWitt Clinton, address on July 4, 1825, in *Trumpets of Glory: Fourth of July Orations, 1786–1861*, ed. Henry A. Hawken, 119–20.

3. Atwater, *History of the State of Ohio*, 267–68; and *Daily National Intelligencer* (Washington, D.C.), July 18, 1825.

4. *National Aegis* (Worcester, MA), July 6, 1825; *Daily National Intelligencer* (Washington, D.C.), July 20, 1825; and *Norwich Courier* (CT), July 27, 1825.

5. Daniel Walker Howe, *What Hath God Wrought: The Transformation of America, 1815–1848*, 5; and Charles Sellers, *The Market Revolution: Jacksonian America, 1815–1846*, 100.

6. For a similar claim, see Michael F. Holt, *The Rise and Fall of the American Whig Party: Jacksonian Politics and the Onset of the Civil War*, 7.

7. For claims that Ohio Federalists were hopeless in their endeavors after 1815, see Jeffrey P. Brown, "Frontier Politics: The Evolution of a Political Society in Ohio, 1788–1814," 411; R. Carlyle Buley, *The Old Northwest: Pioneer Period, 1815–1840*, 2:8; Andrew R. L. Cayton, *The Frontier Republic: Ideology and Politics in the Ohio Country, 1780–1825*, 80, 129; Donald J. Ratcliffe, *Party Spirit in a Frontier Republic: Democratic Politics in Ohio, 1793–1821*, 206–07; and Donald J. Ratcliffe, *The Politics of Long Division: The Birth of the Second Party System in Ohio, 1818–1828*, 19.

8. Buley, *Old Northwest*, 1:125; Cayton, *Frontier Republic*, 112; Ratcliffe, *Politics of Long Division*, 27–28, 32; and Payson Jackson Treat, *The National Land System, 1785–1820*, 407–08. By Buley's figures, land sales north of the Ohio rose from 823,264 acres in 1814 to 2,064,177 acres in 1819.

9. Buley, *Old Northwest*, 1:532–33; Cayton, *Frontier Republic*, 113; R. Douglas Hurt, *The Ohio Frontier: Crucible of the Old Northwest, 1720–1830*, 348; and Ratcliffe, *Politics of Long Division*, 28.

10. Jacob Burnet, *Notes on the Early Settlement of the North-western Territory*, 406–07; Buley, *Old Northwest*, 1:123; Edward S. Kaplan, *The Bank of the United States and the American Economy*, 57; and Ratcliffe, *Politics of Long Division*, 33.

11. For more on the genesis of the Panic of 1819, see Daniel S. Dupre, "The Panic of 1819 and the Political Economy of Sectionalism," in *The Economy of Early America: Historical Perspectives and New Directions*, ed. Cathy Matson, 270–72; Kaplan, *Bank of the United States*, 67–71; and Murray N. Rothbard, *The Panic of 1819: Reactions and Policies*, 1–21.

12. Duncan McArthur to James McDonald, January 24, 1820, Duncan McArthur Papers (VFM 3018), OHS; John C. Short to William Short, November 11, 1818, quoted in Ratcliffe, *Politics of Long Division*, 33; Atwater, *History of the State of Ohio*, 246; John Lauritz Larson, *The Market Revolution in America: Liberty, Ambition, and the Eclipse of the Common Good*, 41; Ratcliffe, *Party Spirit*, 224.

13. Cayton, *Frontier Republic*, 130; Ernest Ludlow Bogart, *Internal Improvements and the State Debt in Ohio*, 14; Ratcliffe, *Party Spirit*, 225–26; and Ratcliffe, *Politics of Long Division*, 35–36.

14. Ohio House Journal, 1819–1820, 11–12, 201.

15. Edward Tiffin, "Rough Draft of a Letter to the Secretary of the Treasury, from the Surveyor General of the United States," June 25, 1818, Edward Tiffin Collection (SC 1541), ALPL; and Philemon Beecher to E. A. Brown, January 22, 1819, Box 7, Folder 2, William Henry Smith Papers (MSS 2), OHS.

16. Duncan McArthur to "Citizens of the Counties of Ross, Pickaway, Fayette and Hocking," June 14, 1824, Duncan McArthur Papers (VFM 3018), OHS; Atwater, *History of the State of Ohio*, 245; and Hurt, *Ohio Frontier*, 373–74.

17. Clinton to Brown, April 21, 1821; March 4, 1822; May 11, 1822; and March 18, 1823, Box 7, Folder 1, William Henry Smith Papers (MSS 2), OHS; and Howe, *What Hath God Wrought*, 218.

18. Atwater, *History of the State of Ohio*, 249–50; Buley, *Old Northwest*, 1:422; Howe, *What Hath God Wrought*, 214; Larson, *The Market Revolution in America*, 55; and Sellers, *Market Revolution*, 132.

19. Allen Trimble, "Autobiography of Allen Trimble," in *Autobiography and Correspondence of Allen Trimble, Governor of Ohio*, 65–68, 80, 99; and Ratcliffe, *Party Spirit*, 238.

20. "An Act, Respecting a Navigable Communication between Lake Erie and the Ohio River," February 23, 1820, in *The Statutes of Ohio*, ed. Salmon P. Chase, 2:1131–32; Clinton to Brown, May 11, 1822, Box 7, Folder 1, William Henry Smith Papers (MSS 2), OHS; Trimble, "Autobiography of Allen Trimble," 100; William A. Trimble to Allen Trimble, February 12, 1820, in Trimble, *Autobiography and Correspondence of Allen Trimble*, 118; and Harry N. Scheiber, *Ohio Canal Era: A Case Study of Government and the Economy, 1820–1861*, 15–29.

21. Trimble, "Inaugural Address of Gov. Allen Trimble," [January 3] 1822, in *Autobiography and Correspondence of Allen Trimble*, 124.

22. "An Act Authorizing an Examination into the Practicability of Connecting Lake Erie with the Ohio River by a Canal," January 31, 1822 [misdated 1832], in *The Statutes of Ohio*, ed. Chase, 2:1220 ; "Ohio 1822 Governor," NNV, https://elections.lib.tufts.edu/catalog/47429b07v (last accessed November 12, 2011); and Ratcliffe, *Politics of Long Division*, 66. Jeremiah Morrow defeated Trimble by a tally of 27,430–24,361, but as Ratcliffe claims, Trimble only lost because the third candidate, William W. Irwin, siphoned away crucial votes in the Scioto valley.

23. Atwater, *History of the State of Ohio*, 254–55; Julia Perkins Cutler, *The Life and Times of Ephraim Cutler: Prepared from His Journals and Correspondence*, 129; Trimble, "Inaugural Address of Gov. Allen Trimble," [January 3] 1822, in *Autobiography and Correspondence of Allen Trimble*, 126; Cayton, *Frontier Republic*, 142, 145; and Clement L. Martzolff, "Caleb Atwater," 256.

24. *Western Spy* (Cincinnati), August 15, 1818, and July 17, 1819; Hurt, *Ohio Frontier*, 267–68; and Martzolff, "Caleb Atwater," 250.

25. Atwater, *History of the State of Ohio*, 262; Ernest Ludlow Bogart, *Financial History of Ohio*, 202; Cutler, *Ephraim Cutler*, 121; and Ratcliffe, *Politics of Long Division*, 68.

26. Holt, *Rise and Fall*, 12.

27. Cayton, *Frontier Indiana*, 252, 267; James E. Davis, *Frontier Illinois*, 204–05; and Josiah Meigs to Henry Eddy, August 28, 1819 (transcription), Box 1, Folder 1, Henry Eddy Papers, ALPL.

28. *AC*, 14th Cong., 2nd sess., 43; "An Act Providing for the Division of Certain Quarter Sections, in Future Sales of the Public Lands," February 22, 1817, in *United States Statutes at Large*, 3:346; and *House Journal*, 15th Cong., 1st sess., 18, 188; 16th Cong., 1st sess., 19; 17th Cong., 1st sess., 9; and Ruth Esther Amos, "The Noble Brothers and Early Public Internal Improvements in Indiana," 12–19.

29. Jonathan Jennings, "Jennings to His Constituents," June 28, 1823, in *Governors Messages and Letters: Messages and Papers of Jonathan Jennings, Ratliff Boon, William Hendricks, 1816-1825*, ed. Logan Esarey, 266.

30. Ninian Edwards to unnamed, September 10, 1818, Folder 2, Ninian Edwards Collection (SC 447), ALPL.

31. Ninian W. Edwards, *History of Illinois, from 1778 to 1833; and Life and Times of Ninian Edwards*, 132.

32. Illinois House Journal, 1st General Assembly, 1st sess. (October 6, 1818), 9–10; Larson, *Internal Improvement*, 71, 110; and Sellers, *Market Revolution*, 72.

33. Jennings, "Regular Message," December 2, 1817, and "Regular Message," December 9, 1818, in *Governors Messages and Letters*, ed. Esarey, 41, 66–67. Jennings estimated that a few years of saving up the three-percent fund would yield $30,000 annually for state transportation projects.

34. *AC*, 15th Cong., 1st sess., 1113–14; and "An Enabling Bill," April 1, 1816, in *Territorial Papers of the United States*, ed. Clarence E. Carter, 7:407.

35. William Hendricks, "Circular Relating to the 15th Congress, 1st Session," March 17, 1818, in "William Hendricks' Political Circulars to His Constituents:

Congressional Period, 1816–1822," ed. Frederick D. Hill, 322–23; and Hendricks, "Circular Relating to the 17th Congress, 1st Session," April 16, 1822, in "William Hendricks' Political Circulars," ed. Hill, 340–41; and *House Journal*, 15th Cong., 2nd sess., 54, 80, 200, 289.

36. *Register of Debates*, Senate, 19th Congress, 1st sess., 690; Amos, "The Noble Brothers," 20–24; and Clement Eaton, *Henry Clay and the Art of American Politics*, 36–37.

37. Journal of the House of Representatives of the State of Indiana, 1st sess., 10–11.

38. "An Act to Enable the People of the Illinois Territory to Form a Constitution and State Government," April 18, 1818, in *United States Statutes at Large*, 3:430; Illinois House Journal, 1st General Assembly, 1st sess. (October 6, 1818), 8–9; and W. G. Walker, "The Development of the Free Public High School in Illinois during the Nineteenth Century," 267.

39. Donald F. Carmony, *Indiana, 1816–1850: The Pioneer Era*, 364–66; and Otho Lionel Newman, "Development of Common Schools of Indiana to 1851," 235–37, 239–41.

40. Judge Hall to Henry Eddy, November 30, 1824, Box 1, Folder 2, Henry Eddy Papers, ALPL; Davis, *Frontier Illinois*, 172; and E. B. Washburne, *Sketch of Edward Coles, Second Governor of Illinois, and of the Slavery Struggle of 1823–4*, 231.

41. Edwards, *History of Illinois*, 104, 132; and Elizabeth Duncan Putnam, "The Life and Services of Joseph Duncan, Governor of Illinois, 1834–1838," 117–18.

42. Larson, *Internal Improvement*, 118, 146; and Sellers, *The Market Revolution*, 73, 80.

43. Ninian Edwards to Eddy, November 22, 1822, (transcription), Box 1, Folder 1, Henry Eddy Papers, ALPL; Hendricks, "Circular Relating to the 16th Congress, 1st Session," April 10, 1820, in "William Hendricks' Political Circulars to His Constituents," ed. Hill, 335; Jennings, "Jennings to His Constituents," April 7, 1823, in *Governors Messages and Letters*, ed. Esarey, 262; and Jennings, "Jennings to His Constituents," June 28, 1823, in *Governors Messages and Letters*, ed. Esarey, 267.

44. W. T. Barry et al. ("Committee of Correspondence" for Society for Domestic Manufactures), circular letter, November 10, 1817, Folder 1, Beatty-Quisenberry Family Papers (MSS A B369), FHS; and Richard Flower to Robert Barnard, January 12, 1825, Box 1, Folder 1, Flower Family Papers, ALPL.

45. Eaton, *Henry Clay*, 20; Robert V. Remini, *Henry Clay: Statesman for the Union*, 57, 61; and Harlow Giles Unger, *Henry Clay: America's Greatest Statesman*, 81, 99.

46. Henry Clay, "On Domestic Manufactures," April 6, 1810, in *The Life and Speeches of the Hon. Henry Clay*, ed. Daniel Mallory, 1:252.

47. Clay to Peter B. Porter, April 14, 1822, Box 7, Folder 3, William Henry Smith Papers (MSS 2), OHS; Buley, *Old Northwest*, 1:499; Eaton, *Henry Clay*, 34–37; Remini, *Henry Clay*, 219, 225–28; and Sellers, *Market Revolution*, 100.

48. Michael Lind, *What Lincoln Believed: The Values and Convictions of America's Greatest President,* 73; and Remini, *Henry Clay*, 225.

49. Clay, "On American Industry," March 30–31, 1824, in *Hon. Henry Clay*, ed. Mallory, 1:443, 457; Freeman Cleaves, *Old Tippecanoe: William Henry Harrison and His Time*, 278; Ratcliffe, *Politics of Long Division*, 60–61; Merrill D. Peterson, *The Great Triumvirate: Webster, Clay, and Calhoun*, 69–71; and Remini, *Henry Clay*, 228, 232–33.

50. Clay, "On American Industry," March 30–31, 1824, in *Hon. Henry Clay*, ed. Mallory, 1:441, 457; Unger, *Henry Clay*, 107; and Harry L. Watson, *Liberty and Power: The Politics of Jacksonian America*, 243–44.

51. *Eastern Argus* (Portland, ME), December 2, 1823; Ratcliffe, *Politics of Long Division*, 57, 77–79; and Eugene H. Roseboom, "Ohio in the Presidential Election of 1824," 163–65.

52. *New-England Palladium & Commercial Advertiser* (Boston), January 7, 1820; Remini, *Henry Clay*, 212, 237; and Rothbard, *Panic of 1819*, 219.

53. *Steubenville Gazette* (OH), August 2, 1823.

54. James Murray Murdoch, "Charles Hammond: Egalitarian-Whig: An Analysis of the Political Philosophy of a Federalist-Whig Editor and Its Implications Concerning the Traditional Concept of Jacksonian Democracy," 131–32; Roseboom, "Ohio in the Presidential Election of 1824," 182, 194; and Barbara Jo Triplett, "A Biography of Charles Hammond," 73.

55. Carmony, *Indiana, 1816–1850*, 452, 463–64, 479–80; Ratcliffe, *Party Spirit*, 246; and Roseboom, "Ohio in the Presidential Election of 1824," 159, 207.

56. Carmony, *Indiana, 1816–1850*, 482; Cayton, *Frontier Republic*, 136; Howe, *What Hath God Wrought*, 208–10; Remini, *Henry Clay*, 248; Unger, *Henry Clay*, 109–10; and Francis P. Weisenburger, "A Life of Charles Hammond: The First Great Journalist of the Old Northwest," 370.

57. Beecher to Cutler, January 19, 1825, in Cutler, *Ephraim Cutler*, 193; *Liberty Hall and Cincinnati Gazette*, March 15, 1825; and Cayton, *Frontier Republic*, 136.

58. Atwater, *History of the State of Ohio*, 262; "Ohio 1824 Governor," NNV, https://elections.lib.tufts.edu/catalog/z029p480m (last accessed November 19, 2011); and Trimble, *Autobiography and Correspondence of Allen Trimble*, 116.

59. Jeremiah Morrow, *Governor's Message, to the General Assembly of Ohio, December 7, 1824*, 3–4, 8–9; and Cutler, *Ephraim Cutler*, 153–54.

60. *Liberty Hall and Cincinnati Gazette*, January 7 and 21, 1825.

61. "An Act Establishing an Equitable Mode of Levying the Taxes of This State," February 3, 1825, in *The Statutes of Ohio*, ed. Chase, 2:1476, 1478. The full act appears on 1476–92.

62. "An Act, to Provide for the Internal Improvement of the State of Ohio, by Navigable Canals," February 4, 1825, in *The Statutes of Ohio*, ed. Chase, 2:1472–76; and Bogart, *Internal Improvements*, 154.

63. "An Act, to Provide for the Support and Better Regulation of Common Schools," February 5, 1825, in *The Statutes of Ohio*, ed. Chase, 2:1466–67; Cayton, *Frontier Republic*, 146; and Cutler, *Ephraim Cutler*, 167, 171.

64. For a full account of Hammond's years in Cincinnati, see Weisenburger, "Life of Charles Hammond," 372–427.

65. Ohio Senate Journal, 1829–1830, 10–12; and Trimble, "Autobiography of Allen Trimble," in *Autobiography and Correspondence of Allen Trimble*, 103.

66. Burnet to W[yllys] Silliman, December 30, 1828, in Jacob Burnet Collection, OHS; and Trimble, "Autobiography of Allen Trimble," in *Autobiography and Correspondence of Allen Trimble*, 103.

67. *Sangamo Journal* (Springfield, IL), August 2, 1832.

68. Carmony, *Indiana, 1816–1850*, 147–48; Noah Noble, "Message to the General Assembly," December 3, 1833, in *Messages and Papers Relating to the Administration of Noah Noble, Governor of Indiana, 1831–1837*, ed. Dorothy Riker and Gayle Thornbrough, 204.

69. Noble, "Message to the General Assembly," December 2, 1834, in *Noah Noble*, ed. Riker and Thornbrough, 319; and Noble, "Inaugural Address to the General Assembly," December 3, 1834, in *Noah Noble*, ed. Riker and Thornbrough, 341.

70. Carmony, *Indiana, 1816–1850*, 156–58, 164, 190–96; and Cayton, *Frontier Indiana*, 284–85.

71. *Indiana Democrat* (Indianapolis), February 13, 1836, quoted in Carmony, *Indiana, 1816–1850*, 195.

72. Illinois House Journal, 9th General Assembly, 1st sess. (December 3, 1834), 26, 28.

73. Abraham Lincoln to Mary S. Owens, December 13, 1836, in *The Collected Works of Abraham Lincoln*, ed. Roy P. Basler, 1:54; and Paul Simon, *Lincoln's Preparation for Greatness: The Illinois Legislative Years*, 50–52.

74. Atwater, *History of the State of Ohio*, 275; Bogart, *Internal Improvements*, v–vii; and Cayton, *Frontier Republic*, 146–47.

75. Carmony, *Indiana, 1816–1850*, 208–11; Cayton, *Frontier Indiana*, 285; Davis, *Frontier Illinois*, 359; and Simon, *Lincoln's Preparation*, 52–53.

76. Carmony, *Indiana, 1816–1850*, 377–78; Cayton, *Frontier Indiana*, 286–87; Logan Esarey, *A History of Indiana: From Its Exploration to 1850*, 291–92; and Simon, *Lincoln's Preparation*, 70.

Epilogue: Up the Capitol Steps

1. *Sangamo Journal* (Springfield, IL), October 15, 1841.

2. William Lee Miller, *Lincoln's Virtues: An Ethical Biography*, 95–96 (emphasis mine); and Joel H. Silbey, "'Always a Whig in Politics': The Partisan Life of Abraham Lincoln," 42.

3. Abraham Lincoln, "Autobiography Written for John L. Scripps," in *The Collected Works of Abraham Lincoln*, ed. Roy P. Basler, 4:61–62; Charles M. Segal, ed., *Conversations with Lincoln*, 348; William E. Bartelt, "The Land Dealings of Spencer County, Indiana, Pioneer Thomas Lincoln," 211–13, 218–21; David Herbert Donald, *Lincoln*, 23–24; Lowell H. Harrison, *Lincoln of Kentucky*, 28; and Louis A. Warren, *Lincoln's Youth: Indiana Years, 1816–1830*, 12–13.

4. Interview with J. K. Dubois, July 4, 1875, in *An Oral History of Abraham Lincoln: John G. Nicolay's Interviews and Essays*, ed. Michael Burlingame, 30; and Michael Lind, *What Lincoln Believed: The Values and Convictions of America's Greatest President*, 94.

5. Hamilton, "Report on Manufactures," Dec. 5, 1791, in *Selected Writings and Speeches of Alexander Hamilton*, ed. Morton J. Frisch, 303; and *Illinois House Journal*, January 8, 1835.

6. Lincoln, "Speech on the Subtreasury," December [26], 1839, in *Collected Works*, ed. Basler, 1:160; *Sangamo Journal* (Springfield, IL), January 3, 1840; and Richard Carwardine, *Lincoln: A Life of Purpose and Power*, 16.

7. Fisher Ames, "Laocoon, No. 1," April 1799, in *Works of Fisher Ames, with a Selection of his Speeches and Correspondence*, ed. Seth Ames, 2:111–12; Lincoln, "Speech on the Subtreasury," December [26], 1839, in *Collected Works*, ed. Basler, 1:164; Lincoln, "Speech in the Illinois State Legislature Concerning the State Bank," in *Collected Works*, ed. Basler, 1:67; and Daniel Walker Howe, *The Political Culture of the American Whigs*, 265.

8. Carwardine, *Lincoln*, 15; and Donald, *Lincoln*, 31.

9. Lincoln, "Communication to the People of Sangamo County," March 9, 1832, in *Collected Works*, ed. Basler, 1:7; Interview with John T. Stuart, June 24, 1875, in *An Oral History of Abraham Lincoln*, ed. Burlingame, 12; John H. Krenkel, *Illinois Internal Improvements, 1818–1848*, 21; and Paul Simon, *Lincoln's Preparation for Greatness: The Illinois Legislative Years*, 35.

10. Daniel Walker Howe, "Why Abraham Lincoln Was a Whig," 30–31.

11. Lincoln, "Remarks In Illinois Legislature Concerning a Bill for Completion of the Illinois and Michigan Canal," Feb. 26, 1841, in *Collected Works*, ed. Basler, 1:244; and Daniel Walker Howe, *What Hath God Wrought: The Transformation of America, 1815–1848*, 525.

12. William H. Herndon and Jesse William Weik, *Herndon's Lincoln: The True Story of a Great Life*, 1:125; Howe, *What Hath God Wrought*, 244; Harvey J. Kaye, *Thomas Paine and the Promise of America*, 119–20; Ward Hill Lamon, *The Life of Abraham Lincoln: From His Birth to His Inauguration as President*, 2:493; and Lind, *What Lincoln Believed*, 48–52.

13. *Illinois House Journal*, January 10, 1835; Olivier Fraysse, *Lincoln, Land, and Labor, 1809–60*, trans. Sylvia Neely, 76–78; Lind, *What Lincoln Believed*, 60, 99; and John R. Van Atta, "'A Lawless Rabble': Henry Clay and the Cultural Politics of Squatters' Rights, 1832–1841," 349–50.

14. Lincoln, "Address before the Young Men's Lyceum," January 27, 1838, in *Collected Works*, ed. Basler, 1:109–11.

15. *Sangamo Journal* (Springfield, IL), Feb. 26, 1841.

16. Lincoln, "Address before the Young Men's Lyceum," January 27, 1838, in *Collected Works*, ed. Basler, 1:112, 115. Emphasis in the original.

17. For example, see Michael F. Holt, *The Rise and Fall of the American Whig Party: Jacksonian Politics and the Onset of the Civil War*, 105–07.

18. National Whig Party, *Proceedings of the Democratic Whig National Convention, which Assembled at Harrisburg, Pennsylvania, on the Fourth of December,*

1839, for the Purpose of Nominating Candidates for President and Vice President of the United States, 42. For the full speech, see 34–42.

19. For particular examples of declaring the Federalists extinct, Jeffrey P. Brown, "The Ohio Federalists, 1803–1815," 281; and Donald J. Ratcliffe, *Party Spirit in a Frontier Republic: Democratic Politics in Ohio, 1793–1821*, 21, 122.

20. *Sangamo Journal* (Springfield, IL), February 28, 1840; *The Old Soldier* (Springfield, IL), May 1, 1840; Burlingame, *Abraham Lincoln: A Life*, 1:148; and Simon, *Lincoln's Preparation*, 207.

21. Donald Richard Deskins et al., *Presidential Elections, 1789–2008: County, State, and National Mapping of Election Data*, 119. The final tallies were in Ohio, 148,030 to 123,905 for Harrison; in Indiana, 65,239 to 51,655 for Harrison; and in Illinois, 47,398 to 45,532 for Van Buren.

Bibliography

Archival Sources

Abraham Lincoln Presidential Library
Duncan Family Papers
Henry Eddy Papers
Ninian Edwards Papers
Flower Family Papers
Edward Tiffin Collection

Filson Historical Society
Beall-Booth Family Papers
Beatty-Quisenberry Family Papers
Bodley Family Papers
Bullitt Family Papers
Arthur Campbell Papers
Samuel McDowell Papers
Isaac Shelby Papers
Hosea Smith Letters
Louis Tarascon Journal

Indiana Historical Society
William Henry Harrison Papers and Documents, 1791-1864
Indiana Territory Collection
John Johnston Records
Harlow Lindley Collection
Noah Noble Letters, 1824-1843
Northwest Territory Collection, 1721-1825
Benjamin Parke Papers, 1816-1818
Albert Gallatin Porter Papers, 1759-1934
George Washington Letters, 1786-1795

Ohio Historical Society
Backus-Woodbridge Family Papers

Jacob Burnet Papers
Thomas Ewing Papers
Charles Hammond Papers
William Henry Harrison Papers
John Johnston Papers
Duncan McArthur Papers
Ohio Company Records
William Henry Smith Papers
Arthur St. Clair Papers
John Allen Trimble Papers

Primary Sources

Abbot, W. W., and Dorothy Twohig, eds. *The Papers of George Washington: Con-
federation Series*. Charlottesville: University Press of Virginia, 1992–1997.
Adams, Charles Francis, ed. *The Works of John Adams, Second President of the
United States: With a Life of the Author, Notes and Illustrations*. Boston:
Little, Brown and Company, 1850–1856.
Ames, Seth, ed. *Works of Fisher Ames, with a Selection of His Speeches and Cor-
respondence*. Boston: Little, Brown and Company, 1854.
Basler, Roy P., ed. *The Collected Works of Abraham Lincoln*. 8 vols. New Bruns-
wick, NJ: Rutgers University Press, 1953–1959.
Benton, Elbert Jay, ed. "Side Lights on the Ohio Company of Associates from
the John May Papers." *The Western Reserve Historical Society* 97 (October
1917): 63–221.
Birkbeck, Morris. *Letters from Illinois*. London: Taylor and Hessey, 1818.
———. *Notes on a Journey in America, from the Coast of Virginia to the Territory
of Illinois*. Second ed. London: James Ridgway, 1818.
Bond, Beverley W., Jr., ed. *The Correspondence of John Cleves Symmes: Founder
of the Miami Purchase*. New York: Macmillan, 1926.
———, ed. *The Intimate Letters of John Cleves Symmes and His Family*. Cincin-
nati: Historical and Philosophical Society of Ohio, 1956.
Brackenridge, Hugh Henry. *Incidents of the Insurrection in the Western Parts of
Pennsylvania, in the Year 1794*. Edited by Daniel Marder. New Haven, CT:
College & University Press, 1972.
Bradley, Daniel. *Journal of Capt. Daniel Bradley; an Epic of the Ohio Frontier*.
Edited by Frazer E. Wilson. Greenville, OH: F. H. Jobes & Son, 1935.
Buell, Rowena, ed. *The Memoirs of Rufus Putnam and Certain Official Papers
and Correspondence*. Boston: Houghton, Mifflin, 1903.
Burnet, Jacob. *Notes on the Early Settlement of the North-western Territory*. Cin-
cinnati: Derby, Bradley, and Co., 1847.
Burton, C. M., ed. "General Wayne's Orderly Book." *Michigan Pioneer and His-
torical Society Historical Collections* 34 (1904): 341–733.
Butterfield, C. W., ed. *The Washington-Irvine Correspondence: The Official Letters which Passed between Washington and Brig.-Gen. William Irvine and*

between Irvine and Others Concerning Military Affairs in the West from 1781 to 1783. Madison, WI: David Atwood, 1882.

Carter, Clarence E., ed. *Territorial Papers of the United States*. 26 vols. Washington: United States Government Printing Office, 1934–1972.

Chase, Salmon P., ed. *The Statutes of Ohio and of the Northwestern Territory, Adapted or Enacted from 1783 to 1833 Inclusive, Together with the Ordinance of 1787; the Constitutions of Ohio and of the United States, and Various Public Instruments of Congress; Illustrated by a Preliminary Sketch of the History of Ohio*. 4 vols. Cincinnati: Corey & Fairbank, 1833–1835.

Clark, William. "William Clark's Journal of General Wayne's Campaign." Edited by R. C. Magrane. *The Mississippi Valley Historical Review* 1, no. 3 (December 1914): 418–44.

Cochran, Thomas C. et al., eds. *The New American State Papers: Indian Affairs*. Vol. 4: Northwest. Wilmington, DE: Scholarly Resources, Inc., 1972.

Cullen, Charles T., ed. *The Papers of Thomas Jefferson*. 21 vols. Princeton, NJ: Princeton University Press, 1983.

Cutler, Ephraim. *An Oration Delivered before the Washington Benevolent Society, at Marietta, on the 22d of February, 1814, Being the Anniversary of the Birth Day of the Immortal Washington*. Zanesville, OH: Putnam & Israel, 1814.

Cutler, Jervis. *Topographical Description of the State of Ohio, Indiana Territory, and Louisiana*. Boston: Charles Williams, 1812.

Cutler, Julia Perkins. *Life and Times of Ephraim Cutler: Prepared from His Journals and Correspondence*. Cincinnati: Robert Clarke & Co., 1890.

Cutler, Manasseh. *An Explanation of the Map of Federal Lands*. Salem, MA: Dabney and Cushing, 1787. New York: Readex Microprint, 1966.

Cutler, William Parker, and Julia Perkins Cutler, eds. *Life, Journals, and Correspondence of Rev. Manasseh Cutler, LL.D.* 2 vols. Cincinnati: R. Clarke & Co., 1888. Athens: Ohio University Press, 1987.

Denny, Ebenezer. *Military Journal of Major Ebenezer Denny, an Officer in the Revolutionary and Indian Wars*. Philadelphia: Historical Society of Pennsylvania, J. B. Lippincott and Co., 1859.

Drake, B., and E. D. Mansfield. *Cincinnati in 1826*. Cincinnati: Morgan, Lodge, and Fisher, 1827.

Drowne, Solomon. *An Oration, Delivered at Marietta, April 7, 1789, in Commemoration of the Commencement of the Settlement Formed by the Ohio Company*. Worcester, MA: Isaiah Thomas, 1789.

Edwards, Ninian W. *History of Illinois, from 1778 to 1833; and Life and Times of Ninian Edwards*. Springfield: Illinois State Journal Co., 1870.

Ernst, Ferdinand. "Travels in Illinois in 1819." Translated by E. P. Baker. *Transactions of the Illinois State Historical Society* IV (1903), 150–65.

Esarey, Logan, ed. *Messages and Letters of William Henry Harrison*. 2 vols. Indianapolis: Indiana Historical Commission, 1922.

————, ed. *Governors Messages and Letters: Messages and Papers of Jonathan Jennings, Ratliff Boon, William Hendricks, 1816–1825*. Indianapolis: Indiana Historical Commission, 1924.

Fitzpatrick, John C., ed. *The Writings of George Washington: From the Original Manuscript Sources 1745–1799*. 39 vols. Washington: United States Government Printing Office, 1931.

Flower, George. *The Errors of Immigrants: Pointing Out Many Popular Errors Hitherto Unnoticed; with a Sketch of the Extent and Resources of the New States of the North American Union, and a Description of the Progress and Present Aspect of the English Settlement in Illinois, Founded by Morris Birkbeck and George Flower, in the Year 1817*. London: Cleave, 1841. New York: Arno Press, 1975.

Ford, Worthington C. et al. *Journals of the Continental Congress, 1774–1789*. 34 vols. Washington: United States Government Printing Office, 1904–1937.

Frisch, Morton J., Ed. *Selected Writings and Speeches of Alexander Hamilton*. Washington: American Enterprise Institute for Public Policy Research, 1985.

Griswold, Bert J., ed. *Fort Wayne, Gateway of the West, 1802–1813: Garrison Orderly Books, Indian Agency Account Book*. Indianapolis: Historical Bureau of the Indiana Library and Historical Department, 1927.

Hawken, Henry A., ed. *Trumpets of Glory: Fourth of July Orations, 1786-1861*. Granby, CT: Salmon Brook Historical Society, 1976.

Heckewelder, John. *The First Description of Cincinnati and Other Ohio Settlements: The Travel Report of Johann Heckewelder*. Edited by Don Heinrich Tolzmann. Lanham, MD: University Press of America, 1988.

————. *Thirty Thousand Miles with John Heckewelder*. Pittsburgh: University of Pittsburgh Press, 1958.

Herndon, William H. and Jesse William Weik. *Herndon's Lincoln: The True Story of a Great Life*. Chicago: Belford, Clarke, & Co., 1889.

Hill, Frederick D., ed. "William Hendricks' Political Circulars to His Constituents: Congressional Period, 1816–1822." *Indiana Magazine of History* 70, no. 4 (December 1974): 296–344.

————, ed. "William Hendricks' Political Circulars to His Constituents: Second Senatorial Term, 1831–1837." *Indiana Magazine of History* 71, no. 4 (December 1975): 319–74.

Hulbert, Archer Butler, ed. *Records of the Original Proceedings of the Ohio Company*. 2 vols. Marietta, OH: Marietta Historical Commission, 1917.

Hutchinson, William T. et al., eds. *The Papers of James Madison*. 17 vols. Chicago: University of Chicago Press, 1962–1991.

Imlay, Gilbert. *A Topographical Description of the Western Territory of North America: Containing a Succinct Account of Its Soil, Climate, Natural History, Population, Agriculture, Manners, and Customs, with an Ample Description of the Several Divisions into which That Country Is Partitioned; to which Are Added, the Discovery, Settlement, and Present State of Kentucky,*

and an Essay towards the Topography, and Natural History of that Import-
ant Country by John Filson. London: J. Debrett, 1793.

Irwin, Thomas. "St. Clair's Defeat." Edited by Frazer E. Wilson. *Ohio Archaeo-*
logical and Historical Quarterly 10 (1902): 378–80.

Israel, Fred L., ed. *The State of the Union Messages of the Presidents, 1790–1966.*
3 vols. Introduction by Arthur M. Schlesinger, Jr. New York: Chelsea House,
1967.

Jackson, Donald, and Dorothy Twohig, eds. *The Diaries of George Washington.* 6
vols. Charlottesville: University Press of Virginia, 1976.

Knopf, Richard C., ed. *Anthony Wayne, A Name in Arms: Soldier, Diplomat,*
Defender of Expansion Westward of a Nation; The Wayne-Knox-Pickering-
McHenry Correspondence. Pittsburgh: University of Pittsburgh Press, 1960.

———, ed. "A Precise Journal of General Wayne's Last Campaign." *Proceedings*
of the American Antiquarian Society 64 (October 1954): 273–302.

Maclay, Edgar S., ed. *Journal of William Maclay: United States Senator from*
Pennsylvania, 1789–1791. New York: D. Appleton and Co., 1890.

Mallory, Daniel, ed. *The Life and Speeches of the Hon. Henry Clay.* 2 vols. New
York: Robert P. Bixby & Co., 1843.

Marder, Daniel, ed. *A Hugh Henry Brackenridge Reader, 1770–1815.* Pittsburgh:
University of Pittsburgh Press, 1970.

Martzolff, Clement L., ed. "The Autobiography of Thomas Ewing." *Ohio Archae-*
ological and Historical Quarterly 22, no. 1 (January 1913): 126–204.

———. "Caleb Atwater." *Ohio Archaeological and Historical Publications* 14
(1905): 247–71.

Miller, Kerby A. et al. *Irish Immigrants in the Land of Canaan: Letters and Mem-*
oirs from Colonial and Revolutionary America, 1675–1815. New York: Oxford University Press, 2003.

Morrow, Jeremiah. *Governor's Message, to the General Assembly of Ohio, Decem-*
ber 7, 1824. Columbus, OH: P. H. Olmsted, 1824.

Ohio Company. *Articles of an Association by the Name of the Ohio Company.*
New York: Samuel and John Loudon, 1787.

Ohio Constitutional Convention. *Journal of the Convention of the Territory of*
the United States North-west of the Ohio, Begun and Held at Chillicothe, on
Monday the First Day of November, A.D. One Thousand Eight Hundred and
Two, and the Independence of the United States the Twenty-Seventh. Chillicothe, OH: N. Willis, 1802.

Ohio University. *Resolutions and Acts Passed by the Ohio and Territorial Legis-*
latures, Relative to the Ohio University, at Athens. Zanesville, OH: Putnam
and Clark, 1816.

Pease, Theodore Calvin, ed. *Illinois Election Returns, 1818–1848.* Springfield:
Illinois State Historical Library, 1923.

Peck, John Mason. *Forty Years of Pioneer Life: Memoir of John Mason Peck, D.D.*
Edited by Rufus Babcock. Carbondale: Southern Illinois University Press,
1965.

————. *A New Guide for Emigrants to the West, Containing Sketches of Ohio, Indiana, Illinois, Missouri, Michigan, with the Territories of Wisconsin and Arkansas, and the Adjacent Parts*. Boston: Gould, Kendall, and Lincoln, 1836.

Philbrick, Francis S., ed. *The Laws of the Indiana Territory, 1801–1809*. Springfield: Trustees of the Illinois State Historical Library, 1930.

Quaife, M. M., ed. *Fort Wayne in 1790*. Fort Wayne, IN: Public Library of Fort Wayne, 1955.

Riker, Dorothy, and Gayle Thornbrough, eds. *Messages and Papers Relating to the Administration of Noah Noble, Governor of Indiana, 1831–1837*. Indianapolis: Indiana Historical Bureau, 1958.

Rossiter, Clinton, ed. *The Federalist Papers: Alexander Hamilton, James Madison, John Jay*. New York: Mentor, 1961.

Rush, Benjamin. *Essays, Literary, Moral, and Philosophical*. Second ed. Philadelphia: Thomas and William Bradford, 1806.

St. Clair, Arthur. *A Narrative of the Manner in which the Campaign Against the Indians, in the Year One Thousand Seven Hundred and Ninety-One, Was Conducted, Under the Command of Major General St. Clair, Together With His Observations on the Statements of the Secretary of War and the Quarter Master General*. Philadelphia: Jane Aitken, 1812.

Sargent, Winthrop. "Winthrop Sargent's Diary while with General Arthur St. Clair's Expedition Against the Indians." *Ohio Archaeological and Historical Publications* 33 (July 1924): 237–82.

Sealsfield, Charles. *The Americans As They Are: Described in a Tour through the Valley of the Mississippi*. London: Hurst, Chance, and Co., 1828.

Smith, Dwight L., ed. *The Western Journals of John May: Ohio Company Agent and Business Adventurer*. Cincinnati: Historical and Philosophical Society of Ohio, 1961.

Smith, James. "Tours into Kentucky and the Northwest Territory: Three Journals by the Rev. James Smith of Powhatan County, Va., 1783–1795–1797." Edited by Josiah Morrow. *Ohio Archaeological and Historical Publications* 16 (1907): 348–401.

Smith, William Henry, ed. *The St. Clair Papers: The Life and Public Services of Arthur St. Clair: Soldier of the Revolutionary War, President of the Continental Congress, and Governor of the Northwestern Territory: With His Correspondence and Other Papers*. 2 vols. Cincinnati: R. Clarke, 1882.

Symmes, John Cleves. *To the Respectable Public*. Trenton: Isaac Collins, 1787.

Syrett, Harold C., ed. *The Papers of Alexander Hamilton*. 27 vols. New York: Columbia University Press, 1961–1987.

Thornbrough, Gayle, ed. *The Correspondence of John Badollet and Albert Gallatin, 1804–1836*. Indianapolis: Indiana Historical Society, 1963.

————, ed. *Letter Book of the Indian Agency at Fort Wayne, 1809–1815*. Indianapolis: Indiana Historical Society, 1961.

————, ed. *Outpost on the Wabash, 1787–1791*. Indianapolis: Indiana Historical Society, 1957.

Thwaites, Reuben Gold, ed. *Early Western Travels, 1748–1846*. 32 vols. Cleveland: Arthur H. Clark, 1904–1907.

———, ed. "The Fur Trade and Factory System at Green Bay 1816–21." *Report and Collections of the State Historical Society of Wisconsin* VII (1873–1876): 269–88.

Trimble, Allen. *Autobiography and Correspondence of Allen Trimble, Governor of Ohio*. Columbus, OH: "Old Northwest" Genealogical Society, 1909.

Turner, George. *An Oration Pronounced before the Washington Benevolent Society of the County of Washington, State of Ohio, on the 22d. February, 1817*. Marietta, OH: Royal Prentiss, 1817.

Twohig, Dorothy, ed. *The Papers of George Washington: Presidential Series*. 12 vols. Charlottesville: University Press of Virginia, 1987–2005.

United States Congress. *American State Papers*. 38 vols. Washington: Gales and Seaton, 1832–1861.

———. *Annals of the Congress of the United States, 1789–1824*. 42 vols. Washington: Gales and Seaton, 1834–1856.

———. *United States Statutes at Large*. Vols. 1–2. Boston: Little and Brown, 1845.

Varnum, James M. *An Oration, Delivered at Marietta, July 4, 1788, by the Hon. James M. Varnum, Esq. One of the Judges of the Western Territory; the Speech of His Excellency Arthur St. Clair, Esquire, upon the Proclamation of the Commission Appointing Him Governor of Said Territory; and the Proceedings of the Inhabitants of the City of Marietta*. Newport, RI: Peter Edes, 1788.

Vattel, Emer de. *The Law of Nations; or, the Principles of the Law of Nature Applied to the Conduct and Affairs of Nations and Sovereigns*. Trans. Joseph Chitty (1834). New York: Cambridge University Press, 2011.

Wallcut, Thomas. *Journal of Thomas Wallcut in 1790*. Edited by George Dexter. Cambridge, MA: University Press, John Wilson and Son, 1879.

Washburne, E. B., ed. *The Edwards Papers: Being a Portion of the Collection of the Letters, Papers, and Manuscripts of Ninian Edwards*. Chicago: Fergus, 1884.

Wayne, Anthony. "General Anthony Wayne's Orderly Book." Introduction by C. M. Burton. *Historical Collections: Collections and Researches Made by the Michigan Pioneer and Historical Society* XXXIV (1905): 341–733.

Whig Party. *Proceedings of the Democratic Whig National Convention, which Assembled at Harrisburg, Pennsylvania, on the Fourth of December, 1839, for the Purpose of Nominating Candidates for President and Vice President of the United States*. Harrisburg, PA: R. S. Elliott & Co., 1839.

Wilkinson, James. "General James Wilkinson's Narrative of the Fallen Timbers Campaign." Edited by M. M. Quaife. *The Mississippi Valley Historical Review* 16, no. 1 (June 1929): 81–90.

Secondary Sources

Amos, Ruth Esther. "The Noble Brothers and Early Public Improvements in Indiana." Master's thesis, Butler University, 1945.

Atwater, Caleb. *A History of the State of Ohio, Natural and Civil*. 2nd ed. Cincinnati: Glezen and Shepard, 1838.

Banning, Lance. *The Jeffersonian Persuasion: Evolution of a Party Ideology*. Ithaca, NY: Cornell University Press, 1978.

Barnhart, John D. *Valley of Democracy: The Frontier Versus the Plantation in the Ohio Valley, 1775–1818*. Bloomington: Indiana University Press, 1953.

———, and Dorothy L. Riker. *Indiana to 1816: The Colonial Period*. Indianapolis: Indiana Historical Bureau and Indiana Historical Society, 1971.

Barr, Daniel P., ed. *The Boundaries between Us: Natives and Newcomers along the Frontiers of the Old Northwest Territory, 1750–1850*. Kent, OH: Kent State University Press, 2006.

Bartelt, William E. "The Land Dealings of Spencer County, Indiana, Pioneer Thomas Lincoln." *Indiana Magazine of History* 87, no. 3 (September 1991): 211–23.

Bayard, Charles J. *The Development of the Public Land Policy, 1783–1820, with Special Reference to Indiana*. New York: Arno Press, 1979.

Beaver, R. Pierce. "The Miami Purchase of John Cleves Symmes." *Ohio Archaeological and Historical Quarterly* 40 (January 1931): 284–342.

Bemis, Samuel Flagg. *Jay's Treaty: A Study in Commerce and Diplomacy*. Revised ed. New Haven, CT: Yale University Press, 1962.

Ben-Atar, Doron, and Barbara B. Oberg, eds. *Federalists Reconsidered*. Charlottesville: University Press of Virginia, 1998.

Bergmann, William H. *The American National State and the Early West*. New York: Cambridge University Press, 2012.

Bickham, Troy. *The Weight of Vengeance: The United States, the British Empire, and the War of 1812*. New York: Oxford University Press, 2012.

Bogart, Ernest Ludlow. *Financial History of Ohio*. Urbana-Champaign: University of Illinois, 1912.

———. *Internal Improvements and the State Debt in Ohio*. New York: Longmans, Green and Co., 1924.

Boggess, Arthur Clinton. *The Settlement of Illinois, 1778–1830*. Chicago: Chicago Historical Society, 1908.

Bond, Beverley W., Jr. "An American Experiment in Colonial Government." *The Mississippi Valley Historical Review* 15, no. 2 (September 1928): 221–35.

———. *The Foundations of Ohio*. Columbus: Ohio State Archaeological and Historical Society, 1941.

———. "William Henry Harrison in the War of 1812." *Mississippi Valley Historical Review* 13, no. 4 (March 1927): 499–516.

Boorstin, Daniel J. *The Americans: The National Experience*. New York: Vintage Books, 1965.

Bowling, Kenneth R., and Donald R. Kennon, eds. *The House and Senate in the 1790s: Petitioning, Lobbying, and Institutional Development*. Athens: United States Capitol Historical Society, Ohio University Press, 2002.

Brown, Jeffrey P. "Arthur St. Clair and the Northwest Territory." *Northwest Ohio Quarterly* 59 (Summer 1987): 75–90.

———. "Frontier Politics: The Evolution of a Political Society in Ohio, 1788–1814." PhD diss., University of Illinois, 1979.

———. "The Ohio Federalists, 1803–1815." *Journal of the Early Republic* 2, no. 3 (Fall 1982): 261–82.

————, and Andrew R. L. Cayton, eds. *The Pursuit of Public Power: Political Culture in Ohio, 1787–1861*. Kent, OH: Kent State University Press, 1994.

Brown, Robert Elliott. *Manasseh Cutler and the Settlement of Ohio*. Marietta, OH: Marietta College Press, 1938.

Buley, R. Carlyle. *The Old Northwest: Pioneer Period, 1815–1840*. 2 vols. Bloomington: Indiana University Press, 1951.

Burgess, Charles E. "John Rice Jones, Citizen of Many Territories." *Journal of the Illinois State Historical Society* 61, no. 1 (Spring 1968): 58–82.

Bushman, Richard L. *The Refinement of America: Persons, Houses, Cities*. New York: Knopf, 1992.

Callahan, North. *Henry Knox: George Washington's General*. New York: A. S. Barnes, 1958.

Calloway, Colin G. *The American Revolution in Indian Country: Crisis and Diversity in Native American Communities*. New York: Cambridge University Press, 1995.

————. *Crown and Calumet: British-Indian Relations, 1783–1815*. Norman: University of Oklahoma Press, 1987.

————. "The End of an Era: British-Indian Relations in the Great Lakes Region after the War of 1812." *Michigan Historical Review* 12, no. 2 (Fall 1986): 1–20.

————. *The Shawnees and the War for America*. New York: Viking, 2007.

Carmony, Donald F. *Indiana, 1816–1850: The Pioneer Era*. Indianapolis: Indiana Historical Bureau and Indiana Historical Society, 1998.

Carwardine, Richard. *Lincoln: A Life of Purpose and Power*. New York: Knopf, 2006.

Cave, Alfred A. "The Shawnee Prophet, Tecumseh, and Tippecanoe: A Case Study of Historical Myth-Making." *Journal of the Early Republic* 22, no. 4 (Winter 2002): 637–73.

Cayton, Andrew R. L. "The Contours of Power in a Frontier Town: Marietta, Ohio, 1788–1803." *Journal of the Early Republic* 6, no. 2 (Summer 1986): 103–26.

————. *Frontier Indiana*. Bloomington: Indiana University Press, 1996.

————. *The Frontier Republic: Ideology and Politics in the Ohio Country, 1780–1825*. Kent, OH: Kent State University Press, 1986.

————. "Land, Power, and Reputation: The Cultural Dimension of Politics in the Ohio Country." *William and Mary Quarterly* 3rd ser., 47, no. 2 (1990): 266–86.

————. "'A Quiet Independence': The Western Vision of the Ohio Company." *Ohio History* 90, no. 1 (Winter 1981): 5–32.

————. "'Separate Interests' and the Nation-State: The Washington Administration and the Origins of Regionalism in the Trans-Appalachian West." *The Journal of American History* 79, no.1 (June 1992): 39–67.

————, and Stuart D. Hobbs, eds. *"The Center of a Great Empire": The Ohio Country in the Early American Republic*. Athens: Ohio University Press, 2005.

————, and Peter S. Onuf. *The Midwest and the Nation: Rethinking the History of an American Region*. Bloomington: Indiana University Press, 1990.

————, and Fredrika J. Teute, eds. *Contact Points: American Frontiers from the Mohawk Valley to the Mississippi, 1750–1830*. Chapel Hill: University of North Carolina Press, 1998.

Champagne, Raymond W., Jr., and Thomas J. Reuter. "Jonathan Roberts and the 'War Hawk' Congress of 1811–1812." *Pennsylvania Magazine of History and Biography* 104, no. 4 (October 1980): 434–49.

Chatelain, Verne E. "The Public Land Officer on the Northwestern Frontier." *Minnesota History* 12, no. 4 (December 1931): 379–89.

Cleaves, Freeman. *Old Tippecanoe: William Henry Harrison and His Time*. New York: Charles Scribner's Sons, 1939.

Conover, Charlotte Reeve. *Concerning the Forefathers: Being a Memoir, with Personal Narrative and Letters of Two Pioneers, Col. Robert Patterson and Col. John Johnston*. Dayton, OH: National Cash Register, 1902.

Contosta, David R. *Lancaster, Ohio, 1800–1820: Frontier Town to Edge City*. Columbus: Ohio State University Press, 1999.

Cornelius, Janet. *Constitution Making in Illinois, 1818–1970*. Champaign: University of Illinois Press, 1972.

Cramer, C. H. "Duncan McArthur: First Phase, 1772–1812." *Ohio Archaeological and Historical Quarterly* 45 (1936): 27–33.

————. "Duncan McArthur: The Military Phase." *Ohio Archaeological and Historical Quarterly* 46 (1937): 128–47.

Cress, Lawrence D. "Republican Liberty and National Security: American Military Policy as an Ideological Problem, 1783 to 1789." *William and Mary Quarterly* 3rd ser., 38, no. 1 (January 1981): 73–96.

Cutler, Sarah J. "The Coonskin Library." *Ohio Archaeological and Historical Quarterly* 26 (1917): 58–77.

Dangerfield, George. *The Era of Good Feelings*. New York: Harcourt, Brace & World, 1952.

Davis, James E. *Frontier Illinois*. Bloomington: Indiana University Press, 1998.

Deloria, Philip J. *Playing Indian*. New Haven, CT: Yale University Press, 1998.

DeLuca, Tom. *The Two Faces of Political Apathy*. Philadelphia: Temple University Press, 1995.

Deskins, Donald Richard et al. *Presidential Elections, 1789–2008: County, State, and National Mapping of Election Data*. Ann Arbor: University of Michigan Press, 2010.

Donald, David Herbert. *Lincoln*. New York: Simon and Schuster, 1995.

————. *Lincoln Reconsidered: Essays on the Civil War Era*. New York: Vintage, 1961.

Dowd, Gregory Evans. *A Spirited Resistance: The North American Indian Struggle for Unity, 1745–1815*. Baltimore: Johns Hopkins University Press, 1992.

Downes, Randolph C. *Council Fires on the Upper Ohio: A Narrative of Indian Affairs in the Upper Ohio Valley Until 1795*. Pittsburgh: University of Pittsburgh Press, 1940.

————. "Ohio's Squatter Governor: William Hogland of Hoglandstown." *Ohio Archaeological and Historical Quarterly* 43, no. 3 (July 1934): 273–82.

————. "Trade in Frontier Ohio." *The Mississippi Valley Historical Review* 16, no. 4 (March 1930): 467–94.

Drake, Samuel Adams. *The Making of the Ohio Valley States, 1660–1837*. New York: Charles Scriber's Sons, 1894.

Durey, Michael. "Thomas Paine's Apostles: Radical Emigrés and the Triumph of Jeffersonian Republicanism." *William and Mary Quarterly* 3rd ser., 44, no. 4 (October 1987): 662–88.

Eaton, Clement. *Henry Clay and the Art of American Politics*. Boston: Little, Brown, 1957.

Edling, Max M. *A Revolution in Favor of Government: Origins of the U.S. Constitution and the Making of the American State*. Oxford: Oxford University Press, 2003.

Edmunds, R. David. *The Shawnee Prophet*. Lincoln: University of Nebraska Press, 1983.

————. *Tecumseh and the Quest for Indian Leadership*. New York: Longman, 1984.

Eid, Leroy V. "American Indian Military Leadership: St. Clair's 1791 Defeat." *Journal of Military History* 57, no. 1 (January 1993): 71–88.

Elkins, Stanley and Eric McKitrick. *The Age of Federalism: The Early American Republic, 1788-1800*. New York: Oxford University Press, 1993.

————. "A Meaning for Turner's Frontier: Part I: Democracy in the Old Northwest." *Political Science Quarterly* 69, no. 3 (September 1954): 321–53.

Esarey, Logan. *A History of Indiana: From Its Exploration to 1850*. 2nd ed. Indianapolis: B. F. Bowen and Co., 1918.

————. "Internal Improvements in Early Indiana." *Indiana Historical Society Publications* 5 (1912): 3–158.

Farrand, Max. "The Indian Boundary Line." *The American Historical Review* 10, no. 4 (July 1905): 782–91.

Ferguson, Gillum. *Illinois in the War of 1812*. Urbana: University of Illinois Press, 2012.

Fischer, David Hackett. *The Revolution of American Conservatism: The Federalist Party in the Era of Jeffersonian Democracy*. New York: Harper and Row, 1965.

Foreman, Grant. "English Settlers in Illinois." *Journal of the Illinois State Historical Society* 34, no. 3 (September 1941), 303–33.

Formisano, Ronald P. "Federalists and Republicans: Parties, Yes-System, No." In *The Evolution of American Electoral Systems*, edited by Paul Kleppner et al., 33–76. Westport, CT: Greenwood Press, 1981.

Fox, Stephen Carey. "The Group Bases of Ohio Political Behavior, 1803–1848." PhD diss., University of Cincinnati, 1972.

Franklin, W. Neil. "Pennsylvania-Virginia Rivalry for the Indian Trade of the Ohio Valley." *The Mississippi Valley Historical Review* 20, no. 4 (March 1934): 463–80.

Fraysse, Olivier. *Lincoln, Land, and Labor, 1809-60*. Trans. Sylvia Neely. Urbana: University of Illinois Press, 2001.

Friend, Craig Thompson. *Along the Maysville Road: The Early American Republic in the Trans-Appalachian West*. Knoxville: University of Tennessee Press, 2005.

Furstenberg, François. "The Significance of the Trans-Appalachian Frontier in Atlantic History." *American Historical Review* 113, no. 3 (June 2008): 647-77.

Gaff, Alan D. *Bayonets in the Wilderness: Anthony Wayne's Legion in the Old Northwest*. Norman: University of Oklahoma Press, 2004.

Greene, George E. *History of Old Vincennes and Knox County, Indiana*. Vol. 1. Chicago: S. J. Clarke, 1911.

Grenier, John. *The First Way of War: American War Making on the Frontier, 1607–1814*. New York: Cambridge University Press, 2005.

Griffin, Patrick. *American Leviathan: Empire, Nation, and Revolutionary Frontier*. New York: Hill and Wang, 2007.

Gruenwald, Kim M. *River of Enterprise: The Commercial Origins of Regional Identity in the Ohio Valley, 1790–1850*. Bloomington: Indiana University Press, 2002.

Gunderson, Robert Gray. "William Henry Harrison: Apprentice in Arms." *Northwest Ohio Quarterly* 65, no. 1 (Winter 1993): 3–29.

Guthman, William H. *March to Massacre: A History of the First Seven Years of the United States Army, 1784–1791*. New York: McGraw-Hill, 1975.

Haeger, John D. "The American Fur Company and the Chicago of 1812–1835." *Journal of the Illinois State Historical Society* 61, no. 2 (Summer 1968): 117–39.

Hall, John A., ed. *States in History*. New York: Blackwell, 1986.

Hammond, John Craig. *Slavery, Freedom, and Expansion in the Early American West*. Charlottesville: University of Virginia Press, 2007.

Harris, William C. *Lincoln's Rise to the Presidency*. Lawrence: University Press of Kansas, 2007.

Harrison, Joseph H., Jr. "The Internal Improvement Issue in the Politics of the Union, 1783–1825." PhD diss., University of Virginia, 1954.

Harrison, Lowell H. *Lincoln of Kentucky*. Lexington: University Press of Kentucky, 2000.

Hatter, Lawrence B. A. "'Divided by a Common Language': The Neutral Indian Barrier and the British-Indian Alliance in the Old Northwest, 1783-1815." Master's Thesis. University of Missouri, 2003.

Hellenbrand, Harold. "Not 'To Destroy but to Fulfil': Jefferson, Indians, and Republican Dispensation." *Eighteenth-Century Studies* 18, no. 4 (Autumn 1985): 523–49.

Hibbard, Benjamin Horace. *A History of the Public Land Policies*. New York: Peter Smith, 1939.

Hickey, Donald R. "American Trade Restrictions during the War of 1812." *Journal of American History* 68, no. 3 (December 1981): 517–38.

———. "Federalist Defense Policy in the Age of Jefferson, 1801–1812." *Military Affairs* 45, no. 2 (April 1981): 63–70.

———. "Federalist Party Unity and the War of 1812." *Journal of American Studies* 12, no. 1 (April 1978): 23–39.

———. *The War of 1812: A Forgotten Conflict.* Urbana: University of Illinois Press, 1989.

———. "The War of 1812: Still a Forgotten Conflict?" *Journal of Military History* 65, no. 3 (July 2001): 741–69.

Hildreth, S. P. *Biographical and Historical Memoirs of the Early Pioneer Settlers of Ohio, with Narratives of Incidents and Occurrences in 1775.* Cincinnati: H. W. Derby, 1852.

Hill, Leonard U. *John Johnston and the Indians in the Land of the Three Miamis.* Columbus, OH: Stoneman Press, 1957.

Hinderaker, Eric. *Elusive Empires: Constructing Colonialism in the Ohio Valley, 1673–1800.* New York: Cambridge University Press, 1997.

Hockett, Leola. "The Wabash and Erie Canal in Wabash County." *Indiana Magazine of History* 24, no. 4 (December 1928): 295–305.

Hoffman, Ronald, and Peter J. Albert, eds. *The Transforming Hand of Revolution: Reconsidering the American Revolution as a Social Movement.* Charlottesville: United States Capitol Historical Society, University Press of Virginia, 1996.

Hogeland, William. *Autumn of the Black Snake: The Creation of the U.S. Army and the Invasion That Opened the West.* New York: Farrar, Straus, and Giroux, 2017.

Hollow, Betty. *Ohio University, 1804–2004: The Spirit of a Singular Place.* Athens: Ohio University Press, 2003.

Holt, Michael F. *The Rise and Fall of the American Whig Party: Jacksonian Politics and the Onset of the Civil War.* New York: Oxford University Press, 1999.

Holton, Woody. *Unruly Americans and the Origins of the Constitution.* New York: Hill and Wang, 2007.

Hoover, Thomas N. *The History of Ohio University.* Athens: Ohio University Press, 1954.

Horn, James, Jan Ellen Lewis, and Peter S. Onuf, eds. *The Revolution of 1800: Democracy, Race, and the New Republic.* Charlottesville: University of Virginia Press, 2002.

Horsman, Reginald. "American Indian Policy in the Old Northwest, 1783–1812." *The William and Mary Quarterly* 18, no. 1 (January 1961): 35–53.

———. "The British Indian Department and the Resistance to General Anthony Wayne, 1793–1795." *The Mississippi Valley Historical Review* 49, no. 2 (September 1962): 269–90.

———. *Expansion and American Indian Policy, 1783–1812.* Norman: University of Oklahoma Press, 1992.

———. *The Frontier in the Formative Years, 1783–1815.* Albuquerque: University of New Mexico Press, 1975.

Howe, Daniel Walker. *The Political Culture of the American Whigs*. Chicago: University of Chicago Press, 1979.

————. *What Hath God Wrought: The Transformation of America, 1815–1848*. New York: Oxford University Press, 2007.

————. "Why Abraham Lincoln Was a Whig." *Journal of the Abraham Lincoln Association* 16, no. 1 (Winter 1995): 27–38.

Hoxie, Frederick E., Ronald Hoffman, and Peter J. Albert, eds. *Native Americans and the Early Republic*. Charlottesville: University Press of Virginia, 1999.

Hurt, R. Douglas. *The Indian Frontier, 1763–1846*. Albuquerque: University of New Mexico Press, 2002.

————. *The Ohio Frontier: Crucible of the Old Northwest, 1720–1830*. Bloomington: Indiana University Press, 1996.

Ireland, Owen S. *Religion, Ethnicity, and Politics: Ratifying the Constitution in Pennsylvania*. University Park: Pennsylvania State University Press, 1995.

Jacobs, James R. *The Beginning of the U.S. Army, 1783–1812*. Princeton, NJ: Princeton University Press, 1947.

James, Edmund J., and Milo J. Loveless. *A Bibliography of Newspapers Published in Illinois Prior to 1860*. Springfield, IL: Phillips Bros., 1899.

Jenks, William L. "Territorial Legislation by Governor and Judges." *The Mississippi Valley Historical Review* 5, no. 1 (June 1918): 36–50.

Jennings, Helen Louise. "John Mason Peck and the Impact of New England on the Old Northwest." PhD diss., University of Southern California, 1961.

Jensen, Merrill. *The New Nation: A History of the United States During the Confederation, 1781–1789*. New York: Vintage, 1950.

Jensen, Richard J. *Illinois: A Bicentennial History*. New York: Norton, 1978.

John, Richard R. "Governmental Institutions as Agents of Change: Rethinking American Political Development in the Early Republic, 1787–1835." *Studies in American Political Development* 11 (Fall 1997), 347–80.

————. *Spreading the News: The American Postal System from Franklin to Morse*. Cambridge, MA: Harvard University Press, 1995.

Jones, Dorothy V. *License for Empire: Colonialism by Treaty in Early America*. Chicago: University of Chicago Press, 1982.

Kalette, Linda Elise. *The Papers of Thirteen Early Ohio Political Leaders: An Inventory to the 1976–77 Microfilm Editions*. Columbus: Ohio Historical Society, 1977.

Kaplan, Edward S. *The Bank of the United States and the American Economy*. Westport, CT: Greenwood Press, 1999.

Kastor, Peter J., ed. *The Louisiana Purchase: Emergence of an American Nation*. Washington, D.C.: CQ Press, 2002.

Katznelson, Ira, and Martin Shefter, eds. *Shaped by War and Trade: International Influences on American Political Development*. Princeton, NJ: Princeton University Press, 2002.

Kaye, Harvey J. *Thomas Paine and the Promise of America*. New York: Hill and Wang, 2005.

Kelsay, Isabel Thompson. *Joseph Brant, 1743-1807: Man of Two Worlds*. Syracuse, NY: Syracuse University Press, 1984.

Kerber, Linda K. *Federalists in Dissent: Imagery and Ideology in Jeffersonian America*. Ithaca, NY: Cornell University Press, 1970.

Kirby, Julia Duncan. *Biographical Sketch of Joseph Duncan, Fifth Governor of Illinois*. Chicago: Fergus, 1888.

Knudson, Jerry W. *Jefferson and the Press: Crucible of Liberty*. Columbia: University of South Carolina Press, 2006.

Kohl, Lawrence Frederick. *The Politics of Individualism: Parties and the American Character in the Jacksonian Era*. New York: Oxford University Press, 1989.

Kohn, Richard H. *Eagle and Sword: The Federalists and the Creation of the Military Establishment in America, 1783-1802*. New York: Free Press, 1975.

Krenkel, John H. *Illinois Internal Improvements, 1818–1848*. Cedar Rapids, IA: Torch Press, 1958.

Kurtz, Stephen G., and James H. Hutson, eds. *Essays on the American Revolution*. Chapel Hill: Institute of Early American History and Culture, University of North Carolina Press, 1973.

Lamon, Ward Hill. *The Life of Abraham Lincoln: From His Birth to His Inauguration as President*. Boston: James R. Osgood, 1872.

Lampi, Philip J. "The Federalist Party Resurgence, 1808–1816: Evidence from the New Nation Votes Database." *Journal of the Early Republic* 33 (Summer 2013): 255–81.

Larson, John Lauritz. *Internal Improvement: National Public Works and the Promise of Popular Government in the Early United States*. Chapel Hill: University of North Carolina Press, 2001.

———. *The Market Revolution in America: Liberty, Ambition, and the Eclipse of the Common Good*. New York: Cambridge University Press, 2010.

Lind, Michael. *What Lincoln Believed: The Values and Convictions of America's Greatest President*. New York: Doubleday, 2004.

Livermore, Shaw, Jr. *The Twilight of Federalism: The Disintegration of the Federalist Party, 1815–1830*. Princeton, NJ: Princeton University Press, 1962.

Mahon, John K. "Anglo-American Methods of Indian Warfare, 1676–1794." *The Mississippi Valley Historical Review* 45, no. 2 (September 1958): 254–75.

Mahoney, Timothy R. *Provincial Lives: Middle-Class Experience in the Antebellum Middle West*. New York: Cambridge University Press, 1999.

Martzolff, Clement L. "Caleb Atwater." *Ohio Archaeological and Historical Publications* 14 (1905): 247–71.

———. "Land Grants for Education in the Ohio Valley States." *Ohio Archaeological and Historical Publications* 25 (1916): 59–70.

Maryland Weather Service. *Maryland Weather Service*. Volume One. Baltimore: Johns Hopkins University Press, 1899.

Matson, Cathy, ed. *The Economy of Early America: Historical Perspectives and New Directions*. University Park: Pennsylvania State University Press, 2006.

Maulden, Kristopher. "A Show of Force: The Northwest Indian War and the Early American State." *Ohio Valley History* 16, no. 4 (Winter 2016): 20–40.

McAlpine, William. "The Origin of Public Education in Ohio." *Ohio Archaeological and Historical Society Publications* 38 (1929): 409–47.

McCormick, Richard P. "Ambiguous Authority: The Ordinances of the Confederation Congress, 1781–1789." *The American Journal of Legal History* 41, no. 4 (October 1997): 411–39.

———. "The 'Ordinance' of 1784?" *The William and Mary Quarterly* 3rd ser., 50, no. 1 (January 1993): 112–22.

McCormick, Virginia E., and Robert W. McCormick. *New Englanders on the Ohio Frontier: Migration and Settlement of Worthington, Ohio.* Kent, OH: Kent State University Press, 1998.

McCoy, Drew R. "An 'Old-Fashioned' Nationalism: Lincoln, Jefferson, and the Classical Tradition." *Journal of the Abraham Lincoln Association* 23, no. 1 (Winter 2002): 55–67.

McMurtrie, Douglas C. *Early Printing in Dayton, Ohio.* Dayton, OH: Printing House Craftsmen's Club of Dayton and Vicinity, 1935.

Merrell, James H. *Into the American Woods: Negotiators on the Pennsylvania Frontier.* New York: Norton, 1999.

Middleton, Stephen. *The Black Laws in the Old Northwest: A Documentary History.* Westport, CT: Greenwood, 1993.

Miller, John C. *The Federalist Era, 1789–1801.* New York: Harper, 1960.

Miller, William Lee. *Lincoln's Virtues: An Ethical Biography.* New York: Alfred A. Knopf, 2002.

Mitchell, Broadus. *Alexander Hamilton: A Concise Biography.* New York: Oxford University Press, 1976. New York: Barnes and Noble, 2007.

Murdoch, James Murray. "Charles Hammond: Egalitarian-Whig: An Analysis of the Political Philosophy of a Federalist-Whig Editor and Its Implications Concerning the Traditional Concept of Jacksonian Democracy." PhD diss., Northwestern University, 1971.

Nelson, Paul David. *Anthony Wayne, Soldier of the Early Republic.* Bloomington: Indiana University Press, 1985.

Newman, Otho Lionel. "Development of the Common Schools of Indiana to 1851." *Indiana Magazine of History* 22, no. 3 (September 1926): 229–76.

Nichols, David Andrew. *Engines of Diplomacy: Indian Trading Factories and the Negotiation of American Empire.* Chapel Hill: University of North Carolina Press, 2016.

———. *Red Gentlemen & White Savages: Indians, Federalists, and the Search for Order on the American Frontier.* Charlottesville: University of Virginia Press, 2008.

Nicholson, John B., Jr. "'The Coonskin Library': A Legend of Books in the Wilderness." *Aspects of Librarianship* 9 (1955/1956): 1–11.

Novak, William J. "The Myth of the 'Weak' American State." *American Historical Review* 113, no. 3 (June 2008), 752–72.

———. *The People's Welfare: Law and Regulation in Nineteenth-Century America*. Chapel Hill: University of North Carolina Press, 1996.

Ohio Historical Society. *History of the Ohio Canals: Their Construction, Cost, Use and Partial Abandonment*. Columbus, OH: Fred J. Heer, 1905.

Onuf, Peter S. "From Colony to Territory: Changing Concepts of Statehood in Revolutionary America." *Political Science Quarterly* 97, no. 3 (Autumn 1982): 447–59.

———. "Liberty, Development, and Union: Visions of the West in the 1780s." *The William and Mary Quarterly* 3rd ser., 43, no. 2 (April 1986): 179–213.

———. *Statehood and Union: A History of the Northwest Ordinance*. Bloomington: Indiana University Press, 1987.

Owens, Robert M. "Jeffersonian Benevolence on the Ground: The Indian Land Cession Treaties of William Henry Harrison." *Journal of the Early Republic* 22, no. 3 (Fall 2002): 405–35.

———. *Mr. Jefferson's Hammer: William Henry Harrison and the Origins of American Indian Policy*. Norman: University of Oklahoma Press, 2007.

Pasley, Jeffrey L. *"The Tyranny of Printers": Newspaper Politics in the Early American Republic*. Charlottesville: University Press of Virginia, 2001.

———, Andrew Robertson, and David Waldstreicher, eds. *Beyond the Founders: New Approaches to the Political History of the Early American Republic*. Chapel Hill: University of North Carolina Press, 2004.

Peake, Ora Brooks. *A History of the United States Indian Factory System, 1795–1822*. Denver: Sage Books, 1954.

Pearce, Roy Harvey. *Savagism and Civilization: A Study of the Indian and the American Mind*. Baltimore: The Johns Hopkins Press, 1967.

Pease, Theodore C. "The Ordinance of 1787." *The Mississippi Valley Historical Review* 25, no. 2 (September 1938): 167–80.

Peckham, Howard H. "Josiah Harmar and His Indian Expedition." *Ohio Archaeological and Historical Quarterly* 55 (1946): 227–41.

Peters, William E. *Legal History of the Ohio University, Athens, Ohio*. Cincinnati: Western Methodist Book Concern, 1910.

Peterson, Merrill, D. *The Great Triumvirate: Webster, Clay, and Calhoun*. New York: Oxford University Press, 1987.

Pocock, Emil. "Popular Roots of Jacksonian Democracy: The Case of Dayton, Ohio, 1815–1830." *Journal of the Early Republic* 9, no. 4 (Winter 1989): 489–515.

Pocock, J. G. A., ed. *Three British Revolutions: 1641, 1688, 1776*. Princeton, NJ: Princeton University Press, 1980.

Pratt, Julius W. "Western Aims in the War of 1812." *Mississippi Valley Historical Review* 12, no. 1 (June 1925): 36–50.

Proctor, Redfield. *Annual Report of the Secretary of War for the Year 1891*. 5 vols. Washington, D.C.: Government Printing Office, 1892.

Prucha, Francis Paul. *American Indian Policy in the Formative Years: The Indian Trade and Intercourse Acts, 1780–1834*. Cambridge, MA: Harvard University Press, 1962.

—————. *Broadax and Bayonet: The Role of the United States Army in the Development of the Northwest, 1815–1860.* Introduction by Edward M. Coffman. Lincoln: Bison Books, University of Nebraska Press, 1995.

—————. *The Great Father: The United States Government and the American Indians.* Lincoln: University of Nebraska Press, 1984.

—————. *The Sword of the Republic: The United States Army on the Frontier, 1783–1846.* Toronto: Macmillan, 1969.

Rae, John Bell. "Federal Land Grants in Aid of Canals." *Journal of Economic History* 4, no. 2 (November 1944): 167–77.

Randall, E. O., and Daniel J. Ryan. *History of Ohio: The Rise and Progress of an American State.* New York: Century History, 1912.

Randall, J. G. *Lincoln: The President.* 4 vols. New York: Dodd, Mead, 1945–1953.

Randall, William Sterne. *Unshackling America: How the War of 1812 Truly Ended the American Revolution.* New York: St. Martin's, 2017.

Ratcliffe, Donald J. *Party Spirit in a Frontier Republic: Democratic Politics in Ohio, 1793–1821.* Columbus: Ohio State University Press, 1998.

—————. *The Politics of Long Division: The Birth of the Second Party System in Ohio, 1818–1828.* Columbus: Ohio State University Press, 2000.

—————. "The Role of Voters and Issues in Party Formation: Ohio, 1824." *Journal of American History* 59, no. 4 (March 1973): 847–70.

Reps, John W. *Cities of the American West: A History of Frontier Urban Planning.* Princeton, NJ: Princeton University Press, 1979.

—————. *The Making of Urban America: A History of City Planning in the United States.* Princeton, NJ: Princeton University Press, 1965.

Robbins, Roy M. *Our Landed Heritage: The Public Domain, 1776–1970.* Lincoln: University of Nebraska Press, 1976.

Rohrbough, Malcolm J. *The Land Office Business: The Settlement and Administration of American Public Lands, 1789–1837.* New York: Oxford University Press, 1968.

—————. *The Trans-Appalachian Frontier: People, Societies, and Institutions, 1775–1850.* New York: Oxford University Press, 1978.

Roney, Jessica Choppin. "1776, Viewed from the West." *Journal of the Early Republic* 37, no. 4 (Winter 2017): 655–700.

Roseboom, Eugene H. "Ohio in the Presidential Election of 1824." *Ohio Archaeological and Historical Publications* 26 (1917): 153–224.

Rothbard, Murray N. *The Panic of 1819: Reactions and Policies.* New York: Columbia University Press, 1962.

Saler, Bethel. *The Settlers' Empire: Colonialism and State Formation in America's Old Northwest.* Philadelphia: University of Pennsylvania Press, 2015.

Scheiber, Harry N. *Ohio Canal Era: A Case Study of Government and the Economy, 1820-1861.* Athens: Ohio University Press, 1969.

—————, ed. *The Old Northwest: Studies in Regional History, 1787–1910.* Lincoln: University of Nebraska Press, 1969.

—————. "State Policy and the Public Domain: The Ohio Canal Lands." *Journal of Economic History* 25, no. 1 (March 1965): 86–113.

Schwartz, Thomas F. "An Egregious Political Blunder: Justin Butterfield, Lincoln, and Illinois Whiggery." *Journal of the Abraham Lincoln Association* 8 (1986): 9–19.

Scott, Frank W. *Newspapers and Periodicals of Illinois, 1814–1879*. Springfield: Illinois State Historical Library, 1910.

Sellers, Charles. *The Market Revolution: Jacksonian America, 1815–1846*. New York: Oxford University Press, 1991.

Sears, Alfred Byron. "The Political Philosophy of Arthur St. Clair." *Ohio State Archaeological and Historical Quarterly* 49 (1940): 41–57.

———. *Thomas Worthington: Father of Ohio Statehood*. Columbus: Ohio State University Press, 1958.

Segal, Charles M., ed. *Conversations with Lincoln*. New York: G. P. Putnam's Sons, 1961.

Shade, William G. *Banks or No Banks: The Money Issue in Western Politics, 1832–1865*. Detroit: Wayne State University Press, 1972.

Sheehan, Bernard W. *Seeds of Extinction: Jeffersonian Philanthropy and the American Indian*. Chapel Hill: Institute of Early American History and Culture, University of North Carolina Press, 1973.

Shepherd, William R. "Wilkinson and the Beginnings of the Spanish Conspiracy." *American Historical Review* 9, no. 3 (April 1904): 490-506.

Shetrone, Henry C. "Caleb Atwater: Versatile Pioneer, a Re-Appraisal." *Ohio Archaeological and Historical Quarterly* 54 (1945): 79–88.

Siddali, Silvana R. *Frontier Democracy: Constitutional Conventions in the Old Northwest*. New York: Cambridge University Press, 2016.

Silbey, Joel H. "'Always a Whig in Politics': The Partisan Life of Abraham Lincoln." *Journal of the Abraham Lincoln Association* 8 (1986): 21–42.

Silver, Peter. *Our Savage Neighbors: How Indian War Transformed Early America*. New York: W. W. Norton, 2008.

Simon, Paul. *Lincoln's Preparation for Greatness: The Illinois Legislative Years*. Norman: University of Oklahoma Press, 1965.

Skaggs, David Curtis, and Larry L. Nelson, eds. *The Sixty Years' War for the Great Lakes, 1754–1814*. East Lansing: Michigan State University Press, 2001.

Slaughter, Thomas. *The Whiskey Rebellion: Frontier Prologue to the American Revolution*. New York: Oxford University Press, 1986.

Slocum, Charles Elihu. *The Ohio Country between the Years 1783 and 1815, Including Military Operations that Twice Saved to the United States the Country West of the Alleghany Mountains after the Revolutionary War*. New York: G. P. Putnam's Sons, 1910.

Smith, Craig Bruce. *American Honor: The Creation of the Nation's Ideals during the Revolutionary Era*. Chapel Hill: University of North Carolina Press, 2018.

Smith, Henry Nash. *Virgin Land: The American West as Symbol and Myth*. New York: Vintage, 1950.

Sosin, Jack M. *The Revolutionary Frontier, 1763-1783*. New York: Holt, Rinehart and Winston, 1967.

Stagg, J. C. A. *Mr. Madison's War: Politics, Diplomacy, and Warfare in the Early American Republic, 1783–1830*. Princeton, NJ: Princeton University Press, 1983.

Sugden, John. *Blue Jacket: Warrior of the Shawnees*. Lincoln: University of Nebraska Press, 2000.

———. *Tecumseh: A Life*. New York: Henry Holt, 1998.

Sword, Wiley. *President Washington's Indian War: The Struggle for the Old Northwest, 1790-1795*. Norman: University of Oklahoma Press, 1985.

Tachau, Mary K. Bonsteel. *Federal Courts in the Early Republic: Kentucky, 1789–1816*. Princeton, NJ: Princeton University Press, 1978.

Taylor, Alan. *The Civil War of 1812: American Citizens, British Subjects, Irish Rebels, & Indian Allies*. New York: Vintage, 2011.

———. *Liberty Men and Great Proprietors: The Revolutionary Settlement on the Maine Frontier, 1760–1820*. Chapel Hill: Institute of Early American History and Culture, University of North Carolina Press, 1990.

———. *William Cooper's Town: Power and Persuasion on the Frontier of the Early American Republic*. New York: Vintage, 1995.

Theriault, Sean M. "Party Politics during the Louisiana Purchase." *Social Science History* 30, no. 3 (Summer 2006): 293–324.

Thompson, Charles Mansfield. "The Illinois Whigs before 1846." *University of Illinois Studies in the Social Sciences* 4 (1915): 1–165.

Tilly, Charles. *Coercion, Capital, and European States, AD 990–1990*. Cambridge, MA: Blackwell, 1990.

Treat, Payson Jackson. *The National Land System, 1785–1820*. New York: E. B. Treat & Co., 1910.

Triplett, Barbara Jo. "A Biography of Charles Hammond." Master's thesis, University of Cincinnati, 1964.

Turner, Frederick Jackson. *Rereading Frederick Jackson Turner: "The Significance of the Frontier in American History" and Other Essays*. Edited by John Mack Faragher. New Haven, CT: Yale University Press, 1994.

Tuttle, Mary McArthur Thompson. "William Allen Trimble: United States Senator from Ohio." *Ohio Archaeological and Historical Society Publications* 14 (1905): 225–46.

Unger, Harlow Giles. *Henry Clay: America's Greatest Statesman*. Boston: Da Capo Press, 2015.

Upham, Charles W. *The Life of Timothy Pickering*. 4 vols. Boston: Little, Brown, 1873.

Utter, William T. *The Frontier State, 1803–1825*. Columbus: Ohio State Archaeological and Historical Society, 1942.

———. "Ohio Politics and Politicians, 1802–1815." PhD diss., University of Chicago, 1929.

Van Atta, John R. *Securing the West: Politics, Public Lands, and the Fate of the Old Republic, 1785–1850*. Baltimore: Johns Hopkins University Press, 2014.

Van Tine, Warren, and Michael Pierce, eds. *Builders of Ohio: A Biographical History*. Columbus: Ohio State University Press, 2003.

Wade, Richard C. *The Urban Frontier: Pioneer Life in Early Pittsburgh, Cincinnati, Lexington, Louisville, and St. Louis.* Cambridge, MA: Harvard University Press, 1959. Chicago: University of Chicago Press, 1972.

Waldstreicher, David. *In the Midst of Perpetual Fetes: The Making of American Nationalism, 1776–1820.* Chapel Hill: Omohundro Institute of Early American History and Culture, University of North Carolina Press, 1997.

Walker, Charles M. *History of Athens County, Ohio, And Incidentally of the Ohio Land Company and the First Settlement of the State at Marietta: With Personal and Biographical Sketches of the Early Settlers, Narratives of Pioneer Adventurers, Etc.* Cincinnati: Robert Clarke & Co., 1869.

Walker, W. G. "The Development of the Free Public High School in Illinois during the Nineteenth Century." *History of Education Quarterly* 4, no. 4 (December 1964): 264–79.

Walters, Raymond, Jr. *Albert Gallatin: Jeffersonian Financier and Diplomat.* New York: Macmillan, 1957.

Warren, Louis A. *Lincoln's Youth: Indiana Years, 1816–1830.* Indianapolis: Indiana Historical Society Press, 1959.

Washburne, E. B. *Sketch of Edward Coles, Second Governor of Illinois, and of the Slavery Struggle of 1823–4.* Chicago: Jansen, McClurg, & Co., 1882.

Watson, Harry L. *Liberty and Power: The Politics of Jacksonian America.* Revised ed. New York: Hill and Wang, 2006.

Weisenburger, Francis P. "Caleb Atwater: Pioneer Politician and Historian." *Ohio Historical Quarterly* 68 (1959): 18–37.

———. "A Life of Charles Hammond: The First Great Journalist of the Old Northwest." *Ohio Archaeological and Historical Quarterly* 43, no. 4 (October 1934): 337–427.

———. *The Passing of the Frontier: 1825–1850.* Columbus: Ohio State Archaeological and Historical Society, 1941.

White, Leonard D. *The Federalists: A Study in Administrative History.* New York: Macmillan, 1948.

White, Richard. *"It's Your Misfortune and None of My Own": A History of the American West.* Norman: University of Oklahoma Press, 1991.

———. *The Middle Ground: Indians, Empires, and Republics in the Great Lakes Region, 1650–1815.* Cambridge: Cambridge University Press, 1991.

Wiebe, Robert H. *The Opening of American Society: From the Adoption of the Constitution to the Eve of Disunion.* New York: Knopf, 1984.

Wilentz, Sean. *The Rise of American Democracy: Jefferson to Lincoln.* New York: Norton, 2005.

Williams, Frederick D., ed. *The Northwest Ordinance: Essays on Its Formulation, Provisions and Legacy.* East Lansing: Michigan State University Press, 1987.

Williams, William Appleman. *The Contours of American History.* Cleveland: World Publishing, 1961. Chicago: Quadrangle Books, 1966.

———. "A Frontier Federalist and the War of 1812." *Pennsylvania Magazine of History and Biography* 76, no. 1 (January 1952): 81–85.

Willig, Timothy D. "Prophetstown on the Wabash: The Native Spiritual Defense of the Old Northwest." *Michigan Historical Review* 23, no. 2 (Fall 1997): 115–58.

———. *Restoring the Chain of Friendship: British Policy and the Indians of the Great Lakes, 1783–1815*. Lincoln: University of Nebraska Press, 2008.

Wilson, Frazer Ells. *Arthur St. Clair, Rugged Ruler of the Old Northwest: An Epic of the American Frontier*. Richmond: Garrett and Massie, 1944.

Winkle, Kenneth J. *The Politics of Community: Migration and Politics in Antebellum Ohio*. New York: Cambridge University Press, 1988.

———. "The Voters of Lincoln's Springfield: Migration and Political Participation in an Antebellum City." *Journal of Social History* 25, no. 3 (Spring 1992), 595–611.

Wood, Gordon S. *The Creation of the American Republic, 1776–1787*. Chapel Hill: University of North Carolina Press, 1969.

———. *Empire of Liberty: A History of the Early Republic, 1789–1815*. New York: Oxford University Press, 2009.

———. *The Radicalism of the American Revolution*. New York: Vintage, 1991.

Young, Alfred F. *The Democratic Republicans of New York: The Origins, 1763–1797*. Chapel Hill: Institute of Early American History and Culture, University of North Carolina Press, 1967.

Index

About the Author

Kristopher Maulden received his PhD in history from the University of Missouri–Columbia. He teaches history at Scheck Hillel Community School in North Miami Beach, Florida.